Feminism and Nationalism in the Third World

Sudhir Kumar Singh

MD PUBLICATIONS PVT LTD
NEW DELHI
www.mdppl.com

Published by :

MD Publications Pvt Ltd
"MD House", 11, Darya Ganj,
New Delhi - 110 002
Phone : +91-11-45355555
E-mail : contact@mdppl.com
Website: www.mdppl.com

ISBN: 978-81-7533-257-7

Published and Printed by Mr. Pranav Gupta on behalf of **MD Publications Pvt Ltd** at Mohit Enterprises, Delhi.

Preface

The term Feminism can be used to describe a political, cultural or economic movement aimed at establishing more rights and legal protection for women. Feminism involves political and sociological theories and philosophies concerned with issues of gender difference, as well as a movement that advocates more gender-specific rights for women and campaigns for women's rights and interests. Although the terms "feminism" and "feminist" did not gain widespread use until the 1970s, they were already being used in the public parlance much earlier; for instance, Katherine Hepburn speaks of the "feminist movement" in the 1942 film Woman of the Year.

Feminism has altered predominant perspectives in a wide range of areas within Western society, ranging from culture to law. Feminist activists have campaigned for women's legal rights (rights of contract, property rights, voting rights); for women's right to bodily integrity and autonomy, for abortion rights, and for reproductive rights (including access to contraception and quality prenatal care); for protection of women and girls from domestic violence, sexual harassment and rape; for workplace rights, including maternity leave and equal pay; against misogyny; and against other forms of gender-specific discrimination against women.

Although third world women have always been engaged in the feminism movement, they criticise it on the grounds that it is ethnocentric and does not take into account the unique experiences of women from third world countries. Third world women accuse mainstream Western feminists of looking at women's experiences as homogenous, based on the perspectives of middle-class white Western women.

This is not to say that there aren't lots of important gender issues to be addressed in poor countries, just as there are in modern democracies. We certainly need a strong awareness of gender roles when analyzing any given society and its problems. However, feminism is too flawed and too one-sided to be the model that guides us in these endeavors, that we will soon reach a point where gender issues are discussed more freely, using research and facts as much as possible.

While an increasing number of individuals are waking up to the problems that feminist policies create in Western democracies, most people still believe that feminism is just the right medicine for Third World nations. After all, isn't feminism exactly what is needed in these underdeveloped countries where men and women still have very traditional gender roles-to bring them into the 21st century? However, it's the very same flawed gender analysis that has led to feminist thinking in the West that leads to feminist thinking regarding Third World policies.

I am very grateful to Mr. Pranav Gupta, Director of MD Publications Pvt Ltd, New Delhi, for his kind cooperation and support for this book.

Sudhir Kumar Singh

Contents

1

Dilemmas in Feminist Fieldwork

Some of the most insightful work in the political economy of the world system area has been produced by deep familiarity with people and locales based on extensive fieldwork. Few other methods are as useful to understand the impacts of structural change on daily life and the ways agents resist, alter, and shape emerging structures. Yet fieldwork has been subject to twin limitations. First, in the majority of instructional materials on field methods, there is a reliance on social constructionist, social psychological, or interactionist perspectives for exemplars and, as a result, discussions of field work problems. Thus, field methods are largely taught as ways to understand the sociological 'micro' with emphasis on micro-level meanings, rather than wider political economic questions.

This bias provides a limitation on pedagogical training. An important exception is feminist scholarship examining the structural impacts of gender and patriarchy. Second, world systems research and writing often privilege either historical methods to highlight long durée structures and dynamics, or quantitative cross-national studies. Although exemplars of fieldwork that successfully contributes to debates and understandings of larger structural processes abound, there is a lack of systematic attention to field methods by much world systems research. In the process, it may also help de-marginalize political economy informed fieldwork.

COMMITMENT TO WOMEN

Feminism is a perspective, not a research method, which is based on the understanding that the construction of gender is a central organising feature of societies. It is a philosophy of the equality of women and is concerned with intervening in cultural practices which are oppressive. The feminist movement attempts to place women's experiences at the centre of analysis and political action. Collectively, it takes the standpoint of women, recognises shared experiences and opposes domination. From this point on, feminism diverges into many forms including Liberal, Radical, Marxist and Socialist depending on emphases and the understood causes of the oppression. Some forms of feminism contradict. However, generally they share the outlook that it is important to centre and make problematic women's diverse situations and the institutions that frame those situations.

Different feminist approaches to research represent different feminist perspectives. Collectively, they are moved by a commitment to women. Though feminist research may not focus entirely on women, it aims to make women's lives and experiences central and seeks to uncover oppression and inequity in everyday experiences. Poststructuralist challenges to feminist research recognise multiple female positions and subjectivities as opposed to a universal female experience. Feminist research is guided by feminist theory. It seeks to benefit or empower the researched population in a direct and personal way. Feminist researchers clearly articulate these commitments and political priorities in their work. For this reason, fieldwork dilemmas can directly challenge the underlying tenets of their feminist beliefs.

FAILURE OF POSITIVISM AND NEUTRALITY

Feminists use a variety of research methods which generally provide a powerful critique of positivism and the level of 'value free' objectivity that must be attained by the researcher in order to uncover facts and truth. Feminists reject the view that any research can be value neutral. Hence, they renounce research methods which participate in the notion of a 'detached objectivity' and distance between the researcher and the researched. Feminist research clearly challenges traditional notions of objectivity and argues that all research in some way is subjective. As a result, reflexivity is understood to be a crucial and ongoing aspect of the research process involving continuous deep reflection and critique.

Feminist researchers aim to investigate a socially constructed world 'from within' and seek to breakdown the hierarchical and potentially exploitive relationships often created within the research process. They strive to cultivate relationships which lead to a richer picture of women's lives. The strength of feminist research lies in its ability to open contradictions and denaturalise what appears to be natural. This approach to research opens further important debates and questions with which feminists continue to struggle, including the kinds of knowledge needed, how best it can be produced and how it can be used to bring about change in women's lives for the better.

The complexity of feminist research has led to a highly reflexive stance among many about: the conduct of research; the researcher's place in the research; the researcher's relationship with participants; the philosophical location and nature of knowledge; the handling of the report; and the impact of the research on the researched. Feminist research tackles the fundamental question of *who* can be a 'knower', referring to women both as participants and as researchers. Ethnography as a method of research shares these aspects with feminist research in that there is an attempt to build theory which is 'grounded' in everyday experiences and lives.

PERSONAL PERSPECTIVE

As a feminist, physical education teacher, and lecturer I have been conscious for many years of a personal struggle to develop in women a commitment to their physical being and to value themselves and their body enough, to participate in lifelong physical activity. Of concern to me also is equity in support, encouragement and opportunity for physical activity. Most alarming has been the decreasing value and time allocation given to anything that is 'physical' within the education system. Whilst fitness and participation levels of children and adolescents continue to decline and numerous inquiries into the state of Physical Education and Health in schools are ignored, the physical space within the curriculum for physical activity is all but disappearing.

Faced with the compelling evidence of girls' lower rates of participation, I felt obliged to ask why girls more involved physically aren't. Why aren't women more interested in being physical? Are they physical in other ways? Why are they excluded? How do young women like to move and what is the nature of the relationship between young women and physical activity? These questions demand a far different research methodology compared to those that solely measure patterns of involvement. Flintoff (1997) also believes that feminist research "must be more than simply a description of women's lives".

Whilst female experiences might establish a starting point for the production of feminist knowledge, it is not sufficient for understanding the processes and social practices though which this is organised. It is the ways in which women's lives are interpreted by feminists that allow feminist knowledge to accumulate and thereby using theory to investigate practice. Being a feminist and committed to educational opportunities for girls I am particularly interested in constructions of gender in Australian society, how this is acted out in school and community settings and what impact it might have on female involvement in physical activity throughout life.

Drawing on gender construction theory, I consider human experience far too complex to accept a positivist approach in which gender differences in relation to physical activity have primarily a physiological base. Being female may in fact be a potentially lifeshaping attribute. From a young age children are nurtured in certain behaviours deemed socially acceptable. These behaviours are both actively and sometimes unconsciously reinforced by adults, media, language, toys, opportunities and role models. Children quickly come to understand gender as opposition and difference. Over time the human mind and personal experience produce biological states which in turn influence skill, confidence and motivation to move.

These ideas have led me to question practices in Physical Education and the appropriateness or perhaps the limitations of 'sport' as a means to educate the physical dimension of the person. It has become apparent to me that while Australian cultural identity is closely connected to its sporting prowess, sport does not necessarily meet all of the needs of ones' desire to be physically active. This may be especially the case with girls and women. However, there is increasing evidence to suggest that many boys and men are also reluctant to be physical or involved in competitive sport.

CONTEXT OF THE FIELDWORK

It was the intention of this research to explore the way in which the lived experiences of gender and attitudes toward the body impact on young women's physicality and commitment to physical activity. In attempting to analyse the social construction of gender in the context of sport, dance and physical activity, observation and storytelling as the main methodological approaches. Through participant observation, conversation and the mutual construction of stories endeavoured to gain an understanding of how my participants came to know their bodies and how they see themselves in relation to physical activity.

In this way, I hoped to identify what motivates and what 'stops' young women being physically active. The body as a feminine construct is a major focus in the study because of its significant role in the social construction of femininity. Via the interpretation of shared stories I intended to illuminate on how gendered ways of being evolve and how girls might be controlled and restricted in relation to physical activity.

The study focused on four categories of senior secondary girls. Those who identified themselves as accomplished athletes in traditional competitive sports, those who participated on a regular basis in non-typical physical pursuits, those who identified themselves dancers, and those who did not involve themselves in any form of physical activity. A survey was initially carried out to identify research participants. Each consenting participant was then involved in a series of guided interviews. Some of these interviews or conversations occurred in the school grounds while others occurred out of hours and in various locations including sporting venues and dance halls. Group interviews were later set up with individuals from each of the identified categories.

The interviews were carried out with a view to drawing out individual interpretations of a range of topics such as perception of physical activity; body image and its impact on involvement in physical activity; how their bodies and desired way of being became gendered; personal experience of physical activity; understanding of femininity; restrictive understandings; experience of physical education and the ways in which physical activity had and had not been made available to them. Through the guided interview process mutual stories were constructed which depicted a memorable event in the life of the participant. These stories were either, initiated by myself and then shared with the participant for comment and development or written entirely by the participant herself.

A key feature of feminist research is the acknowledgment that the production of knowledge is a social process in which the researcher herself plays an important part. Feminists along with other critical researchers concern themselves with what constitutes valuable knowledge and in whose interests it operates. For these reasons, in feminist research the researcher is encouraged to 'place' herself within the research process. The use of 'self as source' presents a very different relationship between the researcher and the researched compared to that of the traditional experimenter and subject. In feminist research, at the very least, both are to be regarded as having the same status as participants or collaborators in the same enterprise.

The researcher carries a responsibility to critically assess her own, as well as the informants', changing positions and subjectivities. Each researcher brings particular values, interests and experiences to the research and has lived through particular circumstances. While these values, interests and experience do not necessarily determine particular points of view they do give researchers perspectives in relation to topics and discussions. The feminist researcher must then be prepared to situate herself reflexively in the research account and provide an analysis of the social relations underpinning the research process.

The importance of this process of reflexivity for both ethnographic and feminist research is in how it makes visible the ways in which the researcher, who is central to the research, both influences and is influenced by the research. Of significance, is an awareness of how feminist researchers participate as subjects in their own research? Interpretation by the researcher of what they see and hear during fieldwork can cause conflict. The researcher must be continually open to reflect on her standpoint and to the possible silences and absences in her data.

The ongoing challenge for feminists is to produce knowledge which accounts for differences between women and yet maintains the overall goal of challenging women's shared oppression. By virtue of my status as a female, dancer and sportswoman I shared many memories and experiences with those of my participants. When studying one's 'own society' questions arise about how one 'knows' and ethical protocols. In this case, it provokes questions such as to what extent did I as a researcher share mutual knowledge with my participants?

Did the fact I was doing research in familiar terrain increase my possibilities of achieving greater understanding of my participant's experiences or did I view their experiences through my own lenses? Then how did this colour my interpretations of the participants who were less like me? These questions are fore grounded as I carry out further interviews. Their impact includes a change in my interview contribution to being more one of clarification and asking for specific details rather than openly conversing and stating my opinions.

POLITICS OF POWER

The most central dilemma for contemporary feminists in fieldwork is power and the unequal hierarchies or levels of control that are often maintained, perpetuated created and recreated during and after the field research (Wolf, 1996, p. 2).

The researcher still maintains control over the research agenda, process and knowledge creation. Power within research can be considered in different ways: namely, power stemming from the different positions of the researcher and the researched; power exerted during the process in terms of unequal exchange or changing positions and; power exerted after the fieldwork, in writing and representing the researched population. In considering the relationship between the researcher and participants as well as the impact of the research on participants the researcher takes on a set of complex interests and seeks to satisfy them all, sometimes without complete success.

Feminists have clearly gained ground in the rethinking of researcher relationships with 'subjects' and with the politics of power that prevail between the researcher and the researched. Field research requires the researcher to engage in a close if not intimate relationship with those she is researching. Crucial to this relationship is acceptance and infiltration. Sameness and difference have important bearing on the acceptance of female researchers by their female informants. Differences between women in terms of their age, class, race, sexuality or physicality for example, may be far more significant than their 'shared femininity'.

Some difficulty in gaining initial access was experienced when defining the purposes and intentions of the research to gain 'informed consent'. I needed to explain the research in a meaningful and open way, but at the same time in a way which would not jeopardise my chances of having the proposal accepted by the four categories of participants. It was very easy to be labelled sport-based or feminist and therefore dismissed as 'biased' from the beginning simply by revealing that you are interested in gender and physical activity. For this reason my introduction of the project to prospective participants was in the broad terms of senior secondary student experiences out of school hours. The fact that I was interested in physical activity indicated to some that I only wanted to talk to physically active participants.

Early attempts to explain the topic of the research were met with reluctance by the non physically active group to participate. They saw themselves as failures in the categories I was researching and chose, as was their right, not to be involved. By slightly altering what the participants 'believed the research was about' I was faced with the dilemma of engaging in a form of deception in order to ensure the involvement of this group. Whilst being assured that most fieldworkers at some point find a measure of dishonesty unavoidable the critical question then became how much harm might I cause in the process. Lying directly contradicts attempts at a more feminist approach to fieldwork. For this to occur at such an early point in the fieldwork I found myself questioning my ethics and practices.

Some researchers suggest that to presume researchers and informants have common identity, interests and backgrounds might impede the capacity to learn about the multiple realities that women have. Certainly in sport related research the assumption that a universal category of physical women is being challenged. While the researcher has an obligation to share her position in the production of the research, this may have different consequences with each participant. In order to capture my participants' 'lived experiences' and diversity I tried to present a clear picture of myself - that of a urban, middle class, academic, dancer and sportswoman. This meant that I was similar in many ways to some and different in many ways from others within the research. As I presented the aims of my study I also talked about my own background.

Whilst in some cases this was a good idea and engaged participants, in other instances I created distance and possibly even intimidation. I felt that my appearance was also a significant factor in developing trusting relations with this age group who, although they wore uniforms were very concerned with clothes and body size. I purposely wore loose clothing in order to make my own body less noticeable. Endeavouring to present myself as a good listener I felt I could engage trust from most if not all of my participants once they had agreed to be involved in the project.

Most of my observations made were of the physically active participants. During the course of the fieldwork I attended sporting events and competitions, practices, dance rehearsals, classes and performances. In most cases my presence was well received and contributed to a more positive and trusting relationship between the participant involved and myself. They were happy that I was interested in them and had taken time to see them outside the context of school. Non active participants did not have the same physical opportunities for me to witness and even though I scheduled some of their interviews outside of school hours I still felt that I was not able to build the same strength of relationship.

The relationships I had developed with participants though at times close and friendly were short-lived. Despite being interested in physical activity, dance and sport, little held our relationships together after the fieldwork had been completed. Age difference may have been a contributing factor. However, the simple fact remains we went back to our respective worlds and our paths weren't likely to cross. Traditional interviewing practices create problems for feminist researchers whose primary aim is towards the validation of women's subjective experiences as women and as people. Oakley (1981) viewed the interview as a one way process in which the interviewer elicits and receives but does not give information. She identified the interview process as a masculine paradigm, one that appeals to the values of objectivity, detachment, hierarchy and science.

For feminists who have a particular orientation to women's subjective experiences there is an illustrated lack of fit between theory and practice. Interviewing women may be a contradiction in terms. What is apparent is that the goal of finding out about people through interviews is best achieved when the interviewer is prepared to invest her personal identity, and the relationship between the interviewer and interviewee is non-hierarchical. Perceptions of power are supposedly minimised when the interviewer and interviewee share the membership of the same minority group. Despite this I found by virtue of my status as an adult and university researcher that power relations were still clearly evident.

In my role as a researcher I felt relaxed, comfortable and respected. As an adult within the school context I was awarded the same status as that of a teacher. Whilst some participants were wary of me at first I felt I could gain their trust quickly. However, in some instances I felt that the participants saw the interview exercise as some sort of test. They responded with statements that I sensed they thought I wanted to hear. This impacted on our conversations at times when I put my opinions or thoughts forward. Participants were quickly ready to agree and accept my ideas without question, even if I was highly suspicious that they personally disagreed.

While conducting interviews I used a guide to focus the conversations though this was never really adhered to. I told participants that I wanted to listen to their stories about their physical and sporting experiences, their experiences of physical education and other things they felt important. During the interviews I attempted to clarify issues without interrupting respondents' personal narrative. At times I was concerned that I was directing the conversations in a way which focused more on their concerns than what I was interested in. I became clearly aware of changing power relations between myself and my participants.

It may have reflected my lack of status and control over the interview process. I became aware of the limitations of semi structured interviews at times when I struggled to stay remotely connected to research topics. As feminist researchers it can be a challenge to try to understand informants' and treat them respectfully when they express opinions that we, as feminists, oppose. My challenge was to evaluate my participants in relation to their backgrounds and lived experiences even when they shared some very traditional and somewhat restrictive views of gender and appropriate physical states.

YOUNG WOMEN'S VOICES

Women's experiences have been historically subject to interpretation by men or there has been an assumed incorporation of women's experiences as the same as men. Feminist researchers seek to benefit or empower the researched population. They are keen to engage voices which have been silenced in the past. Under conditions of more balanced power relations, the research becomes an opportunity to 'tell all'. Hence, the researcher becomes a bearer of many peoples' stories and has a responsibility to value each one accordingly. By dealing in voices and finding voice in research, power relations are affected. To listen to people's stories is to empower them. This implies the need to be a person that someone will talk to as well as creating an atmosphere where the person can speak knowing that they will be heard.

The researched consent to an invasion by a stranger of their personal and intellectual space. It can be personally cathartic to be able to speak about aspects of their lives that have in the past been ignored or normalised. In this way, the research becomes an opportunity to 'set the record straight'. However, in some cases the process may be quite confronting. Nevertheless, there were times when I felt that I was pushing the conversation, times when I succeeded in complicating issues which didn't seem so complicated to my participants, and times when I 'lost the plot'. This was especially the case with participants who tended to agree with my leading statements but lacked confidence to offer further comment. One such participant responded continuously with "I don't know" even after beginning to converse. I became painfully aware that I was failing to give her 'voice'.

On the other hand, she may not have been all that concerned or interested in the topic of conversation. Some felt empowered by their involvement in the research and responded with comments such as "I've never had the opportunity to talk about things like this before". Conversations provided opportunities for consciousness rising and particularly group interviews stimulated a sense of solidarity and shared experience. Two participants reported that since their involvement in the study they had become more aware of 'gendered' situations. Whilst many still felt powerless to change gender relations around them they were prepared to question unfair conditions, especially those connected to their sporting or physical endeavours.

One participant indicated that the most enlightening aspect of her involvement was the realisation (through group interviews in particular) that "girls control each other as much as anything". This seemed to be something that she felt she could control or at least react against. The characteristics of qualitative research can require respondents to disclose and reflect on vulnerable and aspects of themselves in what amounts to an act of faith or trust in the researcher. Faith is integral to this process both from the perspective of the researcher and the researched. The researched reveal personal aspects of themselves and trust that confidentiality will be preserved.

Certain topics covered in the interviews were confronting to some individuals. Issues around body image and physicality for those who did not fit acceptable cultural norms of slim or athletic were problematic and possibly painful. I felt that I had to be extremely sensitive to their feelings whilst encouraging them to reflect and comment on aspects of themselves that were a likely source of lowered self esteem. Other instances involved discussion surrounding physical ability and physical skills. For those who considered themselves 'not sporty' the conversation seemed to contribute towards feelings of inade-quacy rather than empowerment. My supportive comments and objections to their negative responses were futile against entrenched ideas about their personal lack of skill. It was in these contexts that I felt most confronted with the idea that my research was not empowering or contributing to the interests of the researched. In these cases it seemed to be more likely a source of grief.

STORYTELLING

Co-authoring is another method that feminists have employed in order to give up some of the control the researcher has over the research agenda and knowledge produced form it. Storytelling is one example of co-authoring. By capturing much more than numerical scores or mathematical formulae, stories appeal to those who are weary of reducing human experience to variables and quantification. Stories capture the richness and nuances of meaning in everyday human existence. They give insight into the complexity of our experiences and understandings. However, only recently have stories and narrative appeared as legitimate forms of knowledge construction and focus for conducting research.

Narrative is seen as an especially appropriate form of women's expression and allows for the authentic presentation of women's experiences and concerns. Through the mutual construction of a story, I attempted to create a small cameo of a personal yet significant experience in the life of my participant. These varied considerably in both content and style from participant to participant. However, collectively they provided a series of events and scenarios in which many women could see them, myself included.

Through stories, the taken-for-granted ordinary events of women can be explored and critically examined. Stories are a means of making 'visible the invisible'. Storytelling is also a negotiation of power. By giving voice to previously silenced groups, and by describing the diversity of their experiences, readers gain insight into their own practices and life events. A 'narrative persuasion' may be constructed through the use of analogy and repetition. As researchers we often fail to see ourselves as storytellers or to notice the attention we give to some information over other.

Care must be taken not to give the impression that subjective judgement has shaped the story being told. We need to respect the authenticity and integrity our participant's stories, to see them as subjects creating their own history rather than as objects of research. The tendency to draw and code the exotic, the bizarre, or the violent, is great. Often the mundane events are left out as they don't make such interesting reading. The challenge for the researcher is to 'make the familiar seem strange' and take care not to construct narratives 'spiked with only the hot spots'. The construction of stories in this research project was an interesting process.

The starting point for each story was difficult to pinpoint. Somewhere within the interview series I would highlight what seemed to me to be a significant event for my participant and discussed this in depth. At a later date I would suggest that I would like to write a story about such an event with created characters. Engaging my participants to be part of this process provided a series of dilemmas. For some enthusiastic respondents, I have no doubt comfortable with written language, I merely presented a frame of events and they created the entire story by themselves. However, this definitely was not the case with all. Some saw the exercise as yet another assignment in an already crammed academic year and opted out. Others preferred me to begin the process and then contributed to varying degrees to the creation of the final product. In many cases the participants read the story and thought "it was fine". A clear lack of confidence as was similar in the interviews stopped them from being openly critical, making only minor adjustments if any.

As it turns out the stories do present an interesting array of memorable and influential events. Some seemed bland and uninteresting in writing whilst others seemed full of 'hot spots'. Collectively, they have helped me significantly in my analysis and understanding of how young women come to know their bodies and see themselves in relation to physical activity. However, I am unsure as to what effect or how empowering this process has been for my participants. My interests were certainly served but was this just another burden for already busy senior secondary students?

The research process has the greatest potential for feminist process but is the weakest link in feminist research. Wolf suggests here that there is great scope for feminist research. Passion and enthusiasm in the researcher to attain emancipatory outcomes, to meet complex goals and seek social change can only contribute to the interests of the researched population in powerful ways. However, feminist researchers may be hindered by the research process itself. A process often contributes to the development of hierarchical relationships and an imbalance of power. What remains a pertinent question is whether the interests of the research can in fact contribute to the interests of the subject population.

Although feminist researchers may use methods which give research subjects more power it is not clear that they have succeeded. It is difficult to change the power differences that occur in research without radically changing the kind of research that is done, the structure of academia and the way in which research products are judged. Through this exposition of personal experience I have drawn attention to the importance of reflexivity and have revealed some of the struggles that occur at the interface of feminism and the research process. My intention was not to hide from problems and dilemmas but to explore and expose them. The tensions and dilemmas I encountered during field research were very real and confronting to my feminist ideologies. I feel compelled to 'come clean' and reveal the reality of the research process as well as my place within.

Whilst feminist research may give participants the opportunity for supportive discussions and consciousness raising it does little to change the oppressive environment in which individuals exist. At the end of the fieldwork I left my participants to it and I had probably benefited more than them from our relationship. Although an intention of the study was to make young women's lives visible and their voices audible, the paradox is that some young women had a tendency to 'disappear' or stay hidden. These young women may or may not have chosen to stay silent. They may or may not have been motivated to comment. They may or may not have been hindered in their physical pursuits. They may or may not have been interested in my research topic. I am left to contemplate the multiple realities and subjectivities that young women have in relation to their physicality.

Often what goes on in the research process and what is intended may be entirely different. Although I had attempted to change traditional power relationships between myself and my participants, I admit to becoming lost in the changing and multiple relations we sometimes shared. In other instances traditional relations held firm and influenced the research in ways not always intended. Some believe that the relationship between researcher and researched can never be equal or reciprocal or egalitarian. In retrospect I feel that it is far more difficult to change power relationships that previously imagined and prescribed within the feminist paradigm. The researcher may give up some control over the research and empower participants by employing methodologies including co-authoring, consciousness raising, reflexivity and 'coming clean' with the participants. However, no method assures the researcher of success however clear intentions might be.

The dilemmas outlined in this chapter are related to the power relations within research as well as the distinctive description of feminist research in terms of its insistence on challenging patriarchy and improving women's lives. However, as Maynard (1994) notes, there are several different kinds of change which might result from a feminist research project. Whilst women taking part in the research might or might not be empowered, including the researcher herself, there are also the possible longer term effects which the research could make on other women's experiences in the future. Fieldwork is still important and useful.

Whilst it is sometimes difficult to reconcile these deep contradictions between feminist theory and feminist research practice the outcomes of feminist research have much to contribute to a more open and freer existence for women. Clearly, there is a need to confront and interrogate these dilemmas and to face these problems without naiveté and to creatively move forward and rock the epistemological boat. In this way we continue to challenge established notions about what constitutes quality research.

Nearly every writer on the topic agrees that there is no single feminist method, yet there is a substantial literature on "feminist methodology" representing a diverse community of sociologists in lively and sometimes contentious dialogue. This community, and the very idea of "feminist sociology," is products of the "second-wave" women's movement that began in the 1960s and early 1970s, and has grown and differentiated in the years since through specialization, conflict, institutionalization, and cooptation. Many would agree that a method, consciousness rising, was at the heart of this women's movement. In various settings, small groups of women began to talk together, analyze, and act.

The method of consciousness rising was fundamentally empirical; it provided a systematic mode of inquiry that challenged received knowledge and allowed women to learn from one another. Whether caucusing within established organizations or building new connections, women who became feminists began to see an alternative basis for knowledge and authority in a newly discovered community of women and "women's experience." Subsequent developments would reveal the complex fragilities and resiliencies of this construction, which Donna Haraway characterizes as "a fiction and fact of the most crucial, political kind". Though the women's movement began outside the university, feminists in nearly every discipline soon began to apply its methods to their context and work, embarking on a collective project of critique and transformation.

2

Women and War

Feminist Connections with Nationalism

FEMINIST ORGANIZING IN BELGRADE, SERBIA

The campaign of genocide in Bosnia and Herzegovina, initiated by the Serbian regime, moved the women in Belgrade to confront women's human rights violations on all levels, in their neighborhood and in neighboring states. An energetic, committed group of feminists have created a flourishing women's movement in the hostile conditions of nationalism, militarism, and poverty. This chapter will examine a number of the organziations formed from 1990 through 1994.

DEMOCRACY, NATIONALISM AND FEMINISM

Socialism constrained the development of a feminist movement in several ways. First, socialism did grant women significant rights of employment, divorce, contraception, and abortion. Access to these things was to have ended the oppression of women. Second, communism did not allow alternative political groups to form, and specifically, feminism was discredited in all Eastern European countries as an enemy influence from the West. Third, the ideology called for revolution to be made by women and men working together. Women were discouraged from having women-only meetings and often could not justify such meetings even to themselves.

Despite these conditions, a feminist group has existed in Belgrade since 1980. By 1990 visions and opportunities for change emerged with the democratization of Eastern Europe.

Women started talking to one another, organizing, documenting problems and creating strategies for change. Men started to organize also, but in other ways. Soil, blood and surname became the basis of their organizing. They used all their means of power and state institutions to create hatred and fuel the rise of nationalism throughout Yugoslavia. Differences among people - nationalities, ethnicities, religions - were exaggerated and exploited to present other groups as threatening. Hatred of 'the other' was taught by calling upon unresolved conflicts and atrocities from previous decades and even centuries. In June 1991 Slovenia and Croatia declared their independence from Yugoslavia; Bosnia-Herzegovina followed in April 1992. The Yugoslav National Army, controlled by the Serbs, intervened to stop these moves for independence. As Yugoslavia divided, nationalists formed paramilitary groups and fought to control their geographic regions.

Serb military groups - the official army and paramilitaries - possessed greater arms and supplies that enabled them to initiate 'ethnic cleansing,' a genocidal campaign of forced removal, rape and murder against civilian populations. In June 1991 Slovenia and Croatia declared their independence from Yugoslavia; Bosnia-Herzegovina followed in April 1992. The Yugoslav National Army, controlled by the Serbs, intervened to stop these moves for independence. As Yugoslavia divided, nationalists formed paramilitary groups and fought to control their geographic regions. Serb military groups - the official army and paramilitaries - possessed greater arms and supplies that enabled them to initiate 'ethnic cleansing,' a genocidal campaign of forced removal, rape and murder against civilian populations.

This is the environment in which the feminists in Belgrade organized. In an effort to oppose all the forces that foster violence the position of all the groups is anti-nationalist, anti-militarist, multicultural, and feminist. For discussion we have categorized the organizations and activities of the women in Belgrade into five general groups: 1) violence against women, 2) political, 3) anti-war, 4) academic/publishing and 5) lesbian rights.

VIOLENCE AGAINST WOMEN

Feminist organization coalesced around violence against women, which has subsequently influenced all feminist organizing in Belgrade. The SOS Hotline for Women and Children Victims of Violence opened in Belgrade on 8 March, International Women's Day, 1990. The hotline is non-hierarchical and run by volunteers. Since its opening the hotline has received 6000 calls from women who have been threatened with violence, battered, or raped. In May 1993 the SOS Hotline expanded its services to include outreach services to give women direct contact and accompany them to agencies or institutions. Militarism and war increased the violence against women. The SOS started receiving calls from women threatened or assaulted with weapons from war. Wives, partners and mothers called to report assaulted from soldiers returning from war, but they had little hope of getting assistance because the soldiers had the full support of the regime, institutions and the general public.

The United Nations' call for an embargo and sanctions against Serbia for its aggression in Croatia and Bosnia-Herzegovina resulted in economic crisis, hyper-inflation and unemployment and poverty. Most of which fell hardest on women and children as the war(s) expanded refugees arrived in Belgrade. In December 1992 the SOS Hotline formed The Group for Women Raped in War. The volunteers assisted the survivors by providing basic needs, solidarity and sometimes counseling. Shortly thereafter the women decided to form a rape crisis center. One year later the women opened the Autonomous Women's Center Against Sexual Violence. The Center provides a hotline and personal counseling. They also organize humanitarian aid to refugees in Belgrade and have a project called "Packages to Sarajevo" for women of all nationalities in the city under siege. They organize adoptions for children who lost parents in the war.

As the SOS Hotline became more widely known, adolescent girls started calling to talk about incest, abuse and alcoholic parents. To meet the needs of girls some women from the SOS Hotline formed the Center for Girls in 1994. The Center runs a hotline and is a meeting place for girls. It provides workshops and discussion groups about personal experiences with violence. It also provides educational programs about women's bodies, sexuality and awareness and prevention of sexual, domestic and social violence. The Center also has a program for refugee girls. One of the most serious problems for women in Belgrade trying to escape violence is finding a place to go. Housing has always been limited, but with economic crisis, war and a city filled with refugees, there is no where for women to turn.

In Spring 1994 women from the SOS Hotline and the Autonomous Women's Center opened a shelter for battered women. The shelter quickly filled with women from diverse backgrounds - Serb, Gypsy, Muslim, refugee and Belgrade resident. From the opening of the SOS Hotline the founding women viewed violence against women as a social and political issue for women. In addition to helping individual women their mission was to raise the consciousness of the city and campaign for legal and institutional change.

In 1993 a Women's Rights Group formed to analyze the legal status for women in Serbia and within the context of global human rights. In 1994 the group campaigned in the Serbian Parliament for a marital rape law - which only brought them laughs. They were more successful in countering an effort to restrict women's access to abortion. In 1994 the group founded the Women's Advocacy (Law) Center. Its mission is to provide immediate legal counseling to women, to promote women's human rights and to campaign for legal reforms.

POLITICAL ORGANIZATIONS

In the Fall, 1990 women formed the Women's Party (ZEST) with the purpose of improving women's lives through public discussions and projects for women. This organization was short lived. Conflicts arose over nationalism and the position ZEST should take. By the next year, 1991, ZEST had disbanded. The first 'free' multi-party elections were held in Yugoslavia in the Fall 1990. The result was a Serbian Parliament with only 1.6

percent women, the lowest in Europe. In response women formed the Women's Parliament on 8 March 1991. Its purpose was to follow the work of the Serbian Parliament and protest any proposals that would decrease women's rights, especially those that deal with family law and abortion rights.

The Women's Lobby, formed in 1991, is an ad hoc group that has taken the most active role in accusing perpetrators and war criminals. The Lobby has made public statements to the media in opposition to the Serbian regime and its role in the war and the production of hate and nationalism. It has protested Serbian fascism, war, misogyny, nationalism, homophobia and fundamentalism. Since it formed it has organized protests and street demonstrations and issued more than forty public letters of protest and petitions.

ANTI-WAR GROUPS AND PROTESTS

After the start of the war, the political anti-war group Women In Black formed in Belgrade. This group modeled itself on the Israeli women pacifists who protested their government's actions against the Palestinians and the Italian and German women who protested their government's involvement in the Gulf War. Every Wednesday afternoon since 9 October 1991 Women in Black has stood in silence in the Republic Square in Belgrade to protest the war, militarism, nationalism and violence against women. In addition Women in Black have several programs for women refugees. Their goal is to spread the culture of peace among women.

LESBIAN RIGHTS

Lesbians and gay men started meeting informally toward the end of 1990. Officially they became, Arkadia - Lesbian and Gay Lobby in December 1990. The mission of the group is to promote the visibility and rights of lesbians and gay men. There were early conflicts over nationalism. When the decision was made to be non-nationalist, the group became predominantly lesbian. They have organized workshops on lesbian identity, health, families and violence against lesbians. They have promoted lesbian visibility through workshops and media presentations. There is an ongoing campaign, "Lesbian Rights Are Women's Rights," for equality in the education, work, and family.

ACADEMIC ORGANIZATIONS AND PUBLISHING

On 8 March 1992 women opened the Center for Women's Studies Research and Communication. It is an independent collective with no institutional affiliation, with a mission to research and critique patriarchy and teach feminist knowledge. Subjects that have been taught include: literature, linguistics, law, philosophy, and sociology, and anthropology, violence against women, psychology, archaeology and visual arts. In 1994, the Center started publishing own journal. The feminist organizations in Belgrade have done a remarkable job of documenting their work.

The SOS Hotline has published four volumes of the *SOS Bulletin*. Later, along with the Autonomous Women's Center Against Sexual Violence, they started publishing the Feminist Notebooks. Women in Black have published two anthologies on their anti-war work, Women for Peace Anthology and Women for Peace. Arkadia has also issued a booklet entitled Arkadia. In 1994 women started a publishing house, called Ninety-four. Its mission is to publish works by women, children and marginalized writers. One of its first publications is *In Exile* by Jasmina Tesanovic. There are current projects for an anthology of writings by women refugees, a workbook on human rights, and translations of Virginia Woolf and Taslima Nasrin.

ORGANIZATION AND WORK CONTINUES

By the end of 1994 so many organizations each with many projects had formed that an umbrella group was needed to coordinate work. The Women's Network is composed of all the women's groups, initiatives, sections and individuals working against violence against women, militarism, nationalism and for feminist education and publishing. The feminist groups in Belgrade have maintained communications with feminist groups in Zagreb, Croatia. The groups are dedicated to continuing connections among women and refuse to allow men's nationalism and war divide them. The new Women's Network hopes to coordinate more communication and activities with women in other cities.

Nationalism and war has permanently changed the lives of women in Belgrade, some of whom are from war zones. The lives of some of the women have been permanently changed by their response to nationalism and war. A strong influence on the women and their ability to form feminist projects and organizations is the international solidarity of other women's groups and funding. Although no on knows what the future holds, the feminists in Belgrade are dedicated to continuing their efforts to assist individual women and to resist misogyny, nationalism and war.

FEMINISM AND PEACE

One of the early peace groups to draw a connection between feminism and peace was the Garrisonian wing, of the New England Non-Resistance Society in the 1830s, including among its members such prominent early abolitionist-feminists as Maria Weston Chapman, Lucretia Mott and William Lloyd Garrison himself. The group was also responsible for arranging the New England tour of the most prominent feminist abolitionists of the era, Sarah and Angelina Grimke. The Garrisonians based their view on a radical concept of nonresi-stance as conversion to perfection or holiness. They believed that conversion to radical Christian ideals entailed repudiation of all unjust structures of government, including those which subjugated women or which countenanced the enslavement of Negroes.

Christian perfection demands an immediate rejection of war and social injustice, they taught. There is no difference in. this ideal of converted life for men or for women; both sexes are called to the same life of perfection. Thus the Garrisonians both affirmed the connection between nonresistance and women's equality, and repudiated any special gender differences between men and women. Both men and women must be converted to this single ideal, they believed-men from their socialization in patterns of violence and women from their socialization in timidity and acquiescence to unjust social patterns. The connection of many early pacifists and feminists with Quakerism is not accidental.

The Society of Friends offered a congenial environment for both women's equality and nonviolence through a common understanding of a radical Christian ethic of love. The Shaker Society in 19th century America also combined rejection of violence and war with the affirmation of women's equality. For the Shakers, this equality of woman was the revelation of the feminine side of God, or the feminine Christ, the revelation of divine Mother Wisdom. Through this revelation of God's female aspect, woman's full humanity is affirmed and she is able to take her rightful place in the church and in the order of redemption. The leading Shaker eldress of the Mount Lebanon community, Anna White, was an active worker in international peace organizations. She was the vice-president for the state of New York of the International Petition on Disarmament, which White presented to Theodore Roosevelt. For these radical Christians, love and peace were not specifically female qualities, but common ideals for both men and women.

For many 19th and early 20th century women's rights and women's reform societies, the virtues of peace and love were linked particularly with women. These groups believed that men too must be converted to these ideals. But they accepted the current cultural identification of these virtues with women's nature and concluded that the vindication of peace would be linked with the ascendancy of women's influence in the public order. The Women's Christian Temperance Union promoted a department of Peace and Arbitration, headed for many years by Mary Woodbridge. In her oft-delivered speech on Peace and Arbitration in National and International Affairs, Woodbridge saw the day of world peace hastening as women's influence in government grew. Women's influence in the establishment of peace would also hasten Christ's reign as Prince of Peace over the world. Women around the world were seen as joining with American women in the establishment of arbitration as the alternative to settling international conflict through war.

The women's organizations of 1880-1915 generally accepted a close relationship between peace and women's suffrage. To be a suffragist was also to be antiwar. The progress of the human species demanded that war be replaced by arbitration and that there be general disarmament. However, in their view, the male had been socialized through his long association with war to seek violent means of resolving conflict. Male socialization thus preserved regressive and antisocial psychological traits. The enfranchisement of women would bring into political decision-making that half of the human race which had never participated in war as a direct protagonist and which, through its nurturing role, was innately against war. As women gained equal rights and were able to enter parliaments and decision-making bodies in equal numbers with men, their influence would be able to sway societies away from war and toward nonviolent political means of solving disputes.

The suffragists realized that most women throughout history had been the loyal supporters of their husbands' and sons' military activities, but they linked this female support for war with woman's unemancipated condition. As women were liberated from passive dependence on men, they would be able to direct their naturally pacific tendencies into the public arena as an independent force for peace and disarmament. Suffragists and peace activists saw a connection between women's rights, peace and a new concept of citizenship and nationalism. Jane Addams said in *Newer Ideals of Peace,* published in 1907, that the old concepts of citizenship were based on the society of males as warriors. Citizenship was related to the ability to bear arms in war; thus women, excluded from bearing arms, were also excluded from citizenship. Citizenship based on bearing arms fostered a hostile, competitive, chauvinistic concept of patriotism, which precluded international solidarity between national groups.

The giving of citizenship to women would demand a new definition of citizenship based on nonviolent political methods of resolving conflict. These links between feminism, peace and a new internationalism were developed in the Women's Peace Party founded by Jane Addams in 1915; the group later became what is still the oldest women's peace organization, the Women's International League for Peace and Freedom. The

Women's International League, after its founding congress in April 1915 in The Hague, soon gathered national sections throughout Western Europe and began to reach out to found groups in Eastern Europe, the Middle East and the Far East. Much of that small but heroic generation of women who entered their national parliaments or were sent as delegates to the League of Nations in the 1920s and '30s were members of the Women's International League.

The league saw itself as modeling a new internationalism through the relationship of its national sections to each other. National sections of the league were expected to transcend a chauvinist concept of nationalism. Instead, each national group was expected to be the foremost in criticizing the unjust and war-making tendencies of its own national government. American women would take the lead in criticizing the American government, etc. A model of arbitration was set up in which the women from warring sides of a conflict would arbitrate the dispute, with the women from the aggrieved nation defining the situation, while the women from the aggressor nation would accept and announce this criticism of their own government.

The league hoped to present to male statesmen and parliamentarians a new model of arbitration devoted to the international good of the human community, rather than to the narrow advantage of nations at the expense of the whole. Although this model of internationalism became increasingly difficult to practice with the rise of the ideological movements of fascism and communism, even during the darkest days of World War II and the pressures of the cold war, the league has sought to maintain a model of friendly communication and solidarity across national divisions. The secularization of the values of peacemaking left groups such as the Women's Peace Party and the Women's International League with only a quasi-biological link between these values and women's influence, however.

It was presumed that women sought peace because their biological roles as mothers inclined them to biophilic activities. By contrast, males were thought to have fewer loving and peaceful impulses. Thus the women's peace movement was left with an implied doctrine of split natures and split ethics between men and women. Women were urged to gain power and influence in the world in order to counteract the male tendency toward aggression, but there was no longer a basis for a common ethic of peacemaking to which both men and women were called. By contrast, the forms of pacifism based on radical Christianity had not started out with a presumed ethical split between male and female genders. However much those forms recognized that males were socialized more toward war than were women, they featured an ethic of peacemaking based on Christian conversion to God's will for peace on earth that was directed to men and women equally.

With the rise of the new feminist movements of the late 1960s, new rifts appeared in the earlier connections between feminism and peace. The feminist movements of the 1970s could no longer make the connection which many feminists of the 19th century made between women's rights and Christianity:. They found their 19th century forebears in those anticlerical and even anti-Christian feminists such as Elizabeth Cady Stanton or Matilda Joselyn Gage, who suspected that Christianity was basically a religious agent of patriarchy and thus intrinsically hostile to feminism. In addition, contemporary feminists have grown much less sure about the connections between feminism and peace.

Although many feminists continue to believe that males tend toward hostility and violence, they are no longer sure that women s mothering role inclines women to nonviolence. Further, they are not sure that women should pursue a peacemaking ethic as an expression of their true or emancipated humanity as women. Rather, they suspect that women have become pacified through this ideology of woman's pacific nature and thus socialized into being passive victims of male violence. Women must learn to oppose male violence, to fight back by violent means, if necessary. With this assertion of a counter-violence of women against men in self-defense, the last strands in the fabric of the relationship of feminism and peace threaten to become unraveled. Against this background of militant feminism, which did not hesitate to advocate counter violence-at least in self-defense-to male violence against women, pacifists in the women's movement were made to feel isolated and defensive.

Women who advocated nonviolence as the superior social ethic for dealing with conflict felt the need to defend themselves against the charge of antifeminism by the militants. They had to defend and redefine the links between feminism and nonviolence against a new assumption that female nonviolence promoted their passivity and victimization. Thus Kate Millett in her book *Flying* describes herself as approaching the podium with great trepidation during a panel at a 1971 women's conference on "Violence in the Women's Movement." Most of the other speakers-such as Florynce Kennedy, Gloria Steinem, Myra Lamb, Robin Morgan and Ti-Grace Atkinson-as well as most of the audience-seemed either to favor female violence or else to look at it with analytical detachment.

With fear and trembling, Millett declared that she was about to "come out" as something far less acceptable than a lesbian in the women's movement. She was about to come out as a pacifist. "I wait wondering how they will take it. The word is so hated in the Left. To the hecklers 'all I can do is to ask you to be human to me. To listen.' Finally I have said it. . . . 'I want to speak in favor of and as an advocate of non-violence.'" Although the links of an earlier feminism between women and peace seemed totally broken in such a gathering of militant feminists of the 1970s, in fact bits and pieces of the old assumptions still survive today in feminist ideology.

The connections between patriarchy, violence and war which were first explored by feminist pacifists in the first decades of the 20th Century have been revived today. Although contemporary feminists may champion women's self-defense, few are anxious for women to engage in aggressive violence or to emulate male war-making as a way of proving women's equality. Underneath the rhetoric of militancy there still survive presumptions about women's moral superiority-although it is no longer clear on what basis women claim to stand for a superior nature or ethic. In a recent volume of essays, Reweaving the Web of Life: Feminism and Nonviolence edited by Pam McAlister, feminists in the peace movement struggle to find a higher synthesis between the denunciation of patriarchal violence, the advocacy of feminist militancy and a vision of a new humanism that could shape a world without war.

For many women in the peace movements of the '60s, feminist consciousness was sparked by increasing recognition of the sexism of the male leadership in the peace movement itself. Women in peace organizations began to recognize that traditional patriarchal assumptions about male and female roles still prevailed in these groups. Women were expected to do the rote work of typing and filing; men, to have the ideas and make the decisions. One of the most extreme cases was the antidraft movement. Since only males could be drafted, the ritual act of resistance to war, turning in or burning one's draft card, was an exclusively male event. The draft resistance movement cultivated a macho image to counteract the image of the dominant society of draft resisters as cowards.

One slogan of the movement, "Girls say yes to men who say no," revealed the sexist insensitivity of the male leadership of the movement, it was assumed that women working in the movement were simply molls of the male resisters. Consciousness of sexism in the peace movement caused women to form networks and caucuses among themselves; many women split with these peace organizations and joined the feminist movement. Feminists who wished to maintain their connection with older peace organizations struggled to sensitize male leadership to sexist attitudes and to bring about more shared leadership between women and men.

One way of drawing the connection between feminism and peace for many of these women was to demonstrate the continuity between male violence toward women in the home or in the streets, and war. For many men, violence in Vietnam was serious and important, whereas violence toward women was merely private and trivial. Feminists argued that both were expressions of the same mentality of patriarchy. The socialization of women to be victims and men to be aggressors is the training ground for the culminating expression of male violence in warfare, they said. The exaltation of war in male culture has typically been accompanied by a strident sexism. The slogan of the Italian fascist writer Filippo Marinetti in the 1930s, "We are out to glorify war, the only health-giver of the world, militarism, patriotism, ideas that kill, contempt for women," vividly illustrates the emotional and ideological connections between super masculinity, violence and negation of women or the "feminine."

In macho mythology, women stand for a feared weakness, passivity and vulnerability which must be purged and exorcised from the male psyche through the rituals of war. Feminists have pointed out the close connection between military indoctrination and sexism typical of the U.S. Army's basic training. A key element in the rhetoric of basic training is the put-down of women, and, by implication, all that might be "womanish" in the recruit who is being trained. The recruit is shamed by being called a "girl" or a "faggot," thereby inculcating a terror of his own feelings and sensitivities. Through his assault on his fears of weakness, a psychic numbing takes place which is then intended to be turned into aggressiveness toward a dehumanized "enemy."

The emotional identification of the male sexual organ and the gun is a recurring theme in basic training rhetoric. The U.S. Army training jingles "This is my rifle [slapping rifle]; this is my gun [slapping crotch]. The one is for killing; the other's for fun" makes the psychological connection between violence and sexual dehumanization of women clear. The role of rape or the capture of women as part of the spoils of war can be illustrated by virtually every war in recorded history, not the least of which was the Winter Soldier Investigation of combined rape and violence toward captured Vietnamese women in the war in Southeast Asia. Patriarchy turns the sexual relationship into a power relationship, a relationship of conquest and domination. Women are the currency of male prowess, to be protected and displayed on the one hand; to be ravished and "blown away" on the other.

The linking of male sexuality to aggression is the root of both patriarchy and war. For many contemporary feminists, the response of women to male violence cannot simply be a contrary assertion of feminine values of love and nurture. These qualities themselves have become distorted in female socialization into timidity and vulnerability. Women are not so much peacemakers within the present order as they are repressed into passive "kept women." They acquiesce to male violence in the home and accept it in society. The first step for women, therefore, is to throw off these shackles of fear and lack of self-confidence. Feminists have pointed out that, although most women are of slighter build than most men, physique does not mean that women need be passive victims to every random male assault. Training in martial arts could equip women to defend themselves in many situations.

Women who have gone through such training find that the greatest gain is a new sense of self-esteem. They no longer, feel helpless before the possibility of attack. In the very way they now carry themselves, they signal to the male world that they are no longer an easy prey. True nonviolence must be based, first of all, on a secure sense of one's own value as a human being. Violence toward others, far from being an expression of self-worth, is based on a repression of one's sense of vulnerability which then translates into hostility toward others. The most violent men are those with the deepest fears of their own impotence. Training in nonviolence must be based on spiritual or personal development and empowerment of the self. An empowered self will not accept its own degradation, or that of others.

At this point, it becomes possible to forge hew links between feminism and peace. Feminism fundamentally rejects the power principle of domination and subjugation. It rejects the concept of power which says that one side's victory must be the other side's defeat. Feminism must question social structures based on this principle at every level, from the competition of men and women in personal relationships to the competition of the nations of the globe, including the U.S. and the U.S.S.R. We seek an alternative power principle of empowerment in community rather than power over and disabling of others. Such enabling in community is based on a recognition of the fundamental interconnectedness of life, of men and women, blacks and whites, Americans and Nicaraguans, Americans and Russians, humans and the nonhuman community of animals, plants, air and water. Nobody wins unless all win. War-making has reached such a level of destructiveness that the defeat of one side means the defeat of all, the destruction of the earth itself. Feminism today sees its links with the cause of human survival and the survival of the planet itself.

Biophilic values, therefore, cannot remain the preserve of women or women's supposed special "nature" or ethics. As historic victims of violence and repression, as well as those socialized to cultivate supportive roles-but in disempowered sphere-women may have a particular vantage point on the issue. But they are not immune to expressions of hostility, chauvinism, racism or warmongering, even if their role has more often been to be the backup force for the main fighters. Conversion to a new sense of self that wills the good of others in a community of life must transform traditional women as well as traditional men. Both feminism and peacemaking need to be grounded in an alternative vision of the authentic self and human community that was once provided by radical Christianity.

This alternative vision must be clear that we are children of one mother, the earth, part of one interdependent community of life. On this basis we must oppose all social systems that create wealth and privilege for some by impoverishing, degrading or eliminating other people, whether they are the systems of domination that repress or assault women, or the systems that plan nuclear annihilation in a futile search for security based on competitive world power only on the basis of such an alternative vision can men and women join together to rebuild the earth.

WOMEN'S ANTI-WAR ACTIVISM

Globally, women are engaging in actions and conversations in resistance to war and cultures of militarism. In doing so they are simultaneously active at local and global sites of cooperation and community-building. Grassroots-level activism is one means by which antiwar discourses are engaged. Internationally through autonomous and organisational networks women may be seen to be creating an 'imagined community'. The central objective of the thesis is to answer the research question of whether feminist solidarity in the women's antiwar movement is possible, by examining the ways in which women in anti-war movements conceive of solidarity in light of shared discourses and different experiences. It presents an analysis of how solidarity is being enacted in its response to militarism, war and nationalism in a feminist context. The thesis will discuss the limitations of solidarity and the problematic aspects of global 'sisterhood' and contemporary notions of women's collective political mobilisation.

There is a distinct movement globally by many women who have chosen to build alliances and work together under feminist principles across differences, and are thus creating solidarity in practice. Arguments about the substance and very possibility of women's solidarity have consumed feminist theorists for years. Given the myriad collaborative works of women internationally in response to labour rights, environmentalism, women's rights, suffrage and war, questioning the possibility of women's solidarity must explore how discursive conceptions are reconciled with feminist praxis. Solidarity in women's antiwar movement is not only possible but crucial for effective political resistance, despite the problematic presented by engagement across difference.

The emergence of a feminist paradigm of transnational networks is assisting in the construction of discourse and dialogue to enable solidarity, though caution must be exercised in drawing Universalist conclusions or assuming the necessity of this project for all women. I contend that the re-emergence of feminist solidarity in practice is a reconciliation of universalism and difference capable of redressing past criticisms and fashioning more reflexive feminist praxis. Exploring the nexus between the theory and practice of women's antiwar resistance I present a case study of *Women in Black* (WiB), a contemporary women's antiwar movement, to demonstrate how active engagement with antiwar discourses is a form of solidarity in action. WiB is a global network of women opposing war and violence by a shared method of protest based on silent, black-clothed public vigils.

Emerging from the Israel/Palestine conflict, WiB has itself become a method of protest and mobilisation by women in every continent to resist both local and international conflicts. Without naively assuming that practice is exonerated of problematic politics, this chapter will critically analyse the possibility of women's solidarity, given both the current state of theorising and practice. This thesis will assess how feminism has revised past debates over difference and solidarity in the light of international collaborations. Contemporary feminist theory is increasingly attentive to intersectional politics and thus more able to engage with difference and particularity. This has enabled a shift from the preoccupation of a traditional western feminist agenda with 'patriarchal' oppression and suffrage to an analysis of the multiple loci of oppression and the interplay of these with gendered experience.

Emerging paradigms of transnational feminist networks and transversal politics have put a new spin on women's solidarity. The concurrent shift in feminist anti-war theorising has also come to challenge essentialism about the 'innate' peaceability of the category 'women', demanding more awareness of the multiplicity of experiences of women around conflict environments. Appeals to solidarity by feminists in response to the Iraq war has witnessed both the expression of shared identity and an affirmation of difference by way of grounding protests in local subjectivities. Women protesting were doing so generally on a local level, appealing to local political processes and transnational networks. The effects of global feedback loops of interaction mean that standing in solidarity with women across borders also ideally requires those in privileged countries taking responsibility and nurturing awareness of their own positionality rather than claiming the safety of neutrality.

It is impossible to speak out against the 'war on terror' without understanding how 'our' government and populace is implicated, it is similarly premature to decry free trade as a western consumer without an analysis of how we are all embedded in international economic processes often built on the labour of underprivileged women. Contemporary feminism and its search for neo-solidarities is concerned with women interrogating their own positions of privilege and power in reference to interaction with others across race/class/age/ability/sexuality. There is a pressing need to recognise, understand, and reconcile differences in grassroots activism, building this into academic discourses to nurture diversity and remember the necessity of engagement, rather than building walls around them. The research question is significant in addressing a current crisis in feminist theorising, in the troublesome post-identity politics phase, where neither post-patriarchal nor 'traditional' (western) feminist analysis is considered entirely appropriate.

As a feminist actively involved in multiple struggles, I am often confronted by both the frustration of feeling backed into the proverbial corner by postmodernism's focus on the subject's ever-problematic positioning, yet also by the need to be constantly aware of how I am engaging with other women and the complexities of differences between us, and how we can open space for dialogue which is respectful and responsive to this. This is the problematical the heart of feminist political activism; how to engage across differences, and how these alliances are understood and developed as part of an emergent paradigm of transversal politics. The tensions across discourse and experience that I seek to explore in this text are considered critical issues in feminism and the creation of feminist political alliances, as they wrestle with notions of power, difference and unity.

The research methodology is developed from a literature review of contemporary feminist approaches to solidarity. I then conduct a case study of the antiwar activist movement Women in Black as a means of contextualising conceptions of solidarity in arguing that these women are creating a framework of solidarity that draws its legitimacy and strength from the diversity of the movement. It makes possible and tangible the idea of feminist solidarity that is enabled, not precluded, by difference. In the literature review I will analyse different notions of solidarity that have been proposed by feminist writers, although key aspects in recent literature are concerned with how to approach differences in a way that traditional 'westocentric' feminism failed. Transversal politics, reflective solidarity, empathetic cooperation and 'common differences' are some of the proposed progressive methods of feminist organisation across diversity.

A key concern here is regarding how to identify and codify solidarity; I am primarily concerned with an analytical account of the political alliances formed between women and women's networks, and about shared analyses of war and militarism. I recognise there are a considerable number of psychologically-based studies of solidarity and group-identity building in more corporate organisational settings. I do not wish to dismiss these works, but reiterate my concern with the relationships of women primarily via a feminist frame in the context of antiwar activism. It is imperative to ground the case study by analysis of feminist theorising on women's solidarity and its articulation via their transnational networks and anti-war discourses. Accounts dealing with the themes of gender and war are too numerous and complex to analyse in-depth at this point. Key texts include those by Cynthia Cockburn, J. Ann Ticker, Nira Yuval-Davis, Chandra Mohanty, Hannah Arendt, Jean Bethke Elshtain and Cynthia Enloe.

These texts analyse contemporary women's involvement with narratives of gender and war, providing a genealogy of how women have both reinforced and resisted them. One problematic aspect of the issue of women's antiwar activity is the consistently maternalistic and essentialist material that appears around the subject which often fails to address the complexities of such a political agenda. Whether this is by the assumed homogeneity of women's experiences, or in the misrepresentation of women across cultures and societies (speaking for rather than with), exposition which does not explicitly analyse power dynamics within women's movements simply cannot do justice to the deeper issues underlying women's action.

There is certainly a need to heed the words of those such as Chandra Mohanty or bell hooks who analyse the possibilities of alliances, and the impact of subjectivities and boundaries in creating and restricting relationships of principled solidarity within imagined communities. The case study links theory and practice to relate women's experiences and ideas about their involvement in the antiwar movement. My intention is not to develop a universal theory, but to examine how women's solidarity operates in their engagement with antiwar discourses. I analyse the synthesis of feminist theory in the practices of women's global resistance, contingent on the localised understandings and relationships of people involved.

The case study consists of both document analysis and interviews with key informants from WiB chapters globally. Feminist standpoint theory has assisted in developing approaches which value the production of knowledge from experience, centering women's perspectives and creating a space in which this voice is heard directly. An email questionnaire was sent to publicly listed WiB members and internal lists, asking women to respond to a number of questions. They were asked why and when they joined WiB actions, as well as whether they had been engaged in previous antiwar or feminist activism.

They were asked to reflect on the key ideals of their WiB groups, and whether these connected feminist and antiwar discourses for them personally. Further questioning revolved around issues of internationalism; their contact with other WiB groups and what solidarity meant to them. Some issues of differences and conflict resolution were discussed on a number of levels including recognition and working with differences, conflict resolution within and between groups, responses of the general public, and their own experiences of nationalism. These replies gave insights into the issues of political mobilisation by common ideals and differences, and the particularity of local interpretations of an international movement. I received replies from women in Australia, the United Kingdom, USA and Denmark.

The majority are from women living in the US, and their prevalence must be balanced with WiB voices from further afield. Words of the women themselves are used as directly as possible, and interviews based on a less formal structure using an open-ended response style and a participatory method. Through this interviewees demonstrated they were actively involved in a discursive process of understanding their relationships with each other, the movement and the broader social contexts they are part of creating and resisting. Email based interviews were chosen in consideration of physical distance and the already-established major means of online communication between the networks of women in WiB. Melanie Mauthner (2000:293-299) iterated some of the difficulties in interview-based case study research within a feminist framework centered on analysing disagreements and agreements, degrees of disclosure and how to ensure anonymity and confidentiality.

Other possible weaknesses in such a research project include the difficulties of ethical issues and potential for misrepresentation faced by interview and ethnographic research generally, especially given my own limited 'outsider' knowledge in regard to the particular cultural and historical backgrounds of many women in WiB. This is also compounded by the difficulties of 'measuring' solidarity and systematically identifying shared discourses across language and cultural barriers which may affect understanding. The length of this chapter and the time for research is similarly limiting, as is the response-rate and generalisability of online surveys.

Echoing Collins' ideas for researching situated knowledge, this study is based on feminist epistemology to "measure knowledge against concrete experience, test it through dialogue, and judge it in relation to an ethic of personal accountability". I thus approach my research from a qualitative and interpretive approach with a consciously feminist methodology, but have not excluded the use of supplementary quantitative data where it is appropriate and can be adequately analysed in light of its particular socio-historical context. Some literature presents qualitative approaches as more relevant for feminist research based on the direct expression of participants' voices and the possibilities for examining contextual complexities where positivist methods tend towards generalisation (and universalism) and assume an unproblematic 'objective' research perspective.

The literature draws from contemporary feminist theorising and commentary and will situate current feminist actions within broader debates about cross-cultural feminist organisation, seeking to highlight the tensions embroiled in claims for solidarity. The literature review outlines the impact of identity debates on this discourse, identifies key feminist notions of solidarity and then presents the current political paradigm of transnational feminist antiwar movements as a context for the expression of solidarity in shared political critique and resistance. Solidarity, as the notion that some sense of shared identity or aspiration can provide the platform for movement from empathy to political action, is a point of contestation in contemporary feminist debates. Emerging concepts of solidarity by key feminist thinkers attempt to reconcile the crisis of difference/distance and connection which emerge in the local/global nexus of feminist struggles. A key question for feminists engaged in these struggles is how we can nurture transnational feminisms while being cognisant of differences and local contexts.

DIFFERENCE AND FEMINISM

Coinciding with the American civil rights and global independence movements against colonialism, women from various identity-based groups protested their appropriation by a mainstream feminism that failed to recognise their differences and distinct needs. These 'identity debates' in feminism were a difficult, but necessary point of problematising difference of identity and positionality between women, some choosing to politically mobilise on the basis of distinct ethno-cultural identities. An international women's movement historically directed by 'western' organisations has been charged by many contemporary feminists as treating issues and identities as universal and homogenised, or as bipolar and distinguished by a 'core/periphery' divide differentiating 'First' and 'Third' World women.

Mainstream 'First World' feminism, experienced as alienating by those it positions as 'other', is consistently criticised for failing to interrogate its own orthodoxy in terms of whiteness, power, privilege and complicity in global economic processes exploiting women workers in developing states. Differences can inhibit solidarity when left unrecognised and unexplored, or when they are considered an insurmountable barrier to responsible communicative relationships. White western feminism has been charged with myopia around issues of difference; an apparent failure to self-critique compounded by the displacement of 'otherness' as affecting only women elsewhere. Black women are expected to 'own' race against the neutral hegemony of whiteness, as eloquently exposed by feminists working to challenge the subtle historical prejudices of feminism in order to reformulate solidarities across diversity such as bell hooks (1989).

She writes that "[t]he vision of sisterhood evoked by women liberationists was based on the idea of common oppression – a false and corrupt platform disguising and mystifying the true nature of women's varied and complex social reality" (1991 in Yuval-Davis 1997:125), demanding that women take responsibility for their own complicity in the oppression of each other. Aileen Moreton-Robinson (2000:45-71) also offers a rigorous account of feminist politics of difference, drawing attention to the failure of white feminism to acknowledge race privilege. She analyses the racism of mainstream feminism from the perspective of an Australian Indigenous (Geonpul) woman marginalised by a struggle which routinely appropriated black women's voices.

This account makes clear the difficulty feminists encounter around the issues of difference and especially race, fragmented identities threatening a political program built on the category 'woman' that can be engaged only by a small group of women with a specific agenda. Reliance on a universal subject 'woman' suffering from a 'common oppression' is considered a problematic idea. For Eliza Noh (2003:141), women's localised and particular experiences of patriarchal control do not necessitate a reductive notion of women's shared oppression.

Refusing any common ground, subjectively and sociopolitically, between Asian American and white women she comes to the conclusion that any seeming solidarity is artificial, eschewing coalition politics as presupposing sameness (142-4).

Whether differences can be reconciled by communication and engagement are issues that urgently need to be addressed by reconceptions of solidarity. Christine Sylvester highlights the need by Euro-American feminists to self-analyse dynamics surrounding their participation in capitalism and concomitant global political structures effecting women in the Global South before meaningful dialogue is at all possible. Caren Kaplan (1994:139) suggests using Adrienne Rich's 'politics of location' to pay homage to historical reasons for differences and inequities, recognising the asymmetry of relationships without constructing identity itself as authentic and primordial as a method to interrogate the 'whiteness' of North American feminism. Mohanty considers the effects of cultural imperialism in discourse, whereby Third World women are constructed or ignored by western feminism (2003:20-23).

Her analysis that the presupposition of the category 'women' contains a notion of women's homogenous oppression highlights the way it draws a misshapen image of the 'average Third World woman' designated by victimhood and dependency. Representing the 'unheard' voices is not uncomplicated. Understanding may rest on knowledge, but its transmission is imbued with the same power imbalances when subject-researcher relations also cross global North/ South divides. Daphne Patai (1994:21-37) judges academic representation of Third World women by US academics, even by consciously feminist research methods, as exploitative and unethical because the exchange can never be what she considers equal. Rather than foreclose on cross-cultural conversation, Assia Djebar reminds women that differences of freedom affect representation: "don't claim to 'speak for' or worse to 'speak on' barely speaking next to and if possible very close to [another]".

Dian Elam warns of developing hierarchies of difference and identities, and the assumption of sameness within collective identities that leads to the potentially treacherous territory of representation that speaks for a whole people (1994:74). Can myriad differences between women be recognised, articulated and scrutinised in feminist reclamations of solidarity beyond sisterhood?

FEMINIST CONCEPTIONS OF SOLIDARITY

Traditional notions of women's solidarity relied on uncritical claims of universal 'sisterhood', based on 'women' as a clearly delineated category with some comparable experiences of oppression; the postmodern backlash to this is the rejection of shared gender identity. Differential histories and socio-cultural positioning affect experience which may or may not be comparable, however, the strategic political necessity of women's mobilisation, including cross-national collaboration, sidelines philosophical debate about whether 'women' still exist as a meaningful unit of analysis for purposes of this thesis. On a political level, 'women' still constitutes a group distinguished by various gendered discrimination. Mohanty (2003:234) notes that women and girls are globally worst affected by environmental degradation, war, famine and displacement exacerbated by globalisation.

While inequalities of wealth, access to education, resources and socio-political capital affect women's lived experiences differently, the reconfiguration of solidarity thus requires attention to the real disparities between women and the possibility of dialogical approaches to enable exchanges across these. Despite the utility of deconstruction for countering the colonising potential of theory, a complete deconstruction of the subject is not politically viable for feminism given current need for mobilisation and action. Feminism should not, however, fear deconstruction, as it "does not say anything against the usefulness of mobilizing unities.

All it says is that because it is not useful it ought not to be monumentalized as the way things really are", suggesting that the essentialism of (western) feminism must be challenged, while opening the category 'women' to reinterpretation and contestation to allow for new identities and political mobilisation. Elam (1994:82) has attempted to reconcile deconstruction and identity-based feminism via the ethical activism of 'groundless solidarity'; the binding aspect of feminism is that we share collective concern for other women despite the uncertainty of knowing who they are (undecided multiple positions), and the indeterminate political possibilities held. For Elam, groundless solidarity presents "the possibility of a community which is not grounded in the truth of a presocial identity" and the basis "for political action and ethical responsibility".

This does not necessarily mean consensus, potentially crossing national, ethnic, and religious borders, facilitating a political coalition based on shared ethical commitments without exclusion and a commitment to difference which destabilises delineations of self/other; 'groundless' in the sense of not relating to an isolated autonomous subject, but one who is "caught up in a network of responsibilities to others". Elam (1994:114) rejects solidarity based on similarity as assimilation and recommends solidarity explicitly based on difference beyond simply accommodating different beliefs, indicating the women's pro-choice movement as respecting differences of choice over abortion.

STANDPOINT FEMINISM AND LOCALISING VOICES

Standpoint feminist theories reflect particularity of experience informed by gendered identity. Some feminist scholars are convinced that standpoint theories are able to respect diversity because of this. Standpoint feminism is concerned with hearing as many women's individual voices as possible, situating feminist claims in solid locational contexts. Individual knowledge-claims and daily experiences give expression to the feminist principle that "the personal is political" allowing more scope for political fodder as "no social practices or activities should be excluded as improper subjects for public discussion, expression, or collective choice." Standpoint feminism elucidates the relationship between knowledge, experience and identity.

It is criticised as reductive when a 'pure' collective subsumes individual identity, or particular knowledge are held only by 'authentic' directly experience. Converging with emerging postmodern theories, however, standpoint feminism can be receptive to multiple, fragmented identity claims allowing for contradiction and democratic constructions of shared knowledge. Multiple standpoint feminism as the basis for further critical analysis can allow for some generalisation without proposing one vital 'legitimate' notion of women's experience, creating space for spared expressions of experience and opinion between women vital for communicative notions of working solidarily across differences and connecting local activism to global community.

LOCAL TO GLOBAL CONNECTION

Conceptual or material links between the local and global emphasise "relations of mutuality, co-responsibility, and common interests, anchoring the idea of feminist solidarity". Mohanty (2003:224-226) and Dean both emphasise this relationship in that the local 'illuminates' the global, arguing for solidarities based on the differences that constitute localised experience, when "specifying difference allows us to theorize universal concerns more fully". Rather than homogenising some notion of women's shared oppression, difference forms the basis of recognising others' struggles and building bridges between movements. Christine Sylvester (2002:216) also supports the notion that the bounds of feminism are flexible enough to provide for recognition of differences, and brings attention to the multiplicity of lived experience and fractured identities.

Chandra Mohanty's "common differences" is the basis of her "feminist solidarity model" (2003:242-245); not relativism but a recognition of coexisting and interdependent relationships containing both commonalities and differences. Such links include the "multiple, fluid structures of domination that intersect to locate women differently at particular historical conjunctures". In this sense she is interested in similar locations of women via their colonial and post-colonial histories, addressing structural issues of power and resistance. Mohanty (2003:49) is concerned with political alliances built from "the common context of struggles against specific exploitative structures and systems". This is primarily by reference to an alliance, or sense of community, between Third World women and Black women involved with anti-sexist, racist and imperialist struggles (49) and their common interests as workers with shared perspectives gleaned by their specific roles in global economic processes.

COMMUNICATION IS ESSENTIAL

Despite the separation of actors in traditional notions of solidarity (i.e. we feel with them), Jodi Dean (1996:8) reflects on the necessity of difference to enable solidarity and the communicative inflection of the 'we' who express solidarity. She is adamant that communicative internal establishment of group identity helps deal with difference by making it explicit and not necessarily exclusive. Dialogue is vital process of each speaker owning her own subject position and recognising others; it is the key in standpoint feminism where each consciously conveys "partial situated knowledge". From distant points, conversations effect alliances, and the explication of different needs. Yuval-Davis considers feminism effective 'coalition politics' where delineation with others is by aspiration, an articulation of "what we want to achieve", not identity, although differences amongst women are voiced.

Christine Sylvester introduced the idea of empathetic cooperation as a means to reinvigorate feminist engagement with International Relations by bridging the rigidity of standpoint feminism and the ambivalence of postmodern critique. She describes it as "a process of positional slippage that occurs when one listens seriously to the concerns, fears, and agendas of those one is unaccustomed to heeding when building social theory, taking on board rather than dismissing, finding in the concerns of others borderlands of one's own concerns and fears" (2002:247). Empathetic cooperation presents a broader perspective by denying one fixed theoretical stranglehold, adopted in her earlier work (1994:3) by reference to Kathy Ferguson's (1993) 'mobile subjectivities' to disrupt ideas of singular stable identities and truths.

Sylvester reveals empathy as a conversational tool that listens without demanding answers, so that multiple stories can be appreciated, combined with cooperation to enable engagement with "politically difficult negotiations at borderlands of knowledge, experience, differences, and subjectivities". Though specifically formulating empathetic cooperation in regard to theory and discussions in IR, she grounds her ideas as bases for action by reference to the women of Greenham Common peace camp and their commitment to dialogue and cooperation as well as diverse tactics and ideology. For activist and academic Nira Yuval-Davis, the framework of dialogue as scaffolding for empowerment and solidarity is best expressed by 'transversal politics', a concept coined by feminist activists involved with Italian Women in Black, to describe engagement with women from various backgrounds with recognition and respect for difference.

These conversations were based on notions of 'rooting' and 'shifting'. 'Rooting' is speaking consciously from one's subject position while 'shifting' attempts to sympathise with 'others' by listening empathetically, enabling exchange while recognising different values and goals. Yuval-Davis (1997:125) sets transversal politics as an alternative to the immobilising dichotomy between universalism and relativism. She indicates a necessity for contestation of 'the authoritative feminist agenda' and a commitment to solidarity informed by cooperation across differences, honouring partiality as opposed to universality but forewarning the easy blur into relativistic immobility.

Jodi Dean's (1996:13-46) proposed theory of "reflective solidarity" is a means to overcome this divide between universality and the particular, moving beyond the rigidity of conventional solidarity to suggest that awareness and nurturing of dialogue can respond to the dilemma of difference. Critical of both the simple emotionality of "affective solidarity" and the strategic disconnection of "conventional (goal-based) solidarity", reflective solidarity is the notion that we can engage cross-culturally, while being cognisant of differences and the historical contexts informing them. Thus engaging in a dialogue and possibly disagreement to reach a position of solidarity towards a "mutual expectation of a responsible orientation to relationship".

Cautioning the silent reprisal contained in dialogue that neglects an exploration of differences by assuming concurrence, reflective solidarity demands openness to disagreement. Thus feminist agendas cannot be assumed, or continued by deference to traditional concerns or constituency. As a means to feminist solidarity, "we have to be allowed to get messy" via constructive, conflictive discussion, and the more questioning the better, given the potential for group dynamics that lend power to particular individuals and agendas. This 'reflective solidarity' depends on engagement for open membership and self-reflectivity. A self-reflective stance enables both responsiveness to criticism and taking responsibility for the 'other' by ownership of concrete fragmented identities within a communicative universal membership.

Opposing theorists, such as Judith Butler, who condemn discursive universality as totalising and exclusionary, Dean's solidarity wrestles with feminist disagreement in order to nurture community *via* difference, challenging the mutual exclusion of the universal and particular in what she considers part of a vital feminist struggle against dualistic gendered hierarchies. Her embrace of difference becomes reason for inclusion: "we appeal to others to include and support us because our communicative engagement allows us to expect another to take responsibility for our relationship".

PRAGMATIC SOLIDARITIES

Manisha Desai (2002:29) supports reflective solidarity as the product of conversations between women from various women's movements globally around "common goals of freedom, justice, and equality variously defined" bridging multiple identity-divides. She positions women's emerging solidarities in the context of their different experiences of macro-social forces, such as religious fundamentalism and post-colonial nation-building, shared globally yet from within historically and culturally discrete circumstances. Chandra Mohanty (2003:7) defines solidarity by reference to pragmatic decisions to work together and by "mutuality, accountability, and the recognitions of common interests as the basis for relationships among diverse communities."

She reaffirms that solidarity is oriented by practice, by political struggle, not the romantic notion of 'sisterhood' (24). Solidarity is the basis of the transborder participatory feminist democracy she calls for. At grassroots level, there is a documented focus on politically strategic solidarities; "solidarities for survival", for example, between women workers in the informal sectors forming credit cooperatives and networks to exchange ideas and influence policymaking. The Self Employed Women's Association (SEWA), initiated by women in Gujarat, is described as an example of informal sector trade unionism, and one that moves beyond solely providing worker-support to enabling social transformation.

Unionisation is an example of women's solidarity based on common (if contextually distinct) experiences or identity as workers. Chandra Mohanty is especially convinced of the possibility for Third World women's connectivity as workers given their particular experiences within global economic systems. Mary Fonow (2005) concurs those women workers developed solidarity through their trade unions in her analysis of cross national campaigns for human and labour rights as well as union conferences and networks afforded by union-based humanitarian aid organisations. In the interest of inclusivity, however, feminists should heed warnings about limiting solidarity to the domain of a class struggle and the need for women to form their unions given the popular perception of these organisations as controlled by a white male working-class.

TRANSNATIONAL FEMINISM NETWORKS

Solidarity, as discussed briefly above, lends itself to political mobilisation beyond emotional rhetorical synthesis. Solidarity requires action by reason of moral obligation to another. While debates continue over how to represent 'women' as a meaningful identity in feminist academia, the emergence of transnational feminist discourses, networks and actions utilising notions of feminist solidarity indicate reconciliation between theoretical consternation and collective political purpose. Feminist theory, North and South, is often consciously based on ground-work.

The grounded networks of women and feminist organisations enable a sharing of resources, knowledge and discourses between women globally. While some activists working at a grassroots level criticise scholars for being removed from the arena of their study, many feminisms deliberately emerge from praxis, so the false dichotomy of theory versus action is not entirely constructive. It is my contention that feminist networks, such as WiB, are actively creating the discursive space for emerging feminist solidarity theories, becoming part of feminism's paradigm shift. Women's organising is often a complicated endeavour, with the clamour of voices necessary to put into effect feminist ideals for participatory, democratic, non-hierarchical and autonomous engagement.

Less formal than structured organisations (although they may include women involved in different organisations), networks of women can nurture a sense of collective identity, empowerment and solidarity. These are critical in constructing feminist movements that can be inclusive and representative. The network becomes a flexible resource to enact solidarity by sharing support, human resources and information between groups and individuals. Women Against Fundamentalism (WAF), for example, is a network of women mostly active as individuals although each may be involved in multiple other groups. Yuval-Davis notes that these women are not obligated to subsume differences by representing a group identity and consider their own knowledge unfinished and dependent on dialogue (1997:128).

Women's mobilisation without structured organisation enables the direct democracy of autonomous activism, though this relies heavily on a communicative understanding between members rather than an institutionalised recourse for accountability. A safeguard to accountability is accommodated in Dean's theory of reflective solidarity by responsibility to multiple viewpoints, especially that of 'the hypothetical third' as the marginalised 'other'. It is imperative to locate women's solidarity within the emergent transnational paradigm of feminist politics; transnationalism goes beyond notions of simply 'international' by suggesting a "conscious crossing of national boundaries and a superseding of nationalist orientations".

According to Valentine Moghadam (2005:9) Transnational Feminist Networks (TFNs) came to the fore of feminist organising in the 1990s, securing common ground between women activists across divisions previously demarcated by ideology and global North/South political divisions. She proposes that via an expanded agenda, global issues that particularly affect women in developing states, including Structural Adjustment Policies and reproductive rights for example, may be addressed. These networks enable solidarity between women who are working from diverse locations on such agendas as development, labour rights and anti-capitalist struggles by bringing global pressure to bear on local political contexts.

Moghadam regards international attention to the issue of women's rights in Afghanistan in the late 1990s as a successful campaign of women's networking between Women Living Under Muslim Laws (WLUML) and other TFNs circulating and responding to appeals to solidarity by Afghani women such as the Revolutionary Afghani Women's Association (RAWA) and expatriates in Pakistan.

United Nations Women's Conferences have been vital to the emergence of contemporary feminist solidarity and consolidation of TFNs as the contemporary paradigm of global feminism. Though they by no means represent the entire spectrum of women's networking, from Mexico City (1975) to Beijing (1995), women's differences have been voiced and negotiated as part of building a common mode of organising across diverse notions of 'women's issues' that Desai has called "solidarities of difference". Articulated through the conferences is the language of women's human rights, re-embraced by a number of feminist theorists in recent years following decades of criticism as a tool for exporting western enlightenment rationality.

Women's rights, interpreted as including labour rights, rights to reproduction and protection against gendered violence specific to women's broad needs for example, presents a means to both pragmatic solidarities and gender main-streaming in broader agendas of peace, development and democratisation, recovering rights discourses from the domain of public, institutional politics and the masculine universal subject on which they were established. By the same token though, international conferences draw attention to the limited agenda of some feminist political action, and have been an arena whereby some women have expressed resistance to cooption by western feminists in the name of supposed solidarity.

SOLIDARITY IN FEMINIST ANTI-WAR DISCOURSES

Concurrent to feminist theorising which critiques the sentimentality of traditional sisterhood, critical analyses of women's antiwar solidarity are suggesting that multiple roles of women in conflict must be recognised, and antiwar activism framed as part of multiple conversations that connect women differently in conflict. Women cannot be assumed to be peaceful, but feminisms can provide key analytical frameworks for positive peace and analyses linking war and domination. It is critical to analyse how feminist conceptions of war, militarism and nationalism underscore the ways in which women's antiwar activism exemplifies solidarity in action. Such critiques and their prescriptive notions of peace are vital for conversations between women.

This is especially so in response to the 'war on terror' as part of building solidarities to counter the hostile binary 'us' versus 'them' characteristic of the political spin on the war and to reclaim feminist voices from their appropriation as part of the justification of invasion of Iraq and Afghanistan. Women's multiple and diverse roles in conflict position them differently from men and from each other. The normative scripts for women in conflict zones are generally fairly passive and these gendered roles are bound up intimately in the languages of nationalism and militarism.

Cynthia Cockburn (1998:13) has noted that there is always a 'gender war' embedded within war and its architecture of gendered domination and dualism. Militarisation of thought and cultures is a subtle and pervasive process, and though its invasion into the everyday lexicon is not always directly about war, it effectively normalises militaristic presumptions. In a more explicit push for the spotlight, global militarisation has stepped up on a global stage since September 11, reframing international politics around agendas of national security, border protection and hard masculinity. There is a particular symbolic weight that women shoulder as keepers of national identity, purity and longevity that often becomes more pronounced, as do other gendered divisions of labour, during conflict.

The idea of 'women and children' as victims in need of protection is defined in opposition to 'male' roles in the masculinist normative narratives of war. Nationalism can thus restrict women's agency during conflict where social obligations delineating women's behaviours are more pronounced and symbolically charged. When these boundaries are crossed, via public protest, domestic non-compliance, or cross-ethnic organisation, women face charges of being 'traitors'. Reaffirming women's multiple active roles in response to cultures of warfare is an inherently valuable feminist exercise, so centring some women's experiences of resistance is also a bold response to such silences. Feminist theorising has long illuminated connections between patriarchy, domination and war, citing feminist concerns for peace with a shared concern for a reduction of violence across public and private spheres.

In this way, the spectrum of violence against women is recognised as spanning domestic, structural, state and military violations, linking these to advocate for broader recognition of women's rights. This has included demands for the prosecution of the use of rape and violence against women as war crimes in conflict, and the drafting of Resolution 1325 in the UN Security Council to recognise and enshrine the need for women's involvement in peace processes. Zorica Mrsevic (2000:41-42) is concerned that the increase in domestic violence in the former Yugoslavia is the result of militarised nationalism in the region, relating aggressive masculinity to a rise in ethnically defined nationalism and structural violence.

Some feminist critiques that analyse the relationship between militaristic nationalism and gendered oppression and violence can thus provide a basis for dialogue and solidarity despite differences in particular experiences. Although nationalistic masculinity is often experienced as a violent, alienating force, some women in militaries or national liberation movements, report their involvement as empowering. Integrationists equate full citizenship and equality with military service, and belie the assumption that women are naturally peaceful. In response, some feminists question the potential for women's empowerment through involvement in systems built on domination and misogyny.

Women's rights are recognised as an essential aspect of some Third World nationalist resistance movements, although realisation of these rights post-independence is often limited. Even within peace movements, some women activists support the use of violence, especially against property. In one widely publicised antiwar action of October 2002, three Dominican nuns in Colorado vandalised a US Air Force missile silo by painting it with a cross in their blood, cutting cables and fencing and hammering at the missile guiding tracks. Thus it is problematic to base women's activism for peace on their characterisation as the 'Beautiful Souls' who weep for the Warriors' return.

Although women's antiwar organising is increasingly political and strategic, there are still perceptions that peace is a 'women's issue'. Given the socialised gender roles of motherhood, care and nurturing, these sentiments do underscore some antiwar discourse and many women's motivations to activism. Separating 'sex' and 'gender' cannot entirely overcome the connection of women to an 'ethics of care'; women's gendered socialisation is popularly considered the basis of better empathy, support and mediation skills and broader attention to interpersonal dynamics. Traditional feminist appeals to women's peaceful inclinations generally invoked tropes of mothering and nurturing.

Appeals to motherhood as a universal experience that crosses boundaries and can connect them with 'enemy' women, can be both constructive and problematic. Accessing the 'other' by crossing borders and identity boundaries can be politically valuable and subversive. Caring for the 'other' and invoking motherhood to care for the 'other's' children can ameliorate the divisive isolation between conflicting populations. Where women's traditional roles restrict resistance activities, utilising motherhood can enable dissent, such as in the activism of the Mothers of the Plaza de Mayo in Argentina, and the mothers of Russian soldiers in Chechnya. However, the senti-mentalisation of motherhood can be appropriated by nationalistic discourses, and risks alienating women who are not mothers from political activities based on this positionality.

What women appeal to in solidarity with others can be pragmatically and emotionally based? Although contemporary movements are moving away from essentialist conceptions of women's solidarity, evoking a shared discourse of women's peaceful character or motherly love can be powerful but problematic in universalising one approach without regard for local and experiential differences. Postmodern theorist Sandra Harding warns of the discursive dangers of political projects built on meta narratives or presumed truths of shared values. From this perspective it is facile to assume that all women are peaceful, or even speak a common language about peace considering the breadth of their different experiences.

Of course, this is not what I am suggesting, and scholars such as Charlotte Bunch (2004:29) have discussed the site-specificity of women's peace activism, recognising that it is no longer focused on catching the unicorn of 'world peace'. Sylvester criticises the potential for emotionality and maternalism in standpoint feminist's project of connecting women and peace, but suggests that this can be ameliorated by allowing the contradictions of multiple standpoints where knowledge is democratically, not derivatively, constructed. Yuval-Davis (1997:111) argues that feminist analyses of war and militarism have thoroughly interrogated the manipulation of traditional notions of femininity and motherhood as part of nationalist militarisation, so that the majority of women's antiwar mobilisation has attempted to move beyond the essentialism of claiming women as the 'peaceful' sex.

Drucilla Cornell (2004a:318) links the US government's appropriation of feminist arguments for women's rights in Afghanistan to analysis of "how women and symbolic articulations of the feminine lie at the heart of many efforts to consolidate nationalist projects". She reinforces the need to re-establish the role of feminism in the peace movement as it has been appropriated by US official rhetoric (314-315). The misrepresentation of solidarity is particularly sensitive for feminists working towards global advocacy in the wake of the 'war on terror', with the US government's pursuit of an agenda ultimately inimical to women's rights, while using feminism to justify invasion and garner domestic support.

The strategic appeal to US and 'coalition' women's solidarity with Afghani women can be read as particularly cynical in light of Washington's disregard for the long campaign of organisations such as RAWA and their continuing resistance to the apparent repression they still face from the US backed Northern Alliance. Although explicitly appreciative of global feminist support, RAWA have criticised the Feminist Majority organisation as a 'mouthpiece' for the government and for ignoring the long history of feminist resistance by Afghani women. Arguably, the symbolism of the veiling of Muslim women was also manipulated to incite a limited form of solidarity based on victimisation. Shahnaz Khan (2001) discusses the problematic politics of sensationalist stereotyping implicated in depictions "situating the body of the Afghan woman as totally contained by the veil of her oppressive culture/religion".

Projecting western women in the role of liberators, the prevalence of such images presents the interplay of gendered cultural repression and the difficulty of uncritically attaching solidary sentiment to misrepresentations of 'other' women without listening to their articulated demands. In this political climate, feminist resistance is vital to refusing the language of militaristic nationalism that excludes 'others' and thus undermines the possibility of reflective communication. It is evident that women's solidarity in antiwar campaigns requires reflectivity to enable self-analysis by western women on their own positions *vis a vis* those who have been victimised in the war. US feminists are urged to reflect on American historical military involvement and the impact of foreign policy globally before they can engage with feminist antiwar and other progressive dialogues building pragmatic political solidarities.

On a more directly personal level, attention to localised differences and how representations of 'other' women affect political engagement must be part of establishing a sense of solidarity that can be based on engagement and receptivity rather than victimisation. Women's engagement with antiwar discourses is as diverse as the conflicts occurring globally. Working towards a commitment to solidarity that recognises this diversity can utilise the complexities of women's politics, loyalties and abilities to confront the uncompromising delineation of patriots and traitors, allies and enemies, victims and saviours that limit dissent and deny the multiple realities of women resisting violence globally. This literature review has shown that emerging feminist theories of transnational solidarity are being more attentive to differences, although criticism continues around the danger of western bias.

Although there is no definitive account of feminist solidarity, some contemporary theories are concerned with a more equitable engagement than the sentimentality of 'sisterhood'. I have found that the central tenets of these are communication, self-reflection and recognition of personal experience combined with intersectional analysis linking local and global phenomena. Feminist solidarity articulated in political struggles is bound to the practical, pragmatic element of shared ethical commitments. I have proven the possibility for antiwar discourses as a discursive basis to feminist solidarity and I will further demonstrate that pursuant to this, WiB are not simply responding to feminist theory, but are actually making space for new conceptions of solidarity by practicing transnational feminism that is diverse and communicative in its shared critiques of war.

CASE STUDY: WOMEN IN BLACK

Women in Black are an international movement of women against war and violence; the organisations are simultaneously locally based and globally connected. The common elements of the movement are based on a shared mode of protest through silent public vigils where members, mostly women, are dressed in black. They are part of an extensive global feminist movement challenging nationalism and militarism and are adding to the development of feminist theories and cultures of nonviolence. From its roots in the Middle East conflict in 1988 as a group of Israeli women opposed to the occupation of Palestinian territory, WiB has grown to an international membership. Apparently they constitute a fairly informal international network, with a shared general philosophy of pacifism and anti-militarism and similar strategy of protest. Some groups have described it as a movement, others as a "means of communicating and a formula for action" rather than a formal 'organisation'.

Analysis of WiB's activities indicates that the solidary organisation of women globally, informed by feminist critiques of nationalism and militarism, is nurturing both an awareness of differences and a common concern for ending political violence. Further, it is arguable that this solidarity can offer an alternative to the limited traditional roles for women and the demands for political compliance and loyalty in times of conflict. Assessing practices of WiB in terms of previously discussed feminist theorising about solidarity will examine how differences and shared ideals are conceived communicatively, as grounding for solidarity. I analyse how these women engage with discourses of nationalism and militarism to build their antiwar movement. I will do so through analysis of web-based communications made by, and in response to, WiB and also through analysis of email based interviews that were conducted in April and May 2006.

Drawing connections between reformulations of feminist solidarity and the character of WiB, it is apparent that the way the movement is built on minimalist mode of protest with basic undercurrents about shared identity and antiwar ideals makes it able to utilise flexible notions of universality in its local interpretation. Not hegemonic, controlled or rigid, it corresponds to central tenets of feminist solidarity. I will also canvass some problematic aspects of assuming WiB's convergence with modern feminist solidarity theories, including potential maternalism, essentialism and questioning whether the minimal mode of protest can inhibit development of political critique.

DIFFERENCE AND DIVERSITY IN WiB

The number of active sites of WiB vigils is itself testament to a diversity of women involved in the movement. Differences of both identity and ideals become apparent within each group, as well as between vigils, across cultures and borders. From the international lists of WiB vigils, they appear to be active in every continent and with over 240 groups meeting in more than thirty states. Part of their strength is the way in which diversity is conceived of as a basis for solidarity, rather than a reason for fragmentation. Indeed, opening speakers at their 2005 international conference reinforced the commitment of WiB to rejecting not only intolerance of the 'other' but working towards a notion of 'solidarity *in* difference'.

Demographic patterns of women in the movement emerge when looking at a number of sites. Trends of participation in Israel suggest a prevalence of wealthier, educated Ashkenazi women in their forties and fifties with histories of political involvement. Although many women identified as Jewish, and followed similar demographics in its adoption in the US, many others became involved to protest the US military response following September 11, 2001. Of the women surveyed by email, most were older than forty, lived in the US and had past experience in peace activism or women's rights campaigns. Some associated their peace activism with religious beliefs as Christians, Quakers and Buddhists; others had been involved in Vietnam protests or anti-nuclear activism while three declared no past activism. Women in the US chose to participate with WiB generally after September 11, 2001 and the invasion of both Afghanistan and Iraq which followed.

Ellen, who stands with the Asheville vigil, observes that although her group is comprised of Euro-American women, other differences affect political perspectives towards activism. She writes "[t]here are class differences in origin and current circumstances, we are both gay and straight, older and younger, of various religious and ethical persuasions, profession and self-employed, rich and poor". In her opinion, its inclusive membership makes it receptive to differences and a "safe place" for women to "come out" as activists. It is apparent that a number of women active in WiB identify as lesbian, and connections between these women in different groups are documented, particularly Belgium and Belgrade.

The women in one Belgian group, Vrouwen in 'T Zwart, see their sexuality as a basis for understanding the feeling of oppression so consider it as an important part of the politics of their activism. Political analyses that combine gendered analysis of conflict with other intersecting experiences of domination such as homophobia or racism can assist in developing more responsive feminist politics and solidarities. Drucilla Cornell (2004b:111) attests to diversity in identity whereby "[s]traight men, gays, lesbians, and the transgendered are welcomed *as* women" when they engage in the embodied politics of WiB. Although within more developed nation states, membership tends towards educated, wealthier women, the cross-section internationally evidences a broader membership. As a global movement WiB is not entirely reflective of white, western English-speaking feminist mainstream and so has fewer issues of western domination when viewed as a global movement articulating ideals of solidarity.

Diversity within the movement is assisted by its broad mandate for involvement and the flexible interpretation of membership. Some men are included in the public vigils, although this is clearly dependent upon a local and generally collective decision by the women directly involved. Many groups report that some men are involved, either directly participating or as supporters of their actions. One man who responded to the questionnaire said he had stood with the vigil for a number of years but withdrew from direct action when he was asked not to participate in the discussion on an international WiB email list. He resented the rejection from the group and decided that one stream of WiB was characterised by the "same-old (sic) righteous sectarianism" although he did recognise this stemmed from the women's collective desire for a women's only 'safe space'.

This demonstrates both the variation in local interpretation of the modus operandi of the movement and the complexities of projecting these onto a global forum, as well as the continuing inability of some men to grasp the notion of women's separate activism. In the context of embodied protest where men's involvement seems somewhat less problematic, their direct representation as part of a 'women's movement' is indicative of a broadening of feminist principles in which different genders can represent similar political objectives and stand under an explicitly 'womanist' and implicitly 'feminist' banner. Although they began in the Israel/Palestine conflict and initial international momentum was in solidarity with those women, WiB groups have also become active around issues related to other international and local conflicts.

For example WiB have been active in former Yugoslavia and the Balkans, since 1991. They formed in response to the perceived maternalism of the early peace movement in Belgrade, defining themselves as antinationalist, antimilitarist, feminist and pacifist so as not to be associated reductively as protective, peaceful mothers. Some North American groups emerging in the last five years have utilised the momentum of antiwar protesting in the wake of the 'war on terror', combining this platform with local issues and Middle East solidarity. Longer-standing groups, such as those in Italy or France for example, which formed initially in solidarity with the Middle East WiB through the 1990s have continued to expand this support to others including Afghani women and wider campaigns against war, violence and poverty. WiB Sydney has expressed opposition to the war in Iraq, and support for Indigenous Australian, refugee and Palestine/Israel causes.

Cynthia Cockburn provides an interesting profile on a number of groups, also documenting international collaboration and elements that distinguish each group or individuals within the group, to demonstrate unity based on difference and a flexibility of interpretation. One French-language and one Flemish-speaking group comprise Belgium's WiB organisations, with little communication between the two and quite distinct agendas. WiB in India are confronting fundamentalist violence against women, while in Germany neo-Nazism is a concern; an international web of local vigils that are responding to their particular conflicts also extend their scope to other or 'global' conflicts.

Links are made between war and violence against women, comparing experiences between women in different areas. The generalist approach of WiB is based on a core tenet of action against violence which allows for freedom of interpretation while standing to support others, requiring awareness of their struggles. In this way, localisation is able to affect the global recognition and support networks key to progressive feminist solidarity, drawing strength by universal scope without the homogenisation of universality.

COMMUNICATION IS ESSENTIAL

Analysing collaboration and communication between groups spans a number of arenas. Exchange occurs between vigils locally, nationally, and internationally. It can involve the spread of WiB vigils, information, personal and political support, resources and fundraising, standing with other groups and attending conferences. Women were asked about their contact with other WiB groups and their opinion on the role of internationalism in the WiB movement. Of the respondents, Californian resident Adriana became involved with WiB in Serbia and continues to support women's peace activism in the Balkans.

Marlena, from Denmark, similarly met WiB in Serbia. Although she does not identify as pacifist, she sought a method to oppose war without continuing cycles of aggression. Inspired by their protest methods and their "possibilities to reach women in deep crisis", she considers herself a founding member of WiB in her state. Ellen valued the physical exchange of women standing with other vigils whereby "[w]e encounters one another throughout the region in our travels. There are WIB groups in most places where I travel in the southeast USA". Natasha also sought out local WiB groups on her travels within the US, but indicated that language barriers were a potential block to international communication; Adriana, Zehra and Sarah had some contact with geographically close WiB vigils.

Exchanges between groups are part of actualising the 'global' aspect of their networking. Mediation and support have been extended to former Yugoslavian, Israeli and Palestinian WiB, particularly by Spanish, Italian, Belgian and some UK WiB groups. A secondary point of access and communication is via the internet and email, apparent in the considerable web-based presence of WiB by sites, lists and press releases. Although internet access is still limited globally, there is potential for more democratic access and input offered by new technologies and the flow of ideas even from a single point of access to grassroots membership. Mujeres de Negro in Spain was apparently the first to set up an electronic list-serve in Spanish, which was then followed by English lists.

Some of the women respondents primarily communicate with other groups over email and online discussion lists, including Marlena who confirmed that women in Denmark utilise international webs of WiB for discussions and mobilising for demonstrations. Despite the highly localised embodiment of WiB vigils, their networks cross borders, cultures, and languages. They present an embedded practice that utilises the differences between members to engage with a broad spectrum of issues by tapping an undercurrent of solidarity informed by basic common interests of resistance to political violence. This is not a homogenising move assuming a common single cause, but leaves women free to interpret how they will respond.

The international WiB conferences since 1991 demonstrate in a tangible manner the diversity of the movement and exchanges between women. The 2005 conference in Jerusalem brought together women from a vast breadth of cultures and made proceedings accessible to women globally via an online audio-visual feed with linked spaces for comment and interaction. Women often spoke in their own languages so English was not an entirely colonising force for translation at the conference. Speakers referred to other participants as 'sister', a familial, embracing signifier. The potentially narrow scope of affective solidarity is mitigated by the way this very personal term ('my sister'/'our sisters') is subversively extended to include a vast number of women who may never have had contact, or met each other personally.

In this way it concurs with Elam's 'groundless solidarity', extending solidarity because of shared ethics to women who may not be explicitly and intimately known. Signifying other women as 'sister' could possibly escape some of the dilemmas of the notion of 'sisterhood', as the association of these women with this particular organisation suggests a willingness to communicate and self-identify under a broad banner with awareness of differences ("our sisters from Bulgaria"), rather than the assumption captured by unmediated demands of international sisterhood. Involvement in WiB does not assume a single understanding of feminism or preclude wider activity with other political, religious and social groups.

An implicit form of communication is also evident in feelings of support women experience knowing that they are part of a broader movement. Sasha valued the conceptual legitimation conferred by internationalism, believing "even without communication in its usual forms that our efforts are amplified because other like-minded people are also vigilant". In her opinion a "critical mass" effect meant their efforts would be stronger because of an international momentum. In the same vein, while silence may characterise many of the public events, on the whole, this movement is far from uncommunicative.

The use of silence and minimal discussion can be analysed in two different directions. It can be seen as inclusive, not drawing boundaries or limitations, and not excluding others by actively naming and refusing them. It may resist unequal group dynamics or hierarchies because each acts autonomously. There is a concern however, that it may limit political development by not nurturing discussion publicly, or with members who limit involvement to silent vigils.

SOLIDARITY AND THE MODE OF PROTEST

Respondents identified why they became involved with WiB and what they considered its primary ideals. Ellen said she "liked the simplicity. The association without demands of an organization. The public silence. The solidarity". Similarly some identified the simplicity of the mode of protest and the freedom from dictates of a formal organisation and the silence as motivating factors. Others were attracted to the opportunity to be politically expressive in a public forum to raise awareness with other women.

Despite the outward silence of the group it is clear that they are engaged in a program of public awareness and public witness, these ideals likewise confirmed by the women surveyed. Central to each groups' function is to give support and information to other women, and to act as public educators against war. The support role for other groups, and the extension of care to the general public is central to the way in which solidarity is conceived of as extending beyond immediate group boundaries to a sense of universal responsibility so that it is not as limited as in familial and emotionally constructed 'mundane' solidarities.

Clare wrote that she became involved with WiB after September 11, although she has a twenty-five year activist history and recently served a prison sentence for peaceful protest against the US School of America's Military Academy. She says she was drawn to WiB for its simplicity and freedom from the demands of formal organisation that allowed her to express her solidarity publicly and silently. The women involved stand in solidarity explicitly with other WiB activists and with broader women's peace movements in the areas of conflict, and implicitly with the general population.

Although they recognise that they may be unable to change the mindset of someone indoctrinated into militaristic ideologies, appeals may be made to the 'silent majority' or those who may support their peace advocacy but not feel compelled to action. Considering this, the scope of their solidarity is not limited, and supports the Universalist framework of Dean's reflective solidarity which extends the potential for membership and conversation to an unlimited constituency. The minimalist protest format is part of the attraction for many women. However, many WiB groups do more than just public vigiling.

Even within groups that primarily exist for public protesting, there are often internal dynamics of organising, filtering and disseminating information and resources. Some groups, such as the Belgrade WiB which holds NGO status, engage in peace work, performance art and lend assistance to refugee populations, for example. Two symbolically rich aspects of WiB's public protesting are those of celebration, and conversely, mourning. Although a complete analysis of the diversity of methods is beyond the scope of this chapter, it is of interest to note that within the numerous ways in which WiB are active, they are also bound by a common thread, a recognised basic mandate that itself is the clarion call of solidarity that demands we act responsibly towards one another.

One symbolically powerful method of protest adopted by WiB is mourning as a public spectacle. The black robes and silence are part of a performance that they conceive of as grieving for violence 'everywhere'. At first glance this can appear as maternalistic, reinforcing essentialised roles for women built on their passive, protective characterisation, and exclusion from formal political processes. They are however, "visible, unavoidable, inescapably political" in their public protests and a more concentrated analysis throws light on possibilities to disrupt traditional constructs.

By the politicisation of women's roles, spaces and manipulating women's 'traditional' roles in mourning rites as a method of resistance, these women use the symbolic strength of common scripts to enable cross-national readings and adoption of their actions. In the context of conflict when women's traditional obligations are invoked in nationalistic discourse and women's political resistance may thus be limited, making use of 'acceptable' images provides a point of access from which to subvert social orders. WiB do this by accessing a language of grief, that itself crosses many borders, and is traditionally associated with women's roles as mothers or wives, remembering the 'Beautiful Souls' depiction.

The public spectacle of grief and emotion disrupts its association with the arcane private realm. This is made more potent by the extension of mourning for the enemy, recognising the bereavement of the 'other'. In this way the action speaks to not only local and national audiences, but projects acknowledgement and support to people further and unknown; it is not simply an extension of domestic expectations. In these ways it is not only politically potent resistance, which can be less confronting and quite distinct from standard protest mechanisms, but aligns with the persistent aspects of feminist conceptions of solidarity. The public subversion of women's mourning is a refusal to align with notions of a political constituency deemed natural and pre-eminent by the demands of nationalism.

Cynthia Cockburn, who has profiled a number of WiB groups from the dual-positioning of participant and researcher, also supports the assertion that WiB pursues the possibility of ambiguity in political conflicts which would otherwise draw exclusive lines around groups of people and delimit action and resistance (2000). Nationalism, as discussed above, often demands a particular set of loyalties from a population to exclude 'outsiders' and is often, particularly in conflict situations, associated with militaristic nuances. Cockburn (2000) refers to the difficult stance of WiB protests in London around the 1999 conflict in the former Yugoslavia. WiB were shunted into the pro-Serbia camps because they opposed NATO air strikes, yet also opposed the aggressive nationalistic stance of those supporting the Milosevic regime.

The simplistic, rigid dichotomy between those who supported military action from one side or another could not represent the complex perspective of those supporting nonviolent resolution or supporting a people without necessarily pledging allegiance to a regime. Drawing from traditionalist imagery does not necessarily equate to public acceptance. Negative, even violent responses from public audiences are common when the women are perceived as disloyal to the nation. Women in Yugoslavia reported violence from nationalist antagonists, including dirt and stones thrown along with threats of murder. Helman and Rapoport (1997:690-694) canvass numerous instances of verbal abuse towards Israeli WiB, noting that the substance of the invective vehemently combined sexism and nationalism.

Israeli women's protest against the occupation and its violence was perceived socially as tantamount to treason. Although some of the American women surveyed reported favourable, appreciative responses from many people, many had experienced abuse centred on criticisms that equated their antiwar activism with unpatriotic behaviour. Sarah related the negative responses to protesters' perceived "disloyalty" and Natasha commented that her extended family involved in the military had been "indoctrinated into thinking war protestors are anti-American". Nadia also expressed her concern that nationalism has limited possibilities for criticising the validity of military response, as many people are "appalled" by her activism and "see pro-peace as unpatriotic".

In contrast she believes that "pro-peace is the ultimate in patriotism – the people who care enough to be involved in their county's political discourse are the most patriotic". Narissa, Adriana, and Marie received some negative remarks from the public, noting that abuse often came from men; Veronica's group had provoked similar reactions when some "older women have actually stopped to cuss us out and say their son [or] husband is in the military and we are being disrespectful...". Narissa considered these perceptions as a direct "result of nationalism", which Sarah considers a national form of "propaganda" linked to the ways in which "militarism is embedded in the community culture" in the US where military proponents are common in public parks and parades for example.

Through personal experiences and feminist discourses, WiB develop critiques linking militaristic nationalism with violence against women and the discouragement of political dissent and choice. Solidarity is evident in women supporting each other in spite of these reactions and by pressure nationally not to continue. Pressure is applied socially (the angry passer-by, the irate taxi driver) and politically, by governmental condemnation as in the case of WiB Belgrade, or criminalisation as in the US where WiB were reportedly investigated by the FBI as "anti-American" and thus a potential threat to national security.

TENSIONS AND LIMITATIONS

As mentioned throughout the case study, appeals of WiB to notions of international feminist solidarity are not without difficulties and tensions. Helman and Rapoport (1997:689) analysed the minimalism of some women's experiences of communication within the vigils, arguing that the "avoidance of ideological deliberation" throws into question the possibilities for nurturing political debates and democratic development of a more solid organisation. Proclaimed solidarity without communication is inimical to key aspects of feminist solidarity, and it is clear that claims to solidarity are stronger where dialogue is undertaken. Part of a failure to communicate is the failure to self-critique, an essential element of truly reflective solidarity.

Some of the women met with their group only for vigils or did not engage with wider discussions, locally or internationally. It is arguable that the silent, self-contained character of some WiB protest may result in limited political discussion and internal dissent, and may weaken appeals to solidarity. I have, however, previously argued that the women's public silence is only part of their protest method and does not necessarily delimit communicative establishment of their political platforms and wider activities. Zehra grounds her engagement across differences by communication and self-reflection; "first you have to do your own work" where this involved confronting "your own homophobia, your own racism, and you have to be a good listener to bridge that gap" to enable responsible communication.

Helene is similarly conscious of the fact that responsibility to diversity in the movement means recognising "that freedom and feminism... mean very different things in different cultures and to different religions" and the "need to suspend our attachments to how it 'needs to be' and hear each others' stories and needs, and respond to that". It is the occasional conflict within groups that creates part of the necessity for communication, and as I suggested earlier, it is clearly not a homogenous movement. The differences of opinion forwarded in the surveys were generally resolved with "compromise" (Zehra), "consensus" (Sasha) and "creative solutions" (Helene) that sometimes meant accepting differences to "honor each others' needs" (Natasha). I have suggested that the women are actively subverting traditional 'female' tropes, but what of their own conceptions of women's relationship to peace?

Of course, the diversity of experiences and levels of feminist critique within the movement and the highly personalised interpretations of involvement similarly bring a wealth of perspectives about why it is women engaged in the struggle for peace. Some of the women surveyed demonstrated seemingly biologically essentialised understandings of women as the peacemakers, as having "a higher level of consciousness around these issues" (Zehra), or musing on the prospects for peace "if women ran the world" (Narissa) because "the women of the world will work harder to promote peace than men will" (Martha). Natasha refused the image of women as 'soft' but framed women's strength by their relationship with their families and as mothers.

Essentialism is a charge often levelled at women-only organising, and is not entirely fair to apply these concerns to the movement as a whole, when other women presented politically sophisticated, reflective accounts of their activism. Elyse was compelled to work in solidarity with women in Iran given her critique of fundamentalism and the threats to freedom presented by structural violence. For her this involves awareness, information sharing, fundraising and political mobilisation to support women with whom she has developed connections. She is one of many whose activism is not based on a sentimental assumption of sisterhood but the politically aware decision to work with others, across differences.

The Women in Black are accessing symbolic potential for women's collective political mobilisation, as distinct from assumptions of a totalising construct of 'sisterhood' or women's inherent peacefulness. There is however, a continuing difficulty that with the isolation of each group, global connections and other WiB struggles may be ignored. There is a problematic possibility of US WiB becoming more controlling of the movement simply by their access to communications, internet and resources. This can be mitigated by the established global frame of WiB, although comparatively few opportunities exist to redistribute resources internally as the network is generally informal, volunteer-based and not focused on accumulating capital or assets.

The gendered analyses of conflict developed by WiB are simultaneously locally informed and globally connected, reflecting multiple positions on peace and challenging expectations of nationalistic loyalty and the traditional submissiveness of normative gender roles. *Women in Black* is a unique movement built on inclusivity and flexibility within feminist commitments to women's solidarity against war and political violence. They access women's mobilisation by drawing on their collective political aspiration, rather than their essential 'peaceful' nature. Public protest may draw on the symbolic power of women's traditional roles in grieving and caring, yet they subvert the process of mourning by creating public spectacle and in doing so "seek forms of solidarity with the so-called enemy in the name of trying to develop a more sweeping program of anti-militarism".

The lack of specificity in their political mandate may threaten organisational coherence, capacity and longevity, as well as inhibiting development through debate. Minimalist binding principles to end violence against women are, however, broad enough that WiB are able to appeal to a wide audience without victimising a particular population of women. Thus they are capable of offering generalist solidarity in raising public awareness. The freedom to voice local emphases as part of WiB vigils, and the strong support for women's peace actions in the Middle East by the movement internationally see the combining of political objectives. In this way WiB is not exclusive and adopts a flexible notion of women's universal inclusion in the movement where each autonomously brings her own concerns.

As a reflection of progressive feminist solidarity, WiB are self-reflective, communicative and responsive to the 'other', using notions of difference and diversity to create the solidarity of a global movement. They are thus pushing at the boundaries that delimit traditional feminist organisation, helping create the discursive space to support, by their activism, the reconfiguration of feminist 'solidarities in diversity'. Developments in feminist thinking complicate traditional notions of women's solidarity so that it must be reformulated to draw not on the assumed similarity of women under sisterhood, but on an analysis of difference that takes into account the global processes underlying these differences and their inter-connectedness; so that it is self-reflective, communicative and inclusive, and responsible in its commitment to action/mobilisation not simply as a rhetorical stance.

The politics of diversity as they are reflected by women's antiwar movements show that solidarity is critical for effective globally-framed activism and can counter the maternalistic essentialism of past (dominant western) feminist antimilitarism and criticisms of western bias, possibly bridging some of the divides between feminisms emerging from Third World feminists. This is not to assume that all women's movements are reconcilable or peaceful, but to offer a response to the totalising intransigence of past criticisms that have either assumed or denied cooperation by homogenising women's identities and political aspirations or asserting their incompatibility across difference. Many women share antiwar discourses and dialogues based on very different experiences of conflict, and the transnational character of this confounds their isolation within nationalistic political climates.

Evidence of self-reflective solidarities is emerging in some contemporary feminist antiwar activism, but is especially urgent since September 11 and the 'war on terror' given the cross-cultural aspects of the conflict and the unambiguous drawing of boundaries by political leaders which would make such communicative gestures suspect, labelling dissent and solidarity dangerously unpatriotic. Antiwar activism that complicates the 'us'/'them' divide is arguably an extension of traditional feminist concerns to continue challenging oppressive hierarchies and divisions.

Sentimental invocation of women's peaceful sisterhood is unable to convey women's varied analyses of war and peace; such a limited dialectic cannot represent the complex meshwork of women's antiwar dialogues. Women in Black are actively working to enable the consolidation of emerging feminist theories of solidarity by embodiment in women's very physical political resistance. I have deconstructed the common themes of these emerging theories and scrutinised them by reference to WiB's mandate and activities to argue that they are working to create solidarity in diversity through communication networks, reflectiveness and the grounding of their global movement each by their localised interpretation.

Through a flexible set of core ideals they resist the hegemonic dictation of the few, allowing for inclusivity that refuses to designate women across national or cultural borders as the 'enemy' or the 'other'. Although tensions remain, and the informal structure of the movement may yet undermine its longevity, these women are proving that solidarity in resistance to war is possible. Women involved describe the cumulative strength of the movement, in the knowledge that others globally stand 'with' them in witness, in resistance to militaristic national discourses that would deny these connections and the potency of their solidarity through difference.

3

Zimbabwean Nationalism and Feminism

Feminist thinkers often draw inspiration from the history of women's leadership roles in African societies, citing examples of women who ruled kingdoms and led wars of conquest since the earliest epochs of human civilization. Most often cited are the seventh-century Berber queen known as the Kahina of the Maghreb, the ninth-century Magajiyas of Daura, the legendary sixteenth-century Queen Amina of Zazzau, the nineteenth-century Nzinga of Angola, and Nehanda of Zimbabwe. These examples illustrate that African women leaders exercised their authority—often in the distinctly feminine styles of their times—in a manner that spanned spiritual, political, and military realms, and that has served to inspire feminist ideas all over the world. The cultural complexity and dynamism of a region in which so many cultures coexisted and interacted with one another throughout the ages has given rise to quite disparate, at times idiosyncratic, gender relations and philosophies.

There is little commonality between the complex and contradictory gender cultures expressed in Yoruba, Somali, Hausa, or Egyptian oral poetry, yet all of them are African, and all are rooted in conditions and contexts that are African in the sense of having been generated and inspired on the continent. Women's movements on the African continent reflect the gendered cultural, social, and political organization of the numerous African societies in which they are located. There is enough evidence to suggest that African history is replete with diverse examples of mobilization against women's oppression, even though these have often been omitted by historians (Zeleza). Many of these at times phenomenal movements defy a simple definition of feminism. The available evidence suggests that women's movements in Africa reflect the traditions of organization that have characterized spiritual and material life in Africa as far back as recorded history goes.

Few would seriously challenge the idea that gender differentiation has been a key feature of social, cultural, and political life all over the continent as far back as records can be found. Accordingly, African women have long been organized around lineage and kinship groupings, and around women's religious, cultural, and political duties and their productive and reproductive roles. The record also shows that these existing organizations were sporadically activated to defend women's interests. Kenyan women were organized in *mumikanda* (work parties) and in various social and welfare groups—*ngwatio* among the Kikuyu-speaking communities, and *mwethya* among the Kamba-speaking communities.

In Nigeria, Igbo women were organized as in various patrilineage wives and daughters associations, and governed through women's councils. Such networks of women collectively imposed sanctions on husbands who erred (the practice of "sitting on a man"), and proved capable of instigating widespread civil disturbances when they found their interests being compromised. The early-twentieth-century example of the Nwabiola Dancing Women's Movement in colonial Igboland (Eastern Nigeria) illustrates the manner in which apparently conservative organizational forms could become militantly active when women saw their interests being threatened (Mba). All across West Africa business has long been conducted through market women's associations and trading networks that were periodically activated in defense of women's economic interests, and at times their political interests.

As colonialism gained ground, some of the earlier women's associations and groups were redirected by missionary groups and colonial governments, often through volunteers with a degree of Western education. These modern "women's clubs" were often designed to "civilize" and "uplift" African women, usually by instilling western European ideologies of domesticity and offering training in related skills (Tranberg Hansen). Domestication notwithstanding, it is clear that African women exercised enough agency to deploy whatever skills they acquired in innovative ways that empowered them and laid the ground for future involvement in national public life.

Examples of women's groups coming together as larger bodies include the Mother's Union and the Catholic Women's Clubs of Uganda, the Federation of Nigerian Women's Societies, the National Council of Women of Kenya, and the Association of Women's Clubs in Zimbabwe. When nationalist movements gained momentum, seemingly conventional women's groups and associations—charitable and welfare groups, mother's groups, and market women's associations—often directed their energies in support of nationalist goals. The Convention People's Party led by Kwame Nkrumah was among those nationalist movements that benefited substantially from the support of women—in this case the market women of Ghana.

Many of the women who later became leading educators, activists, and politicians were initially involved in the women's clubs of the colonial era, among them Margaret Ekpo of Nigeria, Agatha Constance Cummings-John of Sierra Leone, Mable Dove-Danquah of Ghana, and Gertrude Kabwasingo of Uganda. The more radical among these women—most of whom were elite and educated women—mobilized across the class lines too, as Funmilayo Ransome-Kuti did with such success. Ransome-Kuti was a key player in the Abeokuta Women's Union, which mobilized to oust an oppressive *alake* (chief) in 1948.

In the ensuing decades she became a leading national political figure identified with nationalist, socialist, and feminist causes (Johnson-Odim and Mba). Ransome-Kuti's life is illustrative of African women's vibrant and militant history of resistance to colonial rule and imperialism and highlights the key roles that women activists played in nationalist movements all over the region, long before the second wave of feminism emerged in the Western world. Well-documented examples of more overtly political women's movements include those of Egypt, Nigeria, Ghana, Kenya, Uganda, Algeria, Mozambique, and the anti-apartheid movement of South Africa.

Some were chapters for women in the existing nationalist structures (for example, SWAPO Women's League, ZANU Women's League) or women's battalions in the nationalist militia (for example, the Algerian women in the FLN, the Frelimo Women's Brigade convened by Josina Machel, the short-lived women's detachment in the National Resistance Movement [NRM], or the women fighters said to make up 30 percent of the Eritrean People's Liberation Front). Other political women's organizations derived from party organs but broke away out of frustration, at times to pursue feminist agendas more overtly, as was the case with the Egyptian Feminist Union that broke away from the Egyptian Wafdist Party under the leadership of Huda Sharaawi. In an unspecifiable number of cases, women established new kinds of organizations with varying degrees of autonomy.

The crisis of the state and governance in Zimbabwe has divided Zimbabweans, the country's southern African neighbours and the international community. Given Africa's big challenges - HIV/AIDS, trade, debt, food shortages, environmental crises and unending civil wars ravaging failed states - it is striking that such significant symbolic political investment has been made in the fate of a small country (12 million people) with a rapidly declining economy no particular strategic significance. There is no doubt that the Zimbabwean situation is serious, or that President Robert Mugabe bears responsibility for the deep political crisis pervading the country, state-sanctioned repression and the mismanagement of the economy.

The standard of living in Zimbabwe is worse today than it was in 1980. Some 65% of Zimbabweans are living either in poverty or extreme poverty. By July 2003, Zimbabwe had a currency shortage and an inflation rate of 450%. Its citizens face long queues for everything from bread to petrol. An agriculturally productive country has been reduced to seeking food aid. Further, Zimbabwe has one of the highest rates of HIV/AIDS infection on the continent, giving rise to a staggering 2 000 deaths per week. The pandemic has devastated Zimbabwe's social fabric and its productive and reproductive capacities, a tragic reality that has been aggravated by the sexist and homophobic public policies and practices of the Mugabe regime. From international conference halls to grassroots organisations and trade unions, opposing views on Zimbabwe and the source of its troubles have split the continent.

These divisions might suggest that the main protagonists are destined to re-enact some version of the pre-independence drama in which indigenous people were locked in an anti-colonial struggle against Western imperial powers, but we would do well to reject this formulation and recall Marx's caution: history repeats itself - however, the second time is invariably as farce. At the heart of the matter lies the phenomenon that Frantz Fanon pointed to: venal elite that does the "comprador" bidding of the neo-colonial power centers, while using the politics of patronage, the rhetoric of an imagined nation, the tools of repression available in the security apparatus, and the ideological machinery of a ruling party to intimidate the masses. Horace Campbell's Reclaiming Zimbabwe: The Exhaustion of the Patriarchal Model of National Liberation advances this thesis, in one of the most courageous and comprehensive critiques I have seen of Robert Mugabe and his distorted tradition. Furthermore, Campbell attempts to provide a feminist critique of Mugabe's macho militarism.

In Reclaiming Zimbabwe, Campbell makes it quite clear why reasonable people will avoid the simplistic labels invoked by Mugabe and his supporters; labels that wrap Mugabe in the mantle of a "liberationist", while dubbing those who criticise his regime as "imperialists" or "imperialist collaborators". While it may be tempting to fall back on this easy rhetoric, it does not begin to capture the nuances of the crisis in Zimbabwe. Mugabe's past involvement in the liberation struggle does not legitimate the present state-sanctioned violence against political opponents. Campbell explains why we should look elsewhere, including to the authoritarian impulse of the early liberation movement itself, to explain the crisis of governance and to envision an alternative to the current political disorder in Zimbabwe. The "liberationists versus imperialists" simplification occludes the profound regional and continental implications of the Zimbabwe crisis at an historic juncture when continental leaders are building a new global solidarity and partnership for Africa's development.

South Africa, Nigeria and Algeria have promoted the idea of an African "peer review mechanism" that would affirm the continent's commitment to good governance. Donor countries and international critics have insisted that Zimbabwe is a litmus test of this commitment. Campbell is skeptical of any solution short of Mugabe stepping down, given that the latter's tendency to dismiss or violently repress critics reflects his lack of respect for human life and dignity. Campbell's book is based on over two decades of engaging Zimbabwe's politics, in no small part because as a (Jamaican-born) pan-Africanist, he was once part of Harare's insider intelligentsia.

In an easy-to-read style, the book maps the history of the Zimbabwean state from the liberation struggles to the 2002 presidential elections and beyond. He reminds us of the euphoria that accompanied the successful liberation struggle in Zimbabwe. This optimism resonated across the continent and was reflected in songs such as Bob Marley's "Africans a-liberate Zimbabwe". But this euphoria soon dissipated in face of the challenges of rebuilding an equitable society. One stumbling block was the government's failure to redress the injustices of land distribution and the persistence of a colonial racialised class structure. Consequently, "at the dawn of colonialism those who had seized the most fertile land became the bourgeois land owners", while the vast majority of Zimbabweans had to survive on subsistence wages.

Notwithstanding this background, Campbell rejects the regime's rationalisations for the war veterans' land grab. He argues that it is nonsensical for liberationists to redress the land injustice "by unleashing new injustices". Another reason for the decline in optimism concerning democracy concerns the manifold failures of leadership. Campbell sees "President

Mugabe [as] an excellent example of a leader who has devalued a just cause and the need to repair the injustices associated with the settler seizure of land during colonialism". He argues that Zimbabwe's leaders adopted the repressive apparatuses and practices of the colonial state, as well as creating new intolerances. A concrete lesson that Campbell draws from the Zimbabwean experience is that it is "not enough to Africanize the structures of domination" – in other words, to simply change the cast of characters in leadership structures.

Instead, Campbell maintains, there must be a fundamental opposition to the "excesses of executive lawlessness, homophobia, military adventure … and the concepts of peace that reinforce militarism". The Mugabe regime learned to promote the trappings of electoral or procedural democracy even as it undermined the more substantive aspects of democracy – respect for the rule of law, promotion and protection of human rights, freedom of association, freedom of speech and the like. Campbell suggests that the patriarchal model of liberation in Zimbabwe has reached its apex. Patriarchy is a system of social structures and everyday practices that enables male domination and the subordination and exploitation of women. Campbell draws our attention to "the militaristic conception of liberation and the gender prejudices" held by early liberation leaders, how this was incorporated into the modern African state, and the ways in which African patriarchs "energised a national opposition movement that brought out male violence and greed … hiding behind the masks of economic nationalism".

It is worth noting that Zimbabwe's political and military liberation leaders are presently involved in regional destabilisation and war profiteering. While invoking the principle of state sovereignty to reject international intervention in its own affairs, Zimbabwe has sent its army to intervene militarily in the Democratic Republic of the Congo. Through direct ownership and investments in banking, mining and diamond companies, both Zimbabwe's Defense Forces and ZANU-PF are engaged in extracting resources from the DRC and in accumulating wealth for personal benefit, while ordinary Zimbabweans and Congolese suffer. In light of this kind of masculinist exploitation, Mugabe's liberation credentials of two decades ago offer cold comfort. Given that these patriarchal values characterised the Zimbabwe liberation movement from its inception, appeals to this same liberatory tradition as a means of resolving the current crisis of the state are misguided.

Instead, Campbell offers a critical meditation on how ordinary Zimbabweans and their allies can build "new indices of democratic politics", "reclaim Zimbabwe" and bring about a more inclusive social order. The book looks beyond specific individuals, and the tired leadership of Mugabe, to envisage alternatives to "the masculinist basis of state power that has been inherited from colonialism." Here Campbell turns to movements such as the women's movement in Zimbabwe, asking what practices these can offer as an alternative to the patriarchal model of liberation. As Campbell rightly observes, the trajectory and terrain of women's organising in Zimbabwe is rich and deep. Women's participation in the nationalist struggle for independence served to provide the impetus for post-independence demands that sought gender equity and disrupted pre-existing gender relations and cultural norms.

These demands were responsible for the most tangible gains for women in the first few years of independence, particularly in the form of legislative change. The most significant of these reforms was the passing of the 1982 Legal Age of Majority Act (LAMA), which saw women being granted majority status at the age of 18, paving the way for their further political and economic empowerment. Campbell's analysis however suggests that after a brief spell of lip-service to gender equality, patriarchy reconfigured itself in the post-independence context, and the political will to meaningfully address gender inequality in Zimbabwe diminished rapidly, being replaced instead by the age-old desire to regulate and control women in both the private and public sphere.

Women's political engagement in the new state was systematically eroded not only by the espousal of the development discourse (which often blunted the radical edge of the women's movement), but also through the very sophisticated and powerful invocation of counter-revolutionary nationalist and cultural discourses that tended to interpolate any women's organising as feminist – and feminism as being anti-nationalist pro-imperialism. I would argue that Campbell sometimes glosses over the subtlety and power of the latter narratives. Although Operation Clean Up was perhaps the most blatant example of this discursive move, it was by no means the only one. Further examples include the repeated attempts to repeal LAMA, and the denial of property and inheritance rights to women under customary law.

Yet another example involved the public stripping of women who wore mini-skirts. All these manoeuvres were met by concerted and direct action from women activists, but as Zimbabwe plunged into socio-economic and political upheaval in the late 1990s, the conditions under which women were organising had become increasingly challenging. By this time, the state's unvarnished hostility to gendered discourses meant that women activists became the target of state-sponsored violence. Meanwhile, what feminist analysts refer to as "the deeply uncivil nature of civil society" with regards to gender meant that alliances across sites of struggle in order to further women's rights-based agendas were tenuous, and had to be carefully negotiated. Campbell misses this reading. All the same, in mining social justice movements and the women's movement in this way, he attempts to envision a more radical democratic order shaped by social movements that reject intimidation, violence and the climate of fear that permeates Zimbabwe's body politic at present.

This takes us beyond the simplistic notion that Mugabe and his supporters are struggling against Western imperialists, a false polarisation that detracts from the harsh realities of everyday life in Zimbabwe. Ultimately, Campbell's book is a reflection on the resilience of the people of Zimbabwe (especially its women), and the peace and social justice movements that continue to struggle for an alternative order characterised by social inclusion: "African women, especially those connected to the various organised movements for democracy and women's rights, have emerged as the force with the strongest claim for a new liberation process in Zimbabwe". In his conclusion, Campbell recalls Walter Rodney's assertion that we need to "have confidence in the capacity of our people; if they could have breached the gates of colonialism through their own effort, then it seems to me that they have brought into the neo-colonial period a capacity to breach the walls of imperialism". To this, one must add, the capacity to resist new forms of domination and exploitation.

It is hard to think of a figure more reviled in the West than Robert Mugabe. Liberal and conservative commentators alike portray him as a brutal dictator, and blame him for Zimbabwe's descent into hyperinflation and poverty. The seizure of white-owned farms by his black supporters has been depicted as a form of thuggery, and as a cause of the country's declining production, as if these lands were doomed by black ownership. Sanctions have been imposed, and opposition groups funded with the explicit aim of unseating him. There is no denying Mugabe's authoritarianism, or his willingness to tolerate and even encourage the violent behaviour of his supporters. His policies have helped lay waste the country's economy, though sanctions have played no small part, while his refusal to share power with the country's growing opposition movement, much of it based in the trade unions, has led to a bitter impasse.

This view of Zimbabwe's crisis can be found everywhere, from the *Economist* and the *Financial Times* to the *Guardian* and the *New Statesman,* but it gives us little sense of how Mugabe has managed to survive. For he has ruled not only by coercion but by consent, and his land reform measures, however harsh, have won him considerable popularity, not just in Zimbabwe but throughout southern Africa. In any case, the preoccupation with his character does little to illuminate the socio-historical issues involved. Many have compared Mugabe to Idi Amin and the land expropriation in Zimbabwe to the Asian expulsion in Uganda. The comparison isn't entirely off the mark. I was one of the 70,000 people of South Asian descent booted out by Idi Amin in 1972; I returned to Uganda in 1979. My abiding recollection of my first few months back is that no one I met opposed Amin's expulsion of 'Asians'. Most merely said: 'It was bad the way he did it.' The same is likely to be said of the land transfers in Zimbabwe.

What distinguishes Mugabe and Amin from other authoritarian rulers is not their demagoguery but the fact that they projected themselves as champions of mass justice and successfully rallied those to whom justice had been denied by the colonial system. Not surprisingly, the justice dispensed by these demagogues mirrored the racialised injustice of the colonial system. In 1979 I began to realise that whatever they made of Amin's brutality, the Ugandan people experienced the Asian expulsion of 1972 - and not the formal handover in 1962 - as the dawn of true independence. The people of Zimbabwe are likely to remember 2000-3 as the end of the settler colonial era. Any assessment of contemporary Zimbabwe needs to begin with this sobering fact. Though widespread grievance over the theft of land - a process begun in 1889 and completed in the 1950s - fuelled the guerrilla struggle against the regime of Ian Smith, whose Rhodesian Front opposed black majority rule, the matter was never properly addressed when Britain came back into the picture to effect a constitutional transition to independence under majority rule.

Southern Rhodesia became Zimbabwe in 1980, but the social realities of the newly independent state remained embedded in an earlier historical period: some six thousand white farmers owned 15.5 million hectares of prime land, 39 per cent of the land in the country, while about 4.5 million farmers (a million households) in 'communal areas' were left to subsist on 16.4 million hectares of the most arid land, to which they'd been removed or confined by a century of colonial rule. In the middle were 8500 small-scale black farmers on about 1.4 million hectares of land. This was not a sustainable arrangement in a country whose independence had been secured at the end of a long armed struggle supported by a land-hungry population. But the agreement that Britain drafted at Lancaster House in 1979 - and that the settlers eagerly backed - didn't seem to take into account the kind of transition that would be necessary to secure a stable social order.

Two of its provisions, one economic and the other political, reflected this short-termism: one called for land transfers on a 'willing buyer, willing seller' basis, with the British funding the scheme; the other reserved 20 per cent of seats in the House of Assembly for whites - 3 per cent of the population - giving the settler community an effective veto over any amendment to the Lancaster House terms. This was qualified majority rule at best. Both provisions had a time limit: 1990 for land transfers based on the market principle, and 1987 for the settler minority to set limits on majority rule. The deal sustained illusions among the settlers that what they had failed to achieve by UDI - Smith's 1965 declaration of independence from the UK - and force of arms, they could now achieve through support from a government of 'kith and kin' (as Smith called it) in Britain. In reality, however, the agreement drew a line under settler privilege.

The inadequacy of the Lancaster House provisions for the decolonisation of land ensured that it remained the focus of politics in independent Zimbabwe. The course of land relations and land reform in Zimbabwe has over the years been meticulously documented by Sam Moyo, a professor who directs the African Institute of Agrarian Studies in Harare. Transfers during the first decade of independence were so minimal that they increased rather than appeased land hunger. The new regime in Harare, installed in 1980 and led by Mugabe and his party, Zanu, called for the purchase of eight million hectares to resettle 162,000 land-poor farming households from communal areas. But the ban on compulsory purchase drove up land prices and encouraged white farmers to sell only the worst land. As the decade drew to a close, only 58,000 families had been resettled on three million hectares of land. No more than 19 per cent of the land acquired between 1980 and 1992 was of prime agricultural value.

As the 1980s wore on, land transfers actually declined, dropping from 430,000 hectares per annum during the first half of the decade to 75,000 hectares during the second. The greater land hunger became, the more often invasions were mounted; in response, Mugabe created local 'squatter control' units in

1985, and they were soon evicting squatters in droves. At this point Zimbabwean law still defined a squatter in racial terms, as 'an African whose house happens to be situated in an area which has been declared European or is set apart for some other reason'. By 1990, 40 per cent of the rural population was said to be landless or affected by the landlessness of dependent relations. When the Lancaster House Agreement's rules on land transfer expired in 1990, the pressure to take direct action was intensified by two very different developments: an IMF Structural Adjustment Programme and recurrent drought. Peasant production, which had been a meagre 8 per cent of marketed output at independence in 1980, and had shot up to 45 per cent by 1985, declined as a result of the programme.

Trade-union analysts pointed out that employment growth also fell from 2.4 per cent in the late 1980s to 1.55 per cent in the period 1991-97. The percentage of households living in poverty throughout the country increased by 14 per cent in five years. There was now widespread squatting on all types of land, from communal areas to state land, commercial farms (mainly growing tobacco), resettlement areas and urban sites. The demand for land reform came from two powerful groups at extreme ends of the social spectrum yet both firmly in Mugabe's camp: the veterans of the liberation war and the small but growing number of indigenous businesses, hitherto the main beneficiaries of independence under majority rule. At the end of the liberation war in 1980, 20,000 guerrillas had been incorporated into the national army and other state organisations, and the rest - about 45,000 - had had to fend for them.

They found it difficult to survive without land or a job, which is why land occupations began in the countryside soon after independence. Mugabe and the Zanu leaders tended at first to dismiss complaints from veterans as expressions of resentment on the part of the rival liberation movement, Joshua Nkomo's Zapu, which had been marginalised in 1980. But after Zanu and Zapu signed a unity accord in 1987, former fighters from both groups became involved in land agitation. Their most significant joint initiative was to form a welfare organisation, the Zimbabwe National Liberation War Veterans Association

(ZNLWVA) in 1988, which called for pensions to be paid and land redistributed.

It soon gained a large membership drawn from most sections of Zimbabwean society and from the two ethnic groups - the Shona majority and the Ndebele - which had defined Zanu and Zapu respectively. Its members, about 200,000 of them, came from a variety of classes, employed and unemployed, urban and rural, with positions in different branches of the state and party and the private sector. Although their strength lay in the countryside, the war vets formed the only alliance that was both independent of Mugabe and Zanu-PF, and could claim to have national support, giving them a decisive advantage over the better organised but urban-based trade-union federation in the power struggle that would shortly tear the country apart. War vets were among the first targets of Structural Adjustment, when its effects began to be felt in 1991.

Entire departments and ministries that had been heavily staffed by ex-combatants were disbanded and the stage set for a series of high-profile confrontations between veterans and government. Mugabe accused the vets of being 'armchair critics' at the inaugural conference of the ZNLWVA in April 1992; they went on to organise street demonstrations, lock top government and party officials in their offices, interrupt Mugabe's Heroes' Day speech in 1997, intervene in court sessions and besiege the State House. After the Lancaster House Agreement had expired, the government tried to occupy the middle ground by shifting from the 'willing buyer, willing seller' formula with a new law, the Land Acquisition Act of 1992, which gave the state powers of compulsory purchase, though landowners retained the right to challenge the price set and to receive prompt compensation. By the late 1990s, market-led land transfers had dwindled to a trickle.

So had British contributions to the fund set up to pay landowners, with a mere £44 million paid out between 1980 and 1992, much less than anticipated at Lancaster House? When New Labour took over in 1997, Clare Short, the minister for international development, claimed that since neither she nor her colleagues came from the landed class in Britain - 'my own origins are Irish and as you know we were colonised not colonizers,' she wrote to the Zimbabwean minister of agriculture and land - they could not be held responsible for what Britain had done in colonial Rhodesia. This effective default coincided with a rise inside Zimbabwe of demands for compulsory acquisition. Veterans led land occupations at Svosve and Goromonzi in 1997, clashing with Mugabe and Zanu-PF.

They were joined by local chiefs and party leaders, peasants and spirit mediums (who had played a key role in the liberation war against Ian Smith). The next year, a wave of co-ordinated land occupations swept across the country, with veterans receiving critical support from the Indigenous Business Development Centre (IBDC), an affirmative action lobby set up in 1988 by members of the new black bourgeoisie. From now on, two very different elements huddled under the war vets' banner: the landless victims of settler colonialism and the elite beneficiaries of the end of settler rule. It was largely for his own purposes, but also as a response to pressure from squatters, occupiers and their local leaders, as well as from sections of the new black elite, that in 1999 Mugabe decided to revise the constitution drafted at Lancaster House.

Two major changes were envisaged: one would allow him to stay in power for two more terms and would ensure immunity from prosecution for political and military leaders accused of committing crimes while in office; the other would empower the government to seize land from white farmers without compensation, which was held to be the responsibility of Britain. The proposals were put to a referendum in February 2000 and defeated: 45.3 per cent of voters were in favour. But only a little more than 20 per cent of the electorate had cast a vote. The urban centers of Harare and Bulawayo were three to one against adoption; voting in the countryside was marked by large-scale abstentions. Post-colonial Zimbabwe had reached a turning point. Very early on, the colonial bureaucracy had translated the ethnic mosaic of the country into an administrative map in such a way as to allow minimum co-operation and maximum competition between different ethnic groups and areas, ensuring among other things that labour for mining, manufacture and service was not recruited from areas where peasants were needed on large farms or plantations.

These areas, as it happened, were mainly Shona and so, unsurprisingly, when the trade-union movement developed in Rhodesia, its leaders were mostly Ndebele, and had few links with the Shona leadership of the peasant-based liberation movement (Mugabe belongs to the Shona majority). I remember listening to the minister of labour in Harare in 1981 complain that workers had failed to support the nationalist movement. When I suggested that it might be useful to turn the proposition around and ask why the nationalist movement had failed to organise support among workers, there was silence. The Shona-Ndebele divide so conspicuous in the two guerrilla movements produced great tension after independence between the mainly Shona government and the mainly Ndebele labour movement, with Mugabe's ferocious repression in Ndebele areas in 1986 remaining the bloodiest phase in post-independence Zimbabwean history.

The slaughter in Matabeleland was followed by a 'reconciliation' that paved the way for a unity government in 1987, but Zanu-PF leaders thereafter suspected all protest - from whatever source - of concealing an Ndebele agenda. The Zimbabwe Congress of Trade Unions, formed in 1981 with the blessing of the government, had by the end of the decade distanced itself from its Zanu patrons, purged internal corruption and elected an independent leadership. In the 1990s it spearheaded the national agitation against Structural Adjustment and the one-party state that acquiesced in it. Yet its organisation in the countryside was confined to workers on commercial farms. The ZCTU had at first been an umbrella body for private sector unions. The spectacular growth of ZCTU, its organisation of public sector workers, has been written about by two Zimbabwean social historians, Brian Raftapolous and Ian Phimister.

After independence, workers in the rapidly Africanised public sector had retained close links to the government. But this began to change when the Structural Adjustment Programme led to public sector job losses and many African workers - especially veterans - were dismissed. When government workers came out on strike in 1996, the ZCTU was able to establish a base in the public sector. A general strike in 1997 and mass stay-aways the following year set the trade unions against the government. Civil servants - including teachers and health workers - who had declared allegiance to the ruling party and the state now began to affiliate to the ZCTU. In 1998, it organised a National Constituent Assembly, with the participation of civic, NGO and church groups. By the time Mugabe put forward amendments to the Lancaster House constitution, an impressive alliance of forces - not only trade unions, churches, civic and NGO groups, but white farmers and Western governments - was arrayed for battle. The Movement for Democratic Change was formed a few months before the 2000 referendum, to campaign for a 'no' vote.

The coalition was diverse, containing, on the one hand, public sector workers trying to roll back the tide of Structural Adjustment; on the other, uncompromising free-marketeers such as Eddie Cross, the MDC secretary of economic affairs and a senior figure in the Confederation of Zimbabwe Industries, who was intent on privatising almost everything, including education. The veterans reacted to the defeat of the constitutional proposals by launching land occupations in Masvingo province. This prompted a split in the ruling party. With Mugabe out of the country, the acting president, Joseph Msika, told the police to torch the new squatter shacks. This was consistent with Zanu-PF policy: in the early days, Mugabe had been praised as a 'conciliator' by the international community for ensuring the security and property of those whites who remained in Zimbabwe, and evicting black squatters.

Two decades later the position had changed: the support of the whites was no longer so important to Mugabe, and he was under enormous pressure from the veterans. With much to gain from casting his lot in with the rural insurgency, he returned from his trip and announced that there would be no government evictions. As land occupations spread to every province - 800 farms were occupied at the height of the protests - the split in the government and party hierarchy deepened. Inevitable tension between the executive and the judiciary undermined the rule of law; the executive sacked a number of judges, replacing them with others more sympathetic to land reform, and enacted pro-squatter legislation.

'Fast-track' land reform was now underway. The types of land that would be acquired compulsorily were specified by the government: unused or underutilised land, land owned by absentees or people with several farms; land above a certain area (determined by region) and land contiguous with communal areas. The white owners of around 2900 commercial farms listed for compulsory acquisition and redistribution were given 90 days to move out. Government directives specified that 'owners of farms marked for redistribution will be compensated for improvements made on the land, but not for the land itself, as this land was stolen from the original owners in the colonial era.' The closing date for 'fast-track' land acquisition - August 2002 - came and went, but occupations continued unimpeded until mid-2003, and on a diminished scale for a year or so after that. Chiefs fought for land for their constituents and for themselves, and so did their counterparts in the state bureaucracy and the private sector. In Matabeleland, a minority of pro-MDC chiefs were sceptical of land reform, but later submitted claims.

The black elite made a brazen land grab in direct contravention of the 'one person, one farm' policy, provoking a hue and cry in society at large and within the ruling party; the government set up a presidential commission to determine the facts. Crucially, in 2005 the government passed an amendment declaring all agricultural land to be state land. Land was seized from nearly 4000 white farmers and redistributed: 72,000 large farmers received 2.19 million hectares and 127,000 smallholders received 4.23 million hectares. What land reform has meant or may come to mean for Zimbabwe's economy is still hotly disputed. Recently there have been signs that scholarly opinion is shifting. A study by Ian Scoones of Sussex University's

Institute of Development Studies - in collaboration with the Programme for Land and Agrarian Studies (PLAAS) at the University of the Western Cape - challenges some of the conventional wisdom in media and academic circles within and beyond Zimbabwe.

The problem with this wisdom is that certain highly destructive aspects of reform - coercion; corruption and incompetence; cronyism in the redistribution of land; lack of funds and an absence of agricultural activity - have come to stand for the whole process. In particular, Scoones identifies five myths: that land reform has been a total failure; that its beneficiaries have been largely political cronies; that there is no new investment in the new settlements; that agriculture is in ruins; and that the rural economy has collapsed. Researchers at PLAAS have been quick to point out that over the past eight years small-scale farmers 'have been particularly robust in weathering Zimbabwe's political and economic turmoil, as well as drought'. Ben Cousins, the director of PLAAS and one of the most astute South African analysts of agrarian change - who had previously argued that the land reform would destroy agricultural production - now says that the future of Zimbabwe lies in providing small farmers with subsidies so that food security can be achieved.

According to researchers at the African Institute for Agrarian Studies in Harare, new farms need to receive subsidised maize seed and fertiliser for a few seasons before achieving full production. Some might give up during this period, but not many - partly because the land tenure system doesn't allow land sales; only land permits or leases can be acquired. Zimbabwe has seen the greatest transfer of property in southern Africa since colonisation and it has all happened extremely rapidly. Eighty per cent of the 4000 white farmers were expropriated; most of them stayed in Zimbabwe. Redistribution revolutionised property-holding, adding more than a hundred thousand small owners to the base of the property pyramid. In social and economic - if not political - terms, this was a democratic revolution. But there was a heavy price to pay.

The first casualty was the rule of law, already tenuous by 1986. When international donors pressured the regime in the run-up to the parliamentary elections of 2000 by suspending aid and loans - a boycott favoured by the MDC and the unions - the government simply fixed the result in its favour. In the violence that followed, more than a hundred people died, including six white farmers and 11 black farm labourers. Some of the violence was government-sponsored and most of it state-sanctioned. The judiciary was reshaped, local institutions in rural areas narrowly politicised, and laws were passed which granted local agencies the powers necessary to crush opponents of land reform. Denouncing his adversaries in the trade unions and NGOs as servants of the old white ruling class, Mugabe authorised the militias and state security agencies to hound down opposition, as repression and reform went hand in hand. In 2003, the leading independent newspaper, the *Daily News*, was shut down.

While jubilant government supporters applauded the sweep of the revolution in agrarian areas, the opposition denounced the repression that accompanied it. Land reform had been ruthless, but in 2004, the violence began to abate. There was noticeably less violence surrounding the parlia-mentary elections of 2005. In retrospect, it is striking how little turmoil accompanied this massive social change. The expla-nation lies in the participation of key rural figures in ad hoc but officially sanctioned land committees. When first introduced in 1996, these committees had mixed fortunes, some not functioning at all, others becoming instruments of this or that group of squatters. But a radical change occurred in 2000, when the committees were expanded to include centrally appointed security officials, ruling party representatives and local govern-ment personnel, as well as local veterans and traditional leaders. Charged with implementing fast-track land reform, these committees sidelined the old local administrative structures.

They also had a national impact, since they reported to similarly constituted provincial committees, which in turn reported to the Ministry of Local Government. It was the infusion of veterans that gave the new semi-bureaucratic committees the edge over their wholly bureaucratic counterparts. Local committees usually comprised between 15 and 30 members. The veterans formed 'base camps' represented by 'committees of seven' which took the lead in identifying land for acquisition as well as finding prospective beneficiaries (mostly from veterans' waiting lists and rosters in former 'communal areas'). They also judged disputes, punished petty criminals and allocated farm equipment, seeds and so on and in a word, the committees co-ordinated everything, thus constituting new centers of power.

The second casualty of the reform was farm labourers. There were about 300,000 in all, around half of them part-time. Fast-track reform resulted in a massive displacement of these workers, who were traditionally drawn from migrant labour. Nearly a fifth came from neighbouring states and were regarded with suspicion by peasants in communal areas; even if they'd been born locally, they were often seen as foreigners and denied citizenship rights. Migrants and women (many employed as casual labour) were the weakest links in the rural mobilisation for land reform. Many were thought to have been encouraged by landowners to vote against the government's constitutional proposals, and the anti-land-reform lobby certainly tried to organise farm workers, ostensibly to protect their jobs, but really to protect the white ownership of farms.

When the workers rallied by the MDC, civil society activists and white farmers clashed with veteran-led occupiers, they came off badly. Occupiers held meetings to explain to workers what was at stake and eventually came themselves to distinguish between white farms, not only on the basis of size, proximity to communal areas, and the amount of unused land, but also on the basis of the farmer's attitudes, particularly on race and towards his workers, and whether he had participated in the counter-insurgency during the independence struggle. Some of the 150,000 full-time farm workers threw in their lot with the occupiers, though usually not on the farms where they had been employed. About 90,000 kept their jobs on sugar and tea estates, and on new or already established tobacco and horticulture farms. About 8000 were granted land, but most were denied it on the grounds that they or their elders had come from foreign countries, though some were given citizenship.

Many went from steady employment to contract or casual work; many others were forced to supplement their meagre incomes through fishing, petty trading, theft and prostitution. The best publicised casualties of the land reform movement were the urban poor who hoped to benefit from extending land invasions to urban areas. The veterans spearheaded occupations of urban residential land in 2000-1. Housing co-operatives and other associations followed their lead and set up 'illegal' residential or business sites. But the state feared that it would lose control over towns to the MDC if the land reform movement was allowed to spread and met these occupations with stiff repression, including Operation Restore Order Murambatsvina, a surprise military-style intervention in 2005 in which tens of thousands of families were evicted. Not surprisingly, those who opposed land reform in rural areas were the strongest critics of government efforts to stifle occupations in urban areas.

The final casualty was food production: Zimbabwe, once a food surplus country, is today deficient in both foreign exchange and food. In 2002-3, half the population depended on food aid: this was a drought year and the figures improved in 2004-5. The UN now estimates that nearly half the country's 13.3 million inhabitants will once again be dependent on food aid in 2009, after another drought year. A million of these are poor, urban residents who can't afford imported food. The rest are peasants, most of them hit by drought. Climate change is clearly a factor here, its role most obvious in marginal land: the communal areas worked by millions of small farmers. A 2002 World Food Programme study noted that there had been three droughts in Zimbabwe since 1982 and that the 2002 drought, which also affected several neighbouring countries in Southern Africa, was the worst in 20 years.

The WFP estimated that 12.8 million people in the region would require assistance as a result of that drought and that in Zimbabwe alone, overall production would decline by 25 per cent, with cereal production down 57 per cent and maize, the staple in the diet of ordinary Zimbabweans, down by a devastating two-thirds. To separate out the effect of drought and that of reform - and thus to understand how land reform has hit production - one needs first to distinguish between three groups of agricultural producer: local white farmers, who were the target of the land reform; peasants with farms in communal areas; and foreign corporations, whose large farms (except for small tracts of unused land) remain intact. Harry Oppenheimer, for example, lost most of his private land, but his firm, Anglo American, kept its sugar estates, which it then sold to Tongaat Hulett, a South African firm with 15,000 hectares in Zimbabwe.

In a nutshell, white commercial farmers focused on export crops, whereas communal farmers were the major source of food security. The production of tobacco, hitherto the main source of foreign exchange, is concentrated in large-scale commercial farms; it has seen the most severe decline, almost entirely as a result of land reform. Maize and cotton are peasant crops and have not really been directly affected by land reform, but have suffered badly from prolonged drought - maize production was down by 90 per cent between 2000 and 2003. In contrast, the production of crops - sugar, tea, and coffee - grown mainly by the large corporate plantations has remained steady.

Besides drought and reform, there is a third cause of declining production: the targeted donor boycott. Zimbabwe has been the target of Western sanctions twice in the last 50 years: once after UDI in 1965 (very 'soft' sanctions, which did not stop the country becoming the second most industrialised in sub-Saharan Africa by the mid-1970s) and again after Zimbabwe's entry into the Congo war in August 1998. Zimbabwe's involvement in the war was not well received in the West. Participants in the donor conference for Zimbabwe that year were decidedly lukewarm about committing funds. Britain announced a review of arms sales to Zimbabwe and, after the conference, again disclaimed any responsibility for funding land reform. The following year the IMF suspended lending to Zimbabwe, while the US and the UK decided to fund the labour movement, led by the ZCTU, first to oppose constitutional change and then to launch the MDC as a full-fledged opposition party.

Its enemies have claimed that, by the late 1990s, the ZCTU

was dependent on foreign sources for two-thirds of its income. Once 'fast-track' land reform began in 2000, the Western donor community shut the door on Zimbabwe. The sanctions regime, led by the US and Britain, was elaborate, tested during the first Iraq war and then against Iran. In 2001 Jesse Helms, previously a supporter of UDI, sponsored the Zimbabwe Democracy and Economic Recovery bill (another sponsor was Hillary Clinton) and it became law in December that year. Part of the act was a formal injunction on US officials in international financial institutions to 'oppose and vote against any extension by the respective institution of any loan, credit or guarantee to the government of Zimbabwe'. In autumn 2001 the IMF had declared Zimbabwe 'ineligible to use the general resources of the IMF' and removed it from the list of countries that could borrow from its Poverty and Growth Facility.

In 2002, it issued a formal declaration of non-co-operation with Zimbabwe and suspended all technical assistance. The US legislation also authorised Bush to fund 'an independent and free press and electronic media in Zimbabwe' and to allocate six million dollars for 'democracy and governance programmes'. This was fighting talk, Cold War vintage. The normative language of sanctions focuses less on the issues that prompted them in the first place - Zimbabwe's intervention in the Congo war and the introduction of fast-track reform - than on the need for 'good governance'. In citing the absence of this as a reason for its imposition of sanctions in 2002, the EU violated Article 98 of the Cotonou Agreement, which requires that disputes between African, Caribbean and Pacific (ACP) countries and the EU be resolved by the joint EU-ACP Council of Ministers. Clearly, the old paradigm of sanctions - isolation - has given way to a more interventionist model, which combines punishment of the regime with subsidies for the opposition. So-called 'smart' sanctions are intended to target the government and its key supporters.

In 2002, the US, Britain and the EU began freezing the assets of state officials and imposing travel bans. Only four days after the EU imposed sanctions, the US expanded the list of targeted individuals to include prominent businessmen and even church leaders, such as the pro-regime Anglican bishop, Nolbert Kunonga. Nonetheless, sanctions mainly affect the lives of ordinary people. Gideon Gono, governor of the Reserve Bank of Zimbabwe, wrote recently that the country's foreign exchange reserves had declined from $830 million, representing three months' import cover in 1996, to less than one month's cover by 2006. Total foreign payments arrears increased from $109 million at the end of 1999 to $2.5 billion at the end of 2006. Foreign direct investment had shrunk from $444.3 million in 1998 to $50 million in 2006. Donor support, even to sectors vital to popular welfare, such as health and education, was at an all-time low.

Danish support for the health sector, $29.7 million in 2000, was suspended. Swedish support for education was also suspended. The US issued travel warnings, blocked food aid during the heyday of land reform and opposed Zimbabwe's application to the Global Fund to Fight Aids - the country has the fourth highest infection rate in the world. Though it was renewed in 2005, the Zimbabwe grant is meagre. Agriculture has been affected too: scale matters, but no one disputes that subsidies are vital for agriculture to be sustainable, and sanctions have made it more difficult to put a proper credit regime in place. Despite the EU's imposition of sanctions in the run-up to the parliamentary elections of 2002, Mugabe polled 56.2 per cent of the vote against Morgan Tsvangirai of the MDC's 42 per cent. There were widespread allegations of Zanu-PF violence and last-minute gerrymandering, with polling stations in urban areas - Tsvangirai's electoral base - closing early and extra stations being set up in rural areas, where Mugabe's support was assured.

Nonetheless, it was clear that support for Zanu-PF was higher than in the pre-fast-track elections of 2000. Bush and Blair refused to recognise the outcome, but Namibia, Nigeria and the South African observer team, which had monitored the elections, concluded that the result was legitimate. Whatever the truth of the matter, the Africans could do little in the face of mounting Western pressure, from Britain especially: a three-member panel of Commonwealth countries - Australia, Nigeria and South Africa - was convened to consider the question of Zimbabwe. There were reports of intense pressure from Tony Blair on Thabo Mbeki. The panel suspended Zimbabwe from the Commonwealth for a year. Zimbabwe withdrew from the organisation. The experience of land reform in Zimbabwe has set alarm bells ringing in South Africa and all the former settler colonies where land shortage is still an issue.

In South Africa especially, the upheaval and bitterness felt in Zimbabwe seems to suggest that the 'Malaysian path' to peaceful redistribution and development is not inevitable. An anxious South Africa and less powerful members of the Southern Africa Development Community tend to feel that sanctions, along with other destabilising policies pursued by the West against Zimbabwe, have only made matters worse. SADC states have long tried to reconcile the need to resist Western influence with the fact that they serve as a bridge between Africa and the wealthy Western economies, but South Africa's non-confrontational policy vis-à-vis Mugabe - which Mbeki pursued despite mounting criticism from the ANC and the unions in South Africa - along with its provision of fuel and electricity to its northern neighbour, set it at odds with Western governments. South Africa and the SADC states describe their approach as one of 'non- interference', 'stabilisation' and 'quiet diplomacy', but the West sees it as a deliberate effort to undermine sanctions, and critics in South Africa - most recently Mandela - have found the Mbeki line much too conciliatory.

In 2007, SADC called for an end to sanctions against Zimbabwe and international support for a post-land-reform recovery programme, but earlier this year Western countries brought their influence to bear on key SADC members - Botswana and Zambia - to split the organisation. Ian Khama, the president of Botswana, went so far as to announce publicly that he would not recognise the results of the 2008 elections. The pressure on SADC came not only from Western countries, but from trade-union movements in the region, in particular Cosatu of South Africa, which has strong links with the ZCTU. Here is another striking aspect of the current Zimbabwe crisis: it is not just Western and pro- Western governments that have joined the sanctions regime, but many activists and intellectuals, for the most part progressives, have aligned themselves with distant or long-standing enemies in an effort to dislodge an authoritarian government clinging to power on the basis of historic grievances about the colonial theft of land.

Symbolic of this was the refusal by Cosatu-affiliated unions to unload a cargo of Chinese arms destined for Zimbabwe when the An Yue Jiang sailed into Durban in April. The arguments, which are not new, turn on questions of nationalism and democracy, pitting champions of national sovereignty and state nationalism against advocates of civil society and internationalism. One group accuses the other of authoritarianism and self-righteous intolerance; it replies that its critics are wallowing in donor largesse. Nationalists speak of a historical racism that has merely migrated from government to civil society with the end of colonial rule, while civil society activists speak of an 'exhausted' nationalism, determined to feed on old injustices. This fierce disagreement is symptomatic of the deep divide between urban and rural Zimbabwe.

Nationalists have been able to withstand civil society-based opposition, reinforced by Western sanctions, because they are supported by large numbers of peasants. The tussle between these groups has even greater poignancy in former settler colonies than it had a generation earlier in former colonies north of the Limpopo, for the simple reason that the central legacy of settler colonialism - the land question - remained unresolved and explosive after independence. Southern African leaders have tried, with some success, to put out the fires in Zimbabwe before they spread beyond its borders. It is worth noting that the agreement between Zanu-PF and the MDC signed in September and brokered by Mbeki accepts land redistribution as irreversible and registers disagreement only over how it was carried out; it also holds Britain responsible for compensating white farmers. In the wake of Mbeki's resignation as president of South Africa it is vital that this agreement remains in place. Few doubt that this is the hour of reckoning for former settler colonies. The increasing number of land invasions in KwaZulu Natal, and the violence that has accompanied them, indicate that the clock is ticking.

4

Gender in the Struggle
Rural Women as Agents

THE SITUATION IN THE EIGHTIES

Independence in 1990 provides an important benchmark for measuring change in Namibia. Although the 1985 Nairobi Conference increased awareness of gender issues in the liberation movement, consideration of the status of women took a back seat to the goal of national liberation and racial equity. At that time, race, not gender, was the variable for analysis. Despite their contribution to the struggle, rural women stood in the margins, both in official policy and in the public consciousness. To understand the historical context which affects women farmers at present, it is necessary to look separately at the situation of agriculture and the development of women's movements.

AGRICULTURE: PRE INDEPENDENCE

The apartheid policies and neglect of rural areas of the South African government impeded the social, political and economic development of communal farmers. They were denied access to a range of institutions and resources which supported the commercial sector. In 1980, the government passed legislation to create separate, Second-Tier Authorities to administer each of the nine 'self-governing territories' which had been created out of the Odendaal Commission in 1964.

Thus, separate agricultural support services, together with provision of health, education and rural water supply, were administered and financed for each separate ethnic group. Most farmers had little or no access to extension services outside of sales of fertilizers and seed. Differential resource allocation created great disparities not only by race but by ethnicity. Women were the least served of all.

In general, the least skilled and trained officers were assigned to the communal areas, and they frequently worked on infrastructure projects, such as road construction. Little research, if any, on communal crops and improved farming systems was undertaken. Marketing, inputs and access to credit services were all neglected. In contrast, white farmers, under the Administration for Whites, enjoyed the benefits of a network of credit, marketing and supply institutions, designed to advance their interests and to subsidize the sector. AGRA, the supply and marketing cooperative, only operated centers in the commercial areas. In 1979, the Land and Agriculture Bank was formed to assist farmers in financing the purchase of land and inputs. By requiring farmers to have surveyed, freehold land as collateral, the Bank excluded communal farmers.

The low interest rates served as a readily available subsidy for white farmers, and just prior to independence a 4% long term loan ensured that freehold land would remain in the hands of whites. The Meat Board, Agronomic Board and Karakul Board regulated pricing and exports of meat, wheat, maize and other commercial crops and karakul pelts respectively. Until recently, millet, the main crop grown in the northern communal areas, was not in the purview of the Agronomic Board. Because the veterinary fence cuts off the densely-populated North - and in the absence of quarantine facilities - many communal farmers could not market cattle for export. Communal farmers, whose livestock often did meet the boards' standards, sold them through auctions run by AGRA and Meatco, or to independent buying agents, often at less than market prices. Namibian marketing boards remain closely allied to the Namibia Agricultural Union (NAU), the main body representing white farmers.

One institution which did work in the bantustans was the First National Development Corporation (FNDC), a parastatal set up in 1978. Based on a vision of free market development in the reserves, the FNDC's strategy has been to channel government resources into commercial ventures in the communal areas. For example, the FNDC set up wholesale outlets to supply implements and offer short-term credit facilities. FNDC's operations, which enjoyed tax breaks and government loans, effectively precluded any competition, individual or cooperative. Its agricultural projects, run primarily in the Okavango and Caprivi regions, have primarily been large mechanized and/or irrigated schemes oriented towards individual farmers with entrepreneurial potential. During the 1980s, the Corporation established farmer support programs, supplying technical assistance, inputs and credit, to farmers able to produce commercial crops such as cotton or livestock for market. Thus, the programs targeted elite farmers and were of little benefit to women, who are engaged in small holder agriculture.

The creation of a black farming elite exacerbated the divisions - ethnic, racial, and social - which apartheid carved into rural communities. To weaken its opponents and further fragment rural communities, the government rewarded cooperative individuals and groups of potential supporters with subsidies and infrastructure projects. Resources were often channelled through traditional authorities, some of whom actively collaborated with the South African Defense Force (SADF) and ruling administrations. At the same time, black farmers were inhibited from forming their own groups.

The Cooperative Societies Act of 1964, currently being redrawn, imposed a complicated set of registration procedures and organizational requirements. These cumbersome restrictions precluded the establishment of small, grassroots cooperatives, seen as potential vehicles for political activity, and effectively limited the formation of cooperatives to large-scale agricultural and consumer cooperatives for whites. The absence of indigenous cooperatives helped to marginalise the participation of black groups in the mainstream economy. Importantly, as Independence loomed closer, the FNDC and extension officers worked with more commercially-oriented farmers to establish farmers associations, such as the Likwama Farmers Union in Caprivi. Here again, the focus was on improved marketing, and women's participation was limited. However, these groups have become important models for emergent farmers associations throughout the country.

THE MOBILISATION OF WOMEN

Efforts to improve the status of women differed among exiles outside the country and the women and institutions that remained in Namibia. The demands of the liberation struggle forced men and women both to abandon a rigid division of labour. Women in exile often took on roles and authority not accessible to them within the country. Many fought in combat and trained military cadres. Others took responsibility for running and managing camps, including setting up clinics and kindergartens. Many benefitted from improved access to education. A recent study found that female returnees were 5 times more likely to have Standard 10 levels or higher than stayers of both sexes. They also achieved higher education levels than men in exile. They gained exposure to countries with greater numbers of women in political and professional positions, and many returnees now challenge traditional gender roles and stereotypes.

This has not been without high personal and social costs. The study found that returnee women were considerably more affected by mental stress and other psychological strains caused by life in exile. Although the experience in exile raised awareness of women's issues, the liberation movement did not highlight or press gender issues. Even after the formation of the SWAPO Women's Council, the liberation of women was subsumed under the struggle for national liberation. As one historian notes, "Women's mobilization for the struggle was regarded as strategically important, yet there was no idea that this might imply changes in gender relations or a transformation of the struggle itself."

Only as liberation became achievable did women begin to stress the equality of women as integral and part and parcel of independence. No doubt, participation in the Nairobi conference, where SWAPO participated in the government forum, also heightened the awareness of women in the movement. Inside the country, the war irreconcilably altered the lives of rural women, particularly those in the North. Military recruitment by both sides tore families asunder. The eventual withdrawal of the South African army devastated some households, who had become reliant on the wages of soldiers. Women struggled to survive, as agriculture declined in the wake of crop destruction by the army, severe drought, and the loss of vast numbers of able-bodied young gone into exile or military service.

In the mid 1980s, community organizations began to emerge. Although spurred on by the fight against apartheid, churches and other institutions began to mobilise people around everyday concerns. Self-help groups promoting health, creches and better housing conditions began to crop up in the Windhoek townships and in the South, which was far removed from armed conflict. Some large companies undertook social responsibility programs, resulting in organizations such as the Rossing Foundation, which provided agricultural and skills training to black Namibians. Although these programs were identified with the status quo, their initiatives did enhance the access of Namibians, including women, to training. Sensing the significance of this movement, the South African regime deployed a hearts and minds campaign, which drew on the emergence of community development schemes, to support development projects, such as clinics and schools in the former reserves and, in some areas, to provide highly subsidized agricultural services.

The regime also promoted cultural organisations in an effort to foster ethnic divisions. Ultimately, the arena of grassroots activity did not extend much beyond the efforts of churches and political party organizations; the base for community development work disappeared in a web of political tensions, suspicious motives, and identities along party lines that to a certain extent persist today. It is important to note that within the country, calls for jobs, housing, and education were also couched in terms of race not gender. Gender issues took a back seat in efforts to raise the welfare of poor Namibians.

A group formed in 1985, the Namibian Women's Voice, attempted to bring women together across party-political lines to promote awareness and action around gender issues. Under the weight of tensions within the organization and pressures from outside, the organization dissolved in 1989. White women, although enfranchised to vote, were largely absent from the liberation movement, and did not play the activist and advocacy role as many of their counterparts in South Africa. Even the election campaign, which sought to woo the female electorate, targeted urban women, stressing issues such as improved working conditions. In sum, neither the exiled liberation struggle, nor the internal grassroots movements, gave priority to rural women *per se*.

THE SHARING OF POWER AND DECISION-MAKING

The prospects for women's participation in decision-making has increased considerably since independence, an important step toward ensuring that Namibian women, who comprise over half of the population, both contribute to and benefit from development. However, key leadership and policy-making positions within the government as well as in rural organisations remain the domain of men. Prior to Independence, women were virtually excluded from partici-pation in the ruling government structures. 18 Women are clearly more visible in leadership positions today, but the balance of power has changed little. Only 2 of the 18 ministerial posts are held by women. Women account for only 6 of the 72 members elected to the first house of parliament, the National Assembly.

Although these women have used their positions to advocate for gender equity, their efforts may reinforce the lack of commitment of their male counterparts, who perceive gender concerns as women's issues to be handled by women. Efforts to promote gender equality in decision-making must therefore aim to increase the commitment of male leaders as well as to alter the balance of power between men and women. For rural women, the election of representatives in local and regional government offers the prospect for increased access to power and decision making at the local level. Many have pinned high expectations on these representatives to work to improve conditions in the rural areas and to redress past inequities.

Indeed, an exit poll of the election revealed that an average of two-thirds of voters were aware of their party or candidate's position on such issues as land policy, poverty, education and unemployment. Residents in towns, municipalities and 'villages' (which are in essence, small rural towns) are represented by local authority councils. Importantly, with the active lobbying of the Minister of Regional, Local Government and Housing, one of the two women ministers, the government enacted an affirmative action provision for the first elections of local authorities. By stipulating that party lists must include a minimum number of women candidates, the provision ensured that almost 38% of candidates fielded were women.

In some instances, lists with no women candidates were changed while other lists were revised upwards of the required minimum. The provision did not, however, require that women nominees be given priority for filling seats which were won, and the final results showed a drop to 31.5% of seats filled by women. The provision clearly boosted the participation of women in the elections. However, it will not apply to future elections, which will be contested on the basis of individual candidates rather than party lists. Rural women in constituencies outside of small towns are represented through the 13 regional councils. Each council, in turn, elects two of its members to the National Council, the second house of Parliament.

Although the councils do not undertake service provision, they have the mandate to undertake regional planning and development, and have responsibility for land use planning, economic development and natural resource management within the region. The National Council is intended to amplify the needs of rural constituencies onto the national level. For these elections, no similar affirmative action provision was made and candidates contested the election as individuals. Moreover, parties attached more prestige and power to the regional councils. Interviews with party representatives revealed that many people made gender-based distinctions between the two elections. Respondents attributed political importance to serving on the regional councils. They saw local councils as involved in "non-political" issues such as social and community concerns-more natural extensions of women's work.

As a result, women are extremely underrepresented in regional councils. Only 12 (6%) of the 195 candidates were women. The elections resulted in only 3 women regional councilors (3 %) of the 95 elected. Only one woman was elected to the 26 member National Council. Additional data on local and regional elections is provided in Tables 7 and 8 respectively. In sum, following Independence, women continue to hold few policy-making positions at the ministerial level. They wield little authority over decision-making, including the development of sectoral policies.

Most noticeable is the lack of women in the management cadre of the Ministry of Agriculture itself. Constitutional provisions, together with administrative demands, meant that many Ministries retained employees of the colonial administration. The current composition of MAWRD in part reflects the legacy of the Ministry's almost exclusive focus on white, commercial agriculture. The Ministry of Agriculture recently lost another senior woman, who became the Director of Agriculture at the restructured development parastatal, the Namibia Development Corporation. Her staff includes two departmental leaders and a six-person interdisciplinary consulting team which guides programme directions and design. The sole woman on the team is advising on horticulture.

The drafting of policy and legislation often evolves out of government-appointed committees assigned to explore complex legal and political issues. Here again, women's participation has been limited. Two commissions of direct relevance to rural women farmers have included the Technical Committee on Commercial Farmland, whose recommendations on the acquisition and reallocation of commercial farmland are expected to reach Parliament in late 1994; and the Commission of Inquiry into Traditional Leadership, whose investigation is expected to form the basis of a bill defining the role of traditional authorities in land allocation and customary law. The former boasted only one woman of its nine members; the latter commission of 12 members did not include any women.

After lobbying from concerned staff within the MAWRD, the National Task Force on Agricultural Policy added a woman to the six-man committee. Her involvement has prompted the Task Force, which is drafting a sectoral White Paper, to give greater attention to the role of women farmers and to gender issues in agricultural planning. Women also remain underrepresented in the leadership of institutions outside of government. In communal areas, traditional authorities hold responsibility for allocating land and adjudicating disputes. With the exception of a few female chiefs and "headmen", women have been and remain almost completely excluded from positions of authority under traditional systems. Only through family lines can women hope to influence the decisions of traditional authorities.

Although no statistics are available, discussions suggest that non-governmental organisations have made the most progress in promoting the participation of women in organisational management and leadership. Many organisations have adopted policies, often entrenched in their constitutions, which specify that women must constitute a certain percentage of membership and/or positions on management committees and organisational boards. The forthcoming Co-operative Act includes provisions that cooperatives in which more than a third of the total members are women must have at least one woman on each Management committee and subcommittee. Policies such as these, while not yet balancing power, have helped to diversify leadership structures.

However, the management and field staff of NGOs are primarily men, while the participants in the community groups they serve are mostly women. Some NGO staff feels that extensive travel and overnight stays in the field deter women, who must still tend to household and child care responsibilities. That women often don't have driver's licenses is also seen as an obstacle; this is, of course, easily overcome by supporting driving lessons, and one NGO's recent advertisement for a rural-based position successfully encouraged female applicants by noting that lack of a license would not be a handicap. An overemphasis on secondary or tertiary qualifications may also exclude women, whose qualifications are often more experience based.

Within community groups, farmers associations and other local-level organisations, a gap continues to exist between membership at the community level and participation in decision-making. As one respondent wryly observed, "Women are the foundation, but they are expected to be a quiet foundation." Women are often praised as the backbone of self-help efforts and community development, but this recognition does not always translate into access to leadership and decision-making. In some self-help programs that work with households, although a woman may be the active participant, her husband is the registered member, attending meetings. Some local associations have also drafted statements that guarantee women have one or more places in management structures. However, this may not guarantee meaningful participation.

One observer noted that female committee members are often relegated to be association secretary. Commenting on farmers associations in particular, he noted that news of important issues and opportunities, often channelled through informal networks, frequently bypasses the female members. The level of authority which women wield in community groups differs from region to region. In the Owambo regions of the North, where the war and labour system have torn households apart, women are seen to be more independent and willing to take on positions of responsibility and decision-making within local initiatives.

In contrast, it was noted that in other rural areas, such as the communal areas in the East, women who do attend meetings sit on the sidelines and speak infrequently. This submissiveness was attributed to a lack of confidence and leadership skills on the one hand, and the hostility of men towards their participation on the other. However, a recent survey of women in an Owambo district underscored the reality that organizational meetings and structures do not take adequate account of rural women's workloads, schedules, and distances from rural centers.

INSUFFICIENT INSTITUTIONS AND MECHANISMS TO PROMOTE

Women's groups, NGOs, and government networks have proliferated since the transition period and are bringing awareness of gender imbalances into the mainstream. However, institutions which enhance women's role in agriculture and food production and advocate on behalf of women farmers are few and far between in Namibia. Although widespread information on participation in NGOs and community institutions is sparse, several recent surveys have sobering results. Only 5.9%, 1% and .75% of 1800 women surveyed in the Owambo regions reported involvement in women's groups, literacy groups and self-help groups respectively. Only 12 women in total were involved in committees around village water, health and literacy.

Another survey, covering a district in the Omusati region, showed that 40% of respondents (both sexes) were involved in community structures; these were predominantly church groups and to a lesser extent, school committees. In the Eastern Communal Areas, 81% of respondents (half of whom were women) had not participated in development projects. 24 % were in farmers associations, only one-third of whom were women.

WOMEN'S ORGANIZATIONS

The constellation of national organisations formed around women's issues includes women's wings of the major political parties, nonpartisan groups such as the Namibia National Women's Organisation (NANAWO) and the Federation of Namibian Women, and organisations dedicated to specific issues or sectors, including counselling and violence. Several national nongovernmental organizations and unions have gender coordinators and/or gender-based programmes. Dominated by educated, urban-based women, these organizations have yet to establish a significant presence in rural regions, particularly in the communal areas. Their agenda emphasizes improvements in employment conditions and other goals of more relevance to urban women. Conflict over perceived party loyalties, as well as a sense of territoriality over specific regions have, limited the impact of women's organizations.

GOVERNMENT MECHANISMS

At independence, the government established a Department of Women Affairs (DWA) in the Office of the President. The role of the DWA has been to facilitate the inclusion of gender issues into national development, to advocate for policies and legislation which are gender-sensitive, to coordinate the gender-related activities of government ministries and to provide a point of contact between government, NGOs and donors promoting gender issues. DWA has also coordinated public education campaigns. In part through advocacy by the DWA, the National Development Plan for 1995-2000 will specifically address gender issues sector by sector, rather than in a separate section on Women in Development. Despite its placement in the Office of the President, the DWA lacks a high profile.

Its ability to coordinate efforts on a national scale is limited by a small budget and a staff not well-versed in advocacy and policy issues. The DWA has no representative or observer in the Cabinet, and so must advocate and lobby indirectly. Rural women are partially served by a DWA grant-making programme for income-generating activities. This programme has proven a drain on the time and resources of the staff, who are unable to fully assess the feasibility and impact of the activities-and draw lessons which are relevant to development planning. These constraints have meant that rural women are not in touch with government plans which may not affect them, nor are their priorities fully addressed in policy and development debates coordinated by the DWA.

The DWA is planning to facilitate an interministerial network on gender issues to be comprised of committed individuals within the line ministries. As yet, no ministry has a focal point for promoting gender concerns. However, in MAWRD, the integration of women has primarily been the task of the former Directorate of Rural Development. Established to improve household food security in rural areas, the Directorate has undertaken two main activities: the provision of rural water supply, and the establishment of Rural Extension Officers (REOs) and Promoters. Their task has been to mobilize communities through income generation activities, education campaigns, and projects to improve food security. Gender awareness and the participation of women has been a priority.

However, MAWRD's commitment to the Directorate has not been strong. Despite a 10% share of MAWRD's budget in its first two years, the Directorate received in actuality only 5-6% of the Department of Agriculture's expenditure. The 20 rural extension officers could not properly serve a vast and scattered rural population. There was also overlap and little coordination between REOs, and the Community Development Extension Service, created by MRLGH. Moreover, some MAWRD staff sees rural development as separate (and inferior) to mainstream agricultural activities. In 1993, the rationalization process has merged the Directorate of Agriculture and Rural Development into the Directorate of Extension and Engineering. It has also created a Division of Rural Develop-ment, with the mandate of rural development policy formu-lation, rural development planning, and coordination of rural development activities.

This Division has proposed the creation of a Gender in Development Unit. It is hoped that this strategy will better reorient the agriculture services toward addressing household food security and gender differences. This Directorate has therefore the responsibility for a recently developed initiative to integrate women into agricultural services. Lastly, it is important to again mention local and regional government. Only limited powers have been decentralised to these structures, and the capacity of the councils remains weak Many councillors lack transportation, and so have little contact with their constituencies Regions in which all or most constituencies lie in communal areas do not have the same revenue bases as those regions with municipalities. As a result, they rely primarily on external funding from the central government, which continues to favour more populated, central regions. Clearly, the elections alone have not ensured a mechanism for democratic participation by rural women.

RURAL INSTITUTIONS

Restrictive legislation, war and migration, and divisions fostered by apartheid stunted the emergence of community organisations and a grassroots movement. Group activities, such as digging wells, are common, particularly in the North. However, formal local-level organisation is a new phenomenon. The establishment of community based organisations is hampered by the lack of experience and resources, as well as the expectation that government must direct development and provide most services. This dependency was fostered by the apartheid regime, which built infrastructure and provided free or subsidized services in order to make the reserve system work.

Within the current government, highly visible development schemes, usually publicized with a great ceremony, have only intensified expectations. Community organizations, although receiving support from donors, NGOs or churches, tend to exist in isolation. They are not linked up to larger networks which could help women voice their priorities, experiences and ideas. Regional development networks of NGO and of line ministry staff have been established in the North. Although primarily seeking to coordinate activities, these groups could play a role in bringing the concerns of women farmers into regional and national decision-making fora.

FARMERS ASSOCIATIONS AND RURAL CO-OPERATIVES

Farmers unions and other rural organizations emphasize the interests of male members and do not sufficiently target rural women. The Namibia Agricultural Union recently established a wing for communal farmers associations. Like their white counterparts in the commercial sector, it is mostly large-scale stock holders, and therefore, men, who are represented. No numbers are available on the levels of membership by women in the associations affiliated to NAU, but few women, mostly widows, own commercial farms in Namibia. In June 1992, the Namibia National Farmers Union (NNFU) was established to provide a voice and organizational base for communal farmers.

Women comprise an estimated 30-60% of affiliate associations. However, the activities of farmers associations stress marketing and surplus production.

Absent are programmes aimed at improved food production and food processing for women farmers. NNFU's policy voice on behalf of the needs of its women members has been overwhelmed by the priority given to commercially-oriented agriculture. Recognising that women's interests are not advanced in the regional farmers union, some NGOs have encouraged women to form separate associations and co-operatives, with the view that they will have more control and gain more leadership experience through their own organisation. The fledgling co-operative movement is also proving to be a significant force for empowering women to participate and for advancing their interests. Currently, an estimated 200 co-operatives nationwide will register upon passage of the Act.

CHURCHES

Of all organizations, churches boast the highest numbers of rural women. For example, 83.7% of women surveyed in the Owambo regions had active ties to the church, particularly the Catholic and Evangelical Lutheran churches. Many church activities, such as Bible classes, aim to offer moral guidance and social interaction. However, on their own and through the Council of Churches of Namibia (CCN), churches have been running development projects since the mid 1980s. The activities of church-based organizations have tended to be welfarist in orientation and limited in scope. Their ability to empower women is hindered by the patriarchal attitudes of the churches themselves, which continue to shape narrow attitudes about marriage and pregnancy, and the role of women in leadership.

Nevertheless, the churches do provide an important foundation for bringing women together. The Women's Desk of the CCN, and the Young Women's Christian Association (YWCA) have considerable experience with rural women and are well-integrated into national-level gender networks. The recently formed Ecumenical Church Group of Namibia, with membership from 74 denominations, reaches both rural and urban women. The importance of the scattered projects of churches and NGOs should also not be underestimated. The Government has been able to build on these foundations to expand national initiatives aimed at promoting health care and literacy. CCN, in particular, has gained considerable experience relevant to women farmers through its drought relief programmes and agricultural development centers.

CURRENT LEGAL PROVISIONS

Upon independence, Namibia put into place a democratic constitution which promotes the advancement of women. For example, the Constitution prohibits sexual discrimination and guarantees equality between men and women in all aspects of marriage, including at its dissolution. An affirmative action provision enables Parliament to enact legislation for policies and programmes to redress past imbalances and specifically notes that "women in Namibia have traditionally suffered special discrimination and that they need to be encouraged and enabled to play a full, equal and effective role in the political social and economic and cultural life of the nation." The principles of state policy include a commitment to promote the welfare of the people by, inter alia, enactment of legislation to ensure equality of opportunity for women to enable them to participate fully in all spheres of Namibian society.

The Constitution also commits Namibia to the promotion of a legal system open to all, improved public health and access to education, and maintenance and sustainable utilization of ecosystems and biological diversity for the benefit of all Namibians. Namibia has also endorsed various international conventions in support of women's rights, including the Convention on the Elimination of All Forms of Discrimination Against Women (UNCEDAW) and the UN Convention on the Rights of the Child. The Constitution, together with the UN Conventions, provides an important framework for promoting and evaluating gender equality. However, to date, constitutional provisions have made few tangible changes in the lives of women, particularly rural women. Provisions such as the affirmative action clause merely serve as guidelines and lack the force to require Parliament to enact legislation.

With the exception of the first local authority elections, the affirmative action provision has had limited application, within the government service and in the private sector. Parliament has passed several laws which enhance the status of women workers, including the Labour Act, which prohibits gender discrimination, offers protection for domestic workers and farm labourers and outlines procedures for establishing minimum wages. However, the Act has little relevance to the majority of rural women who are self-employed or operate in the informal sector. More significantly, the Constitution provides that all laws in force at independence remain in force until repealed or amended by an Act of Parliament or declared unconstitutional by a competent court.

Moreover, customary and common law also remains valid, so long as it does not conflict with the Constitution or statutory law. The legacy of people's isolation from the legal system has resulted in few, if any, challenges on the basis of constitu-tionality. Thus, many discriminatory laws remain in tact. Only through a long process of reform are laws likely to be brought in line with the Constitution and the UNCEDAW. Discrimi-natory marriage laws exert the greatest limitations on women's authority over children, control over property, and access to land and credit. Indeed, under both civil and customary system, women are treated as de facto minors. For example, in the absence of an ante nuptial contract, most civil law marriages are in community of property. Married women cannot register property in their own name.

This gives husbands control over the purchase and disposal of property. Marriage in community of property also restricts women's access to credit; wives require husband's consent and signature to enter into contracts and to initiate law suits. Not recognised as property owners, women are also unable to pledge property as security for credit. The husband is also recognised as the guardian of all children born to the marriage. Similarly, under common law marriages, the upbringing of minor children, including decisions about their education, legally falls under the authority of the father.

Under customary systems, traditional authorities allocate land, adjudicate disputes and rule on criminal acts, and make judgement over traditional divorce. It is important to stress that customary law was largely influenced by colonial interpretation and intervention. With the cooperation of elites and tribal leaders, colonial authorities saw customary law as "a tool to control resources" including the labour and reproductive capacity of women and the stability of the reserve system hinged on these measures. A confusing web of legal provisions continues to govern marriage for most rural women, as colonial marriage laws have been overlaid onto the customary system. Women in customary marriages are also dependent on husbands' authority to sell property or to enter into contracts.

As a legacy of colonial law, a separate matrimonial property regime for blacks in the northern communal areas further entrenches customary law by denying men the right to devise cattle and other movable property by will to wives and children. In some communities, husbands are seen to "own" their wife by virtue of paying 'lobola', or bride price. More research needs to be done to assess the scope and implications of this practice, but a survey of the Owambo Regions highlighted considerable variation. In two of three districts, husbands simply gave gifts, such as the purchase of the wedding dress, as part of a civil marriage ceremony. Bride price was uncommon. In contrast, a majority of men in a neighbouring region paid bride price of 1-5 cattle.

While legislation is required to ensure women equal rights in marriage, it will be more difficult to eradicate the patriarchal attitudes and power which underpin both legal systems. Divorced women and women with children out of wedlock garner little support, and the church requires the mother to attend a rehabilitation course if her child is to be baptized. A relatively small percentage of rural women are married under customary law. Nevertheless, many women married under civil law in the rural communal areas are subject to traditional systems of land allocation and inheritance. Societies in Namibia follow matrilineal or patrilineal lines of descent. In either system, a male, be it the husband or a relative on the mother or father's side of the family, is the locus of authority. Thus, in some regions, unmarried women, who do not gain access to land by virtue of marriage, can only obtain land through male relatives.

Divorce proceedings can also discriminate against women, who face hearings chaired by men and are often prevented from speaking. Elsewhere, in the Eastern and Southern Communal Areas, or in the Okavango Region, women can be allocated land in their own right, but still face discrimination. For example, headmen may give priority to the applications of men, who are seen to be more productive. Alternatively, women may be granted smaller or degraded portions. Women also have little recourse to challenge encroachment of grazing land by larger stock holders or to fight back against stock theft. Some have suggested that judgements favour men in grazing disputes involving both sexes. Discriminatory inheritance traditions further contribute to women's tenuous position.

In the Eastern Communal Areas, a widow's right to keep her home and maintain access to grazing land depends on the goodwill of the deceased's male relatives. Should she return to her family, the relatives will claim her husband's livestock and may or may not permit her to keep her own. Death of the husband often leaves wives in polygamous marriages with virtually no property. In the South, widows appear to be better off, inheriting grazing cards (which regulate rights to use grazing land), livestock and immovable property. In the Okavango Region, the man's family determines who will inherit cattle, typically granting only part of the herd to the widow. Cropland reverts to the widow. A study for a consultative conference on land reform, held in June 1991, found that women in the Northern crop areas were particularly at risk of losing land and other assets upon the death of husband or fathers.

Divorces are also problematic, as many women must turn over assets and property which they have helped to build or purchase. The most drastic examples of discrimination have been reported in the Owambo Regions. The widow does not automatically inherit the land and homestead. Rather, she must pay a fee to the headman to "repurchase" the land. In some instances, even widows who raise the money are forced off the land by the husband's family, who, under customary law, can claim the land and all joint property, including the homestead, any joint enterprise such as a small shop, livestock, and even grain stores. These women return to their families or purchase an inferior plot of land. Women in the region feel strongly that this discrimination must end, and in a 1994 gender-based survey, respondents clearly agreed that: women should inherit husbands' land, not families; headmen should not charge widows for land; and, in divorce, property should be split equally.

MEASURES TO INCREASE AWARENESS

Legislation to enhance the status of women has sorely lagged behind the tenets of gender equality espoused in the Constitution. However, government groups and NGOs together have stepped up efforts to educate men and women on the rights of women, to press for legal reform, and to enable women to promote their interests through the legal system. For example, the Law Reform and Development Commission include a Women and Law Committee, which will seek to reform civil and customary law in line with the Constitution. This process is being supported by an NGO-based Gender Research Project, which aims to assess gender aspects of the law and evaluate proposals for reform. One breakthrough occurred in late 1993, when a chief in the Owambo Region agreed not to force widows off the land or to charge fees for them to remain on their land.

This agreement was achieved through patient consultation by members of government and representatives of legal organisations including the Women and Law Committee. When a local headman did not follow the new ruling, widows, with support from members of NGOs, organized a demonstration. However, many villagers and headmen remain uninformed of the proclamation, and past practices continue. The effort to reform customary law is part of an ongoing programme, coordinated by the Namibia Development Trust, and the Law Faculty at the University of Namibia, to improve the legal and socio-economic situation of women in Namibia. This process has included the gender-based survey, cited earlier, of three districts in the North.

The organizations are now undertaking educational campaigns and workshops to provide information on the difference between being married in and out of community of property-over half of the women surveyed admitted to not knowing the distinction. Importantly, the survey showed that the majority of respondents rely on their future husbands for advice prior to the marriage, while others seek information from parents and friends. The Law Faculty has conducted several workshops for rural communities to show how a properly prepared will can help widows secure rights to (non movable) property and land. However, it is proving difficult to change attitudes and misconceptions of traditional authorities and men. Moreover, some customary systems do not recognize wills.

In addition to the Gender Research Project, programmes are underway to educate women about their rights and how to assert them. One NGO, the Legal Assistance Centre (LAC), is running a legal education project, working closely with the Department of Women's Affairs and non-governmental groups. The project has produced pamphlets for use in schools and communities and a manual for paralegals on the rights of women and children. The rights and procedures which have been or will be covered include maintenance, abortion, rights of single mothers, domestic violence and marriage and divorce. Several other groups have cooperated to produce a booklet on women and rape. The project is also running legal education workshops in townships and rural centers.

The DWA is also working with government departments and partner agencies to communicate the UNCEDAW, and to generate strategies for action and implementation. The booklet has been produced in seven local languages. Rural women remain underserved by the judiciary system. Magistrate courts have yet to be established in several of the regions, following the new delimitation in 1992. The legal profession is male-dominated and largely urban-based. It is likely that many rural women are not reached by education campaigns. For example, the LAC has been actively encouraging women to invoke a pre-Independence law, the Maintenance Act, to claim their entitlement to maintenance.

The Centre has also supported efforts to improve the enforcement of the Act for men who default on payments. However, while increasing numbers of women in the Windhoek area are taking up maintenance procedures, few women in rural areas appear to be utilising it. In addition to its Windhoek office, the Legal Assistance Centre has established branches in five regional centers. Paralegals advise or refer people on cases, most of which concern divorce, maintenance and custody. However, the director of the Legal Education Project is the only woman of ten paralegals involved in the Centre's advice and education functions. Women are often reluctant to bring up concerns about violence, marriage or divorce with men, particularly in light of persistent tolerance towards domestic violence.

A significant initiative is the pilot Women's and Children's Abuse Centre, a hospital-based centre which caters for rape, violence and abuse of women and children. Although the Centre is Windhoek-based, it is anticipated that similar centers will be established in towns serving the communal areas. This lack of self confidence underscores the importance that, in addition to legal reform, women must be empowered socially and economically to challenge unjust measures. Indeed, one important process which has increased the awareness of rights has been the exposure to democratic values, both in national elections and through participation in organizations.

THE STATUS OF RURAL POOR WOMEN

The health and well-being of the majority of children in Namibia is integrally tied to women's roles as farmers and food producers. To date, no national-level statistics on levels of poverty exist, and the country is in the process of establishing a poverty datum line to monitor changes in the ability of poor Namibians to meet basic needs. However, recent regional studies suggest that as many as 40% of households are food insecure. In Namibia, household food security derives from two sources: the production and food stores of the household from agriculture and food gathering; and the ability of households to purchase or acquire food, either from cash income, food transfers or bartering.

The disparity between rich and poor is extreme. There is growing differentiation within rural regions, as well as between households at village level. One measure of this is disparity in the ownership of and access to livestock, an important agricultural asset. In Namibia, the decline in crop production and food availability, together with a reduction in cash income, are further entrenching many households in poverty.

FEMALE-HEADED HOUSEHOLDS

Households headed by women constitute a significant portion of the food insecure. Definitions of what constitutes a household, as well as criteria for determining if the head is a female, vary widely. Some surveys have distinguished between de jure heads, women recognized within civil or customary law as the official head, and de facto heads, women who are in charge in the absence of a male head. Although comprehensive data is limited, regional figures and the national census suggest that between 30-50% of households are effectively female-headed. Far from homogeneous, female-headed households display a range of composition patterns and socio-economic characteristics.

It must also be stressed that a focus on female-headed households masks the vulnerability of single mothers and young married couples, often part of male headed households. A number of factors contribute to the precarious situation of rural women in general, and female headed households in particular. For example, ongoing migration continues to affect the structure of households. In the Northern regions, this pattern is reflected in the noticeable gender imbalances in the productive adult population. Migration has created many female headed households with a shortage of adult labour, often resulting in a decline in food productivity. Women must often make up the loss through additional work in the field, including intensive tasks such as tilling and clearing.

Data on land holdings is sparse, but several recent surveys in the Owambo Region show that although size of land between male and female headed households is comparable, the amount cultivated is often lower for the latter. Even in regions where gender ratios are equal, women still outnumber men in agriculture. In the South, labour shortages are less problematic; however, many able-bodied youths do not contribute fully to agricultural activities. Shortage of labour is exacerbated by the higher dependency ratios present in female headed house-holds. According to the 1991 census, female-headed households are comparable in size to those headed by males but support more children. Similarly, the household subsistence survey found the average size of a rural household headed by a man to be 9.4, while that headed by a female is 7.4.

In contrast, female-headed households have on average 1.9 dependents (those under 16 or over 60), male headed households only 1.4. Thus, while female headed households support more dependents, they have smaller households and therefore fewer able-bodied members to assist with agricultural and domestic tasks. Although school children do contribute to household chores, they are likely to be a net drain. Households who can send their children away to school further benefit from school feeding programmes. Yet another factor affecting women's ability to procure food is the declining natural resource base.

The quality of land is deteriorating, women lack fertiliser, implements and the technical know how to boost the productive potential of their fields. Drought is an ever present threat for communal farmers, whose harvests, in the absence of agricultural inputs, depend even more directly on good rainfall. In the non-crop producing regions, stock-farming households must contend with drought and poor grazing which directly reduce the availability of milk for home consumption. Wild fruits and vegetables, riverine fish, and small animals enhance food security during times of relatively good supply and provide an important buffer for poor households during times of food shortage. However, increasing deforestation and erosion, including along rivers, unsustainable harvesting, and increasing population pressure are shrinking the availability of these foods.

Particularly affected by environmental change, as well as by historical land dispossession are women and their families in traditionally nomadic pastoral or hunting-gathering communities. Bushmen peoples have faced considerable social disruption, caused by restricted access to land and by the influence of the military. Many now live on the margins, squatting in small towns or as overexploited shepherds or maids in the households of communal farmers. Those employed in the military found themselves in precarious circumstances with the withdrawal of the South African Defence Force and the loss of wage income. One group, the Ju/'hoansi, have resettled on traditional grounds, and are working with outside groups to develop a mixed economy including horticulture, cattle-rearing, and craft production in addition to foraging. It remains to be seen how new economic patterns will alter gender roles.

HOUSEHOLD FOOD SECURITY

As a result of these conditions, few households, whether male or female-headed, produce enough food to be self-sufficient. The gender survey of the North found that less than 5 % of all households surveyed had produced a surplus of millet; the majority did not have enough grain in storage to stretch between harvests. Protracted drought no doubt contributed to this extreme situation? but many Northern households must regularly supplement the millet or maize harvested with meal from elsewhere. Even in the best of years, agricultural production is inadequate to meet basic food needs. Since women are the majority of farmers, they are most likely to bear the risk and uncertainty of agriculture.

To meet basic food needs, households therefore augment production from subsistence agriculture with cash or in-kind income from other sources. In addition to purchasing food, cash is also needed to pay for school fees and uniforms, medical bills, clothing and special events. Needs for cash can be severe, and households are occasionally forced to sell food stores or important assets to meet expenses. Although almost three-quarters of the population participate in agriculture, the main contributor to subsistence across households is cash income directly from formal employment or by way of cash and non-cash remittances from an absentee member.

Access to formal employment is the most important distinction between the absolute poor and those able to meet food and income needs. Female headed households have fewer members employed formally or informally than male headed households. Interestingly, a survey in the Omusati Region found that absentee members of male headed households were more likely to be formally employed than those in female headed households, who were almost twice as likely to be looking for work. There are few financial returns to offset the absence of labour. Moreover, rising unemployment and social breakdown of the family have shrunk the amount and frequency of remittances. The gender-based survey of Owambo districts found that less than 15% of households receive cash remittances, often assumed to be the mainstay of incomes in that area.

Similarly, a study of coping strategies in the Erongo Region found that remittances are in decline. 45% of households interviewed had at least one member who had lost his or her job since 1991. Many have taken up ad-hoc employment, earning barely enough to survive. One of the most vulnerable groups is women employed on farms or who are in households in which the principal breadwinner is a labourer on a commercial farm. Over 36,000 farm workers support an estimated 230,000 dependents, on wages ranging between N$80380/month. Many labourers receive few leaves of absence, and like migrants in the cities, may start second families or lose contact with their rural household. Female workers on farms are in a more precarious position, as their work is often on a casual basis, and they lack job security.

Wives resident on the farm have often found themselves evicted upon the death of their husbands. A newly formed farm workers union and several local associations aim to represent farm workers and to encourage enforcement of the Labour Act. However, it must be noted that some of the worst abuse and exploitation of farm workers occurs on communal farms, where immigrants, marginalised peoples such as the Bushmen, and even poor relatives work for little or no pay. In the absence of income from remittances or formal employment, women rely more heavily on cash or barter from informal sector trading, such as beer brewing or crafts. Casual labour or piecework is also increasing in importance.

A day of weeding can earn some much needed cash or ensure several cups of maize meal for food-poor households. However, this transfer of labour, by reducing a household's agricultural productivity, increases dependence on the largesse of wealthier households. The reliance on cash is even greater in stock-farming regions. Two recent surveys of the Southern and Eastern Communal Areas found that the majority of households, regardless of wealth, get their food from shops. Purchasing power, then, is the principal determinant of food security. Although inclined to maintain high numbers of livestock, wealthier households own herds large enough to support at least the occasional sale of animals.

In contrast, 88% of female headed households in the South receive no cash income from the sale of animals. These and other poor households, live on drought relief transfers, the charity of relatives, or senior citizen pensions. The extended family is an important network for food distribution, and in turn, household food security. Food gifts, such as cups of maize meal or gifts of fish thus enable poorer relations and their households to survive food shortages and to defer the impacts of drought or other crises. The shift towards nuclear family patterns appears to be increasing the prospects for joint management of the household on one hand, but is eroding the social and economic support system of the extended family on the other.

Some observers have noted that the Namibian Constitution implicitly recognizes the nuclear family as the main family pattern, and so might not fully promote the rights and security of women in other family situations. Among households without another source of cash income, access to a pension is the primary determinant of food security. Namibia and South Africa are the only two countries in Africa which offer universal pensions for all citizens over the age of 60. The income from the pension, paid out bimonthly, is intended to provide a safety net for the elderly, many of whom lack the security of savings and other financial resources.

Historically, it formed part of the strategy of the South African regime to ensure a minimum level for survival in the reserves. However, pensions have become a critical element for survival in many rural households across the country. 41% of respondents in the survey of the southern communal areas cited pensions as their predominant cash source. Over 50% of surveyed households in two Northern districts have members who receive pensions. Although those with pensions are more secure than households without a regular source of income, the social and economic dependence on female pensioners is high. In Namibia, senior women undertake many household and agricultural tasks, and often bear primary responsibility for childrearing. This responsibility, along with the bimonthly pension, enables adult members to leave children in the care of seniors and migrate to urban areas.

Relying on this support, young women are now increasingly moving out of rural areas to follow their partners or to seek employment or informal sector work in cities and rural towns. Interestingly, even as pensioners, women are more likely to use the income for the family, and a recent survey showed that grandmothers were almost twice as likely as grandfathers to contribute to the payment of school fees in their household. Ironically, the pension system has reversed the social security system prevalent in most of Africa, whereby children are responsible for supporting elderly parents. Rather than enhancing the well-being of elderly women, the pension system may be increasing their vulnerability. Complacency around pensions may account in part for the decreased flow of remittances and paternal maintenance. Indeed, by accommodating the migration of adult labour, pensions appear to inhibit increased agricultural productivity.

MALNUTRITION

Households unable to produce or purchase food often ration basic foods and forego essential sources of protein such as meat or fish. Female headed households have more dependents but less means to obtain food, and so face the greatest risk of poor nutrition among children, nursing mothers and the elderly. Data is inconclusive, although a 1990 survey of rural centers in Owambo found that undernourishment and stunting were more prevalent in children of female headed households. In the Southern Communal Areas, female headed households feed more people but obtain less food, including essential components such as meat and milk.

As noted above, many households are unable to produce enough food for the whole year. Storage problems, including the loss of crops or dried food to pests, affect food availability and nutrition value. Furthermore, employment and casual labour opportunities often do not parallel periods of food shortage. Lack of cash income and food shortages are further compounded by high prices for maize meal and basic food stuffs in the shops. In the South and East, where food is purchased, cash flow determines the abundance of food; as a result, the number of meals typically declines over the course of a month, or for pensioners, a two month period. In crop producing regions, the "hungry season" before harvest is a period of intense labour, which strains the health of nursing mothers. Thus, nutrition levels in Namibia are particularly prone to seasonal and crisis (drought) related food shortages. A 1992 national health survey found that Namibian children have high levels of wasting as a result of acute food shortages.

The survey showed that levels of malnutrition in children differ little by gender, although females are slightly more likely to be stunted. Education of the mother is a factor only at the secondary school level or higher. Mothers at this level are half as likely to have children who are stunted. They also have fewer wasted or undernourished children. While higher levels of education might enhance awareness of nutrition, this difference probably reflects the increased access to employment enjoyed by women with higher educational qualifications. Although there has been little work on food preferences and consumption, the diets of many Namibian groups include foods rich in protein and vitamins.

In the Northern crop areas, women grow and gather several

varieties of leafy greens. The Namibia Development Trust survey found that almost 93% of households grow beans, and 36.7% grow ground nuts, while a recent survey of Okavango found that over 80% of households consume fish. In the Eastern and Southern regions, milk is an important dietary staple. These practices enhance nutrition levels and suggest that agricultural research and extension must look beyond productivity to incorporate nutritional needs and diversity.

DIVISION OF LABOUR AND DECISION-MAKING

The health and well-being of household members not only rests on the availability of food; rather, household food security is also related to distribution of food and income within the household. Indeed, the very notion of the household as a production unit tends to gloss over competing interests and the uneven access and control over resources within the household. The right and ability of women to control the products of their own labour is central to the advancement of rural women in Namibia. Namibia is no exception to the gender division of labour which characterises rural communities throughout the world.

Women carry out the bulk of domestic and agricultural duties, while men are responsible for specific spheres of activity, such as herding and marketing livestock, ploughing fields, or constructing homes. Men are more likely to allocate or share specific tasks with others, or take on tasks that utilise higher levels of technology, such as animal-drawn traction. In contrast, women are more likely to be engaged in the actual work itself. One survey found that women in the Owambo Regions are twice as likely as men to work in the field. Children share in domestic and agricultural tasks while still young, but soon get tracked into gender-based divisions as they grow older.

Few studies have assessed the allocation of time and work responsibility within rural households, and information on the division of labour among different ethnic groups remains somewhat superficial. The economic value of women's work remains underrepresented in research. In contrast, the growing system of casual labour offers some evidence of the productive value of women's labour (although this is clearly not reflected in amounts of payment). Even less consideration is given to women's roles as mothers and caretakers. These roles not only exert physical demands, but entail ongoing planning, attention, and emotional demands.

A gender-based division of labour is arguably complementary. This has been observed of Ju/'hoan society, in which male and female domains are seen to reflect the mutual interdependence of the two sexes. While this interdependence may have been a feature of pre-colonial societies, the division of labour currently present in most Namibian groups has been distorted by ongoing social and economic change. For example, the transformation of rural economies from agriculturally-based to income-based has increased the work load of women. As noted above, women often make up for the lost input of absentee husbands or family members by taking on additional tasks.

Interestingly, as the participation of men in farming activities decreases, the authority of women over agricultural processes may increase. More information is needed to understand the role of men and women in making choices concerning field preparation, seed selection, or care of livestock. Even in male-headed households, Northern women appear to have some say in deciding which crops to grow and when to plant. Women are increasingly responsible for livestock production, traditionally a male domain: the NDT survey found that in 22 % of households, women are the principal person in charge of cattle. In the Southern and Eastern Communal Areas, women are responsible for milking and lambing and exercise control over these processes. In the South, where small stock predominates, women also make decisions about herding and grazing.

Women and children in all rural regions collect water for domestic use and wood, the principal source of fuel for the majority of rural households in Namibia. Routine tasks such as these, as well as collecting wild foods, fruits, and materials, are made more difficult by a shortage of resources. Some households walk more than 5 km to obtain wood. In regions lacking water infrastructure, households must travel well over one hour to fetch water during the dry season. In addition to hindering agricultural work, labour shortages affect the frequency and distance of trips which poor households can make for water and fuel. Thus, poor households must ration out supplies and/or continue to exploit resources located near to the homestead, contributing further to the spiral of environmental degradation.

Men participate in these tasks only if transportation, such as a donkey cart, ox sledge, or truck, is used, or if the household has ready access to a tap or pipeline. Thus, improving access and supply of water not only reduces time but increases the likelihood of men's participation. It is in the home that male participation is most lacking, and men benefit by having greater leisure time as a result. Child rearing, food preparation and maintaining the homestead all place considerable demands on a woman's time; in the North, over an hour of each woman's day is spent pounding grains, while women in pastoral systems devote much of their mornings to milking and tending livestock. As discussed above, households are increasingly relying on purchased foods. This eliminates processing and preparation work but affects nutrition and constrains cash flow.

The entry of rural households into commercial activities also increases the labour burden of women in households able to achieve marketable surpluses. Women must ensure subsistence output and contribute to cash crop production. If women have access to the additional income, then the returns to increased labour can be worthwhile. However, rural women in Namibia continue to have an unequal say in decision-making over agricultural production. Women are expected to utilise their harvest to feed the family, and in some regions, women even farm both individual plots for subsistence and common plots in which men control the harvest. In *de facto* female headed households, the husband's absence does not necessarily increase a woman's freedom to make decisions. She might be entitled to sell produce on an informal scale, but for more significant decisions, such as hiring labour, she defers to her husband.

Women exert even less authority over the sale and disposal of livestock. Men dominate the marketing and slaughter of stock, and although they may confer with their wives, it is men who negotiate prices. In a husband's absence, a woman is expected to consult with his relatives. Reportedly, many women in the Eastern and Southern Communal Areas still wield no control over the sale of animals they themselves own. Moreover, if her animals are sold in a lot, her husband can determine the share she receives. Women's participation in decisions over the allocation of cash income appears to vary by the composition of the household and the marital relationship. In general, female headed households are more likely to make financial and other decisions jointly with family members.

In male-headed households, authority over income and resources is generally vested in the head, but joint decision-making is also commonplace, particularly among nuclear families. There is little work on different areas of responsibility, but women appear to participate more in decisions about health, education and childrearing. Of course, authority is not clear cut, and women employ a number of strategies to enhance their control. For the most part, women are entitled to spend income they have earned through casual labour or non-farm production as they choose. Some women prefer to work for income in kind, since they know that men are less likely to make claims on maize meal than on cash. Not surprisingly, it is women who also dominate food for work programs, while men hold out for opportunities for cash.

Efforts by the government to boost the production and marketing of traditional crops, such as millet, or of livestock, particularly goats, must take care not to marginalise women. Elsewhere in Africa, crops which women traditionally grow and sell on a small scale have come under the control of men as commercial prospects improved. Schemes initiated by the First National Development Corporation (FNDC) appear to mirror this pattern. Male headed households utilise the labour of wives and families to produce surpluses and to diversify into crops such as cotton and groundnuts. Men have also been able to resettle and participate in special farming ventures managed by the Corporation, knowing that their wife will maintain the family and homestead. Women lose twice, as they see few benefits from the surplus production and contend with dwindling incomes from small-scale marketing. In short, women work more but get less.

Agricultural policies and programmes continue to overlook the central role of women in agriculture and reinforce inequality in women's access to: 1) productive resources, including land, labour, inputs and technology; and 2) support services, such as credit, extension and research. Moreover, the failure to acknowledge women's agricultural knowledge and experience makes gender divisions over decision-making even more pronounced. Ultimately, policies must go beyond simply improving services to exploring ways to enhance women's legal and social ability to take up services.

LAND AND ASSETS

On a national level, the constitution maintains the distinction between commercial land and communal land. Historically, legal control of the communal areas was placed in the colonial government or the reserve administrations. At independence, this ownership transferred to the new government. Property held under private title, including commercial farms, is seen as lawfully owned and therefore exempt. Thus, since the majority of black farmers continue to reside in communal areas, they remain disadvantaged by inequitable distribution of land. In June 1991, the Prime Minister convened a national conference on land reform and the land question. Background papers and debates showed that the affects of dispossession, the nature of land problems and attitudes towards land reform and policy differed by region.

The constraints facing women across the nation to obtain land also vary and cannot be generalised. However, conference recommendations made special note of ensuring rights and support for women. In its recommendations, the Technical Committee on Commercial Farmland (TCCF), mandated to evaluate land policy options, has recommended improving women's access to and control over land, through improved rights, affirmative action programmes, repeal of discriminatory statutory and customary laws, and representation on regional or district level land bodies, should they be formed. The recommendations of the TCCF are still under review. In the absence of legislation, customary allocation of communal land by traditional authorities prevails, with households gaining usufruct rights to residential land, for crop production or grazing as well as access to common pasturage.

As discussed earlier, rural women still gain access to land through men, as wives, daughters, sisters. The security of their tenure is also jeopardized by discriminatory marriage customs and inheritance systems. There is no accurate data on landlessness in Namibia. While it is commonly assumed that most households do have access to land under customary law, some landless widows have been forced to move into the households of relatives. The conference recommendations accept that ancestral land claims will not form the basis of restitution and so preclude large-scale land reform. Current strategies target increasing the Land available to communal farmers and improving the productivity of the existing land base, through improved range management, crop production or alternative uses. Without careful consideration, these options will yield few benefits for women farmers, and may diminish their access to land even further.

For example, efforts are underway to increase land availability by opening up communal lands which are under-utilized due to a lack of surface water. In Okavango, the drilling of boreholes is enabling farmers to resettle and to graze livestock away from the river, which currently supports the densest population in the country. Others have moved their herds but maintained homesteads and some stock near the river. However, women are less likely to take up opportunities to resettle or to cultivate new fields. Their child care and domestic responsibilities preclude settlement in marginal areas, which continue to lack basic infrastructure and health care and education facilities. Moreover, the benefits gained by increased crop production are offset by reduced access to fish, veil foods or other natural resources. The distance of fields away from the homestead adds to the time and labour of travelling and transporting harvests, inputs and equipment back and forth.

It is wealthier households and those who own more stock, who most benefit from newly opened grazing lands. These households have the resources to hire herders, and can readily maintain existing lands and keep herds in the new grazing areas. Female headed households lack these resources. In marginal areas, control over water can also dictate access and use to land. In some regions, individuals effectively control water points. Of note, MAWRD is encouraging the formation of village water point committees. To date, the participation of women in the committees has been limited, particularly in regions where men tend to control water infrastructure.

A second strategy aims to relieve pressure on communal lands, particularly in stock producing areas, by enabling communal farmers to purchase commercial farms through a low interest loan programme. No gender-disaggregated data is available, but to date, a small number of farmers, primarily large stockholders, have been granted loans under the scheme. For many farmers the financial incentives of relocating are low, as grazing and water in the communal areas is free. Ostensibly, the scheme should indirectly benefit poorer households, including those headed by women, who would gain by improved grazing due to lower numbers on the range. However, as has happened elsewhere, farmers with commercial farms continue to graze livestock on communal lands.

Elite farmers are also fencing the communal grazing areas at an alarming rate. Many enclose prime grazing areas and dominate water sources. This is effectively privatising the communal lands and reducing the access of poorer households to land. Some farmers are consequently cut off from dry season grazing, a severe constraint to productivity, which rests in part on a strategy of opportunistic and flexible grazing patterns. Illegal fencing has also inhibited the migration of game, an important source of meat for the Ju/'hoan and other groups which actively hunt. The TCCF recommends immediate legislation to stop the fencing, but to date; the government has taken little action against it.

SHORTAGE OF LABOUR

When asked if they would like more land, 89% of respondents in a survey for the land conference naturally answered positively. On the surface, this response would suggest increased pressure on land. According to one report, for example, average land holdings in the Owambo Region have dropped from 6.3 ha in 1968 to 2.6 ha in 1980. However, this drop also reflects the declining importance of agriculture. Households engage in a range of other income activities and so cultivate for consumption rather than surplus production. Ultimately, for many households, the problem is not access to land but rather the ability to utilise it efficiently.

Female headed households particularly lack the labour and inputs to cultivate what they do have, and one observer noted that some households farm only 112-1/3 of their arable land. Households, in turn, are unable to farm cultivated areas efficiently. For example, many households only weed once, although two weeding are preferable.

OWNERSHIP AND ACCESS TO LIVESTOCK

Livestock provide milk, meat and dung for fertilizer. Income from the sale of animals, meat and by-products enhances food security and provides a 'nest egg' to cover unanticipated expenses, such as medical costs. In Namibia, cattle are also imbued with social and cultural importance. There is growing differentiation in the ownership of cattle and other livestock among rural households. Unequal access and control of grazing enables wealthy households to expand their herds, while poor households face a decline in herd size. Recent studies suggest that female headed households on average own fewer animals and are more likely to own no cattle at all. The cattle they do own tend to be lower-value.

In the Northern regions, a shortage of draught power poses a barrier to crop production. Many female headed households do not own or have free access to draught animals and ploughs. Cash-strapped households further lack the option of hiring labour and so till the land. Households often use two methods of ploughing in order to maximise available resources. In contrast, households with draught animals can tap into an added source of income by renting out animals and ploughs. Those forced to hire must wait and so run the risk of late ploughing. Recent droughts have compounded the situation, killing many donkeys and reducing the availability of draught power throughout the North.

CREDIT

As inputs are becoming more available through government schemes, farmers coops and private outlets, the demand for credit is growing. Small-scale farmers have historically been unable to access credit through banks and government institutions, which require titled land as security. Banks in the rural areas only operate in administrative centers and cater to those who earn salaries. Prior to Independence, the development parastatal, the then First National Development Corporation (FNDC), had the mandate to provide loans in the Bantustan areas. These loans were granted primarily to urban-based entrepreneurs to set-up non agricultural businesses; although a few loans were granted to commercially orient agricultural enterprises. Only an estimated 10% of the loans have been granted to women. Few financial institutions have been willing to bear the added costs and risks of administering loans in small amounts.

The largest obstacle to credit faced by women continues to be the restricted rights of marriage in community of property. Married women still require the consent of their husbands to enter into contracts and loans. Few institutions have sought to address this problem. To a limited extent, programmes run by non-governmental organizations have enhanced women's access by targeting small loan programmes to them. The Private Sector Foundation, which supports informal and small business development, has a loan programme specifically for women. Also important is the fledgling credit union movement. Credit unions have been established in the SCAs and Owambo regions, where an estimated 70-80% of the members are women.

Several farmers associations are also supporting credit schemes for their members. The unions provide an opportunity for farmers to access loans without collateral restrictions. The process has been one of trial and error, and NGOs continue to explore models appropriate to Namibia. However, credit unions of necessity serve people with income and so are concentrated in rural centers. The women who participate are those with a reliable income, such as government employees or those engaged in small enterprise. The Namibia Development Corporation (NDC), restructured from the FNDC, has also run a mini-loan programme for entrepreneurs in the small business and informal sector. This programme, too, has served urban residents, who seek support for petty trade and small ventures such as hair salons or shops.

Farmers involved in NDC agricultural projects can obtain small sums of money for the purchase of inputs such as seeds through an informal loan programme. It is not known if women have been able to benefit from this service. Since late 1992, over 450 small-scale communal farmers have also been able to obtain loans through a special scheme administered by MAWRD. Over three quarters of the total amount granted has been for the acquisition of stock, with the remainder for crop production and infrastructure. In the absence of conclusive gender-based data, this suggests that women may be underrepresented, as the purchase of stock often falls to men. The cost and burdensome administration of the programme has led to considerable delays in loan approval and pay out.

Its success has also been hampered by the fact that many extension officers remain unaware of the scheme or lack experience with credit. Currently, MAWRD is developing an agricultural bank equipped to administer a loan programme designed for small-scale communal farmers. The programme would support those farmers who can use loans to increase their productivity, and, in turn, their incomes, through the purchase of inputs, permanent improvements, or the introduction of perennial crops. The programme would make loans to individual farmers organised into informal groups and to formally registered cooperatives. It is anticipated that these approaches will promote shared responsibility for loans and increase the prospects of repayment. The proposed model does not consider affirmative action for women, but it is hoped that loans managed through cooperatives will reach women.

Training in gender aware approaches and the hiring of female staff are recommended. Standard credit schemes cannot meet the needs of the poorest, whose incomes are too low to invest. As a result, vulnerable households resort to informal mechanisms, to meet immediate cash and food needs. For example, households may put up a portion of the future harvest as 'collateral' for loans or as payment for ploughing services. In some regions, a system of loaning cattle, known as mafisa, enables poor households or those with sudden losses to replenish their herds. The borrower tends the animals in return for draught power, milk, and ownership of any calves born. Local shops often allow customers to purchase goods on credit or through barter.

In the southern communal areas, an estimated half of households maintain accounts with shop keepers. People also buy clothes, furniture, and large items on lay bye and payment plans from larger retail chains. While helping rural residents to overcome shortfalls in food and cash, these mechanisms also increase the likelihood of indebtedness, thereby exacerbating food security over the long term. 105 involvements of women in these mechanisms should be examined and considered when designing credit programmes. Finally, households save in order to make investments or as protection against unexpected expenses.

In Namibia common wisdom holds that for most households, savings are in the form of cattle, seen as stored wealth. No doubt true, but as noted above, women have little control over the disposal of livestock and so lack access to this form of savings. However, households can and do save cash earnings, although those headed by females face greater difficulties in saving. Nevertheless, a survey in an Owambo district found that 45% of female headed households and 73 % of male headed households save.

The mean amount saved differed greatly with the former saving only N$ 227, usually keeping it at home. The latter saved an average of N$ 966 and was more likely to save at a bank.

These results, although inconclusive, underscore the need for women to gain information and access to savings institutions, including the bank, post office, and community savings groups. Programmes that promote resource-sharing, such as shared control of draught animals and ploughs, or revolving seed banks, can also address the needs of women farmers with limited access to cash income.

AGRICULTURAL EXTENSION AND INPUTS

Many interventions could enhance the productivity of small-scale farmers. For example, improved application of dung and seed bed preparation could increase harvests of staple crops. However, agricultural extension and services have historically served the interests and needs of commercial farmers. Although steps have been taken to reorient support towards subsistence farmers, many programmes fail to take account of the activities and priorities of women farmers. Initiatives that would benefit women often do not reach them. The legacy of neglect toward communal areas under the apartheid era continues to hinder the effectiveness of extension and veterinary services.

There are too few staff overall to serve the vast numbers of farmers. For example, 25 extension officers in the Owambo Regions serve a population of over 84,000 farmers, resulting in only one officer for over 3,000 farmers. Not surprisingly, many households have little if any contact with extension services. A survey of Okavango Region found that only 1/5 of households had received extension. The NDT survey found that only 13 households of 1365 total had been visited by agriculture or rural development extension officers. Time-consuming administration of the sale of inputs and other commercial services compounds this problem.

A review of extension in an Owambo district found that not a single extension officer had spent more than 30% of his or her time with farmers and so reached only an estimated 18% of farmers. Farmers who purchase seeds or fertiliser from extension offices often do not receive any advice about the use of inputs. In the Northern regions, regional agriculture staff spent as much as 90% of their time administering the tractor scheme. MAWRD has been unable to meet the high demand for the programme which may constitute unsustainable financial drain on the Ministry, which subsidizes an estimated 94% of the actual cost.

Women are less able to take advantage of these services, which, for the most part, are provided out of regional centers. Branch extension offices do not have the infrastructure to supply seeds, fertiliser and other services. Veterinary services, including the provision of medicine, are also centralised. Some extension officers lack transportation. Consequently, farmers must expend time and money to reach the central offices. This disadvantages women who are considerably less mobile than men. In many regions, women lack access to transportation and so usually walk. In some areas, such as the East, cultural norms dictate that women stay close to home; as a result, they have little contact with government institutions.

Although ownership of donkey carts is comparable, female-headed households in the South are less likely to own trucks or cars, important for travelling the long distances between settlements. In the Northern areas, female headed households are less likely to own bicycles or cars, and so make fewer journeys to towns. Lack of mobility also limits the involvement of women in auctions and marketing. Extension and veterinary officers do not record the number of farmers contacted by gender. Men comprise the majority of extension and veterinary staff. In some regions, where women must defer to men, there are few female extension officers to encourage and support their involvement. Extension officers often communicate with male farmers and do not seek out women farmers, who consequently rely on second-hand information from husbands or male relatives.

Clearly, the gender of extension officers alone will not guarantee that women are better served. However, the approach of male officers is often shaped by training and cultural proscriptions which value livestock production over agronomy and commercial production over subsistence and household food security. Despite the merger of rural development and agricultural extension, many officers lack exposure to concepts of household food security and integrated development. Women farmers often have different priorities. Recent studies in the Owambo Region highlighted the interest of women farmers in getting advice on planting and fertiliser techniques and crop rotations. They also stressed the need for reasonably priced seeds, implements, and pesticides, as well as access to millet processing and other technologies to reduce their workload.

Similarly, for women who till by hand, access to draught animals and ploughs would boost their productivity. They might be better served by programmes to support ploughing services, rather than the more costly and technical approach of tractor services. Agricultural services also do not take adequate account of the knowledge and experience of women farmers. Veterinary services and extension for livestock particularly fail to address women's role in the care of animals. Advice and support often stress cattle, with little comparable assistance on small animals, including chickens, which for some households is a more frequent source of protein than beef. Similarly, veterinary services and extension often overlook women's responsibilities for milking and lambing. Emphasizing meat production to the detriment of milk production can affect the nutritional status of households. Moreover, the health and growth rate of young stock is directly linked to milking practices.

During the recent drought, small holders benefitted least from government subsidies. In order to encourage off take, the programme included paying an extra amount for each goat or head of cattle sold. While some households waited too late to sell, many small holders took advantage of the cash incentive. However, the government also subsidized the price of fodder so that farmers could sustain herds through the drought. Wealthy stock owners could afford to purchase the fodder and maintain their large herds, while small owners found their herds reduced to dangerously low levels. Ultimately, well-targeted interventions to increase lambing rates, milk production, animal health and small-scale marketing will have relatively greater benefit to female-headed and other vulnerable households.

AGRICULTURAL AND RURAL DEVELOPMENT CENTERS

The Ministry of Agriculture is in the process of establishing Agricultural and Rural Development centers (ARDC's) to coordinate research extension and training of farmers and to coordinate inputs and marketing. In a pilot programme, the Council of Churches in Namibia (CCN) has established a handful of similar centers, which are being incorporated into the MAWRD extension service. Of note, the CCN programme especially hired women who had received agricultural training in exile. Over 20 of 28 officers are women, which will considerably boost the representation of women on the MAWRD staff.

By decentralising agricultural services through the communal areas, the ARDCs represent an important step in making extension and support more accessible. The ARDCs also provide an opportunity for the government to reduce unsustainable subsidies and to promote and support farmers associations and rural cooperatives to design and implement agricultural activities.

AGRICULTURAL TRAINING AND RESEARCH

Programmes by MAWRD, together with NGO initiatives have resulted in considerable progress in improving research and training oriented towards small-scale farming. An NGO project resulted in a quick-growing, drought resistant millet cultivar-an important development for small-scale farmers whose livelihoods are tied to unpredictable rainfall. The variety has been distributed and taken up by farmers, who plant it along with local varieties to minimise risk. When able, women have also planted the new cultivar. However, many women lack the cash to purchase seeds or do not know where to buy them, and so rely on seed from their own stock or from that of neighbours. Currently, a millet seed multiplication programme is encouraging local farmers to grow seed stock for sale.

The programme aims to increase the local availability of seed stock and enable farmers to generate income. Research must be tailored to the needs of small-scale farmers, through on-farm crop trials and livestock research that mirror local farming systems. Indeed, there has been little research and information on local farming strategies, including local knowledge and systems of decision-making. The introduction of new varieties to farmers must also include management of planting harvesting and storing the variety.

Training is also being reoriented. In 1992, a new curriculum for a 3 year diploma in agriculture was introduced. In addition to technical subject's extension, rural sociology and agricultural economics are taught. Admission policy at the Ogongo Agricultural College emphasizes regional balance and more representation of women in the student body. However, men still outnumber women in enrolment in the colleges. This gap is even more noticeable when compared to enrolment in agricultural subjects at the secondary level. Boys and girls are present in equal numbers in both agricultural science and agricultural production and farming throughout the various grade levels. Interestingly, in grades 10 and 11, there are more girls taking the two subjects, while at grade 12 (matriculation), boys outnumber girls.

Since admission into the agricultural college requires grade 12 math and science, boys are more likely to gain entry. This pattern suggests that as youths begin to choose vocational paths, girls are less likely to continue to pursue professional agricultural careers (although they may return to farming). Although gender stereotypes are one cause, another likely factor is the dearth of women teaching agricultural subjects, as well as in extension, who might serve as mentors to young girls. The curriculum for agricultural subjects at both the junior secondary and senior secondary levels is under revision, in part, through the introduction of the Cambridge system of secondary education.

Classes will include a greater emphasis on practical experience and will be made more relevant to Namibian agro-ecological zones. Horticulture and gardening will form one option of the new curriculum for grades 4-7 at the primary level. However, improving agricultural training at the secondary level faces several obstacles. Many agriculture teachers have their teacher certificate but lack training in agriculture. Plans are underway to include agriculture in-service courses and a new basic education teacher diploma. Agriculture also suffers from the stigma of being a vocational subject, and so gains less attention and resources than academic subjects. Lastly, few schools have the implements, demonstration plots and laboratory facilities needed to integrate practical experience with theoretical learning.

TECHNOLOGY

Namibia particularly lags behind on the development and use of labour saving technology. The vast majority of women continue to pound grains, farm, and collect water and wood by slow, physically-demanding methods. Technology is needed to enhance agricultural productivity as well as to reduce the burden and time of routine household tasks. Freeing up women's time on laborious activities can better enable them to take advantage of economic opportunities. The manufacturing and management of technologies can also provide income opportunities. A rural electrification programme has reached rural regions in Owambo and Okavango. Although the programme greatly benefits government offices, schools, clinics and missions, few households can afford the cost of supplying electricity to their homes.

The availability of electricity could support small scale manufacturing and agricultural processing in rural communities. Agricultural technology has been confined to costly, mechanized equipment, such as spray irrigation systems and tractors. Tractors and improved traction benefit men and women, who both undertake field preparation. Few technologies are available to women to enhance tasks for which they have almost sole responsibility, such as planting, weeding and harvesting. Any programme that addresses ploughing services should also explore options such as line makers that will make weeding and planting more efficient.

Any introduction of technology must also evaluate if the device will displace women from casual labour or employment, important sources of cash income. Improved food storage is also needed to prevent losses and nutritional decline. Large baskets are the granaries for many Northern households, but these are inadequate for keeping stores dry or for keeping out insects and rodents. Training women in alternative processing and drying techniques could also increase the longevity of food. In the Okavango and Caprivi regions, the supply of protein is jeopardized by problems with drying and storing fish. In stock producing regions, spoilage of milk is a problem. Only a small proportion of women have enjoyed access to food processing machines.

The desire is high for these devices, as women and girls spend approximately 50 hours month processing millet. One survey found that 75% of the poorest households would be willing to pay for processing.' Mills exist at centers in the Okavango and Caprivi Regions, primarily for farmers who are marketing their grains. They have had little success since the design was inappropriate for millet. In the Owambo Regions, a dozen community mills have been established as income generation activities. Poor management has hampered the success of the mills. Expensive milling fees, together with the cost of transportation to the mill are a disincentive for households, particularly those with small amounts to mill. Several reports have also noted that machine milling reduces the taste and shelf life of millet.

The Rural Development Centre, located in the Oshana Region, is actively involved in the development of appropriate technology. Alternative energy sources are one focal point of the Centre. Pilot programmes will assess the effectiveness of biogas, locally-made charcoal bricks, solar energy, and energy-saving ovens, to reduce reliance on fuel wood and evaporation cool-boxes. Also underway are efforts to improve transportation, such as donkey carts designed to improve transportation of water and harvests. One innovation of benefit to women has been the aqua roller, a water barrel that can be pushed. Tested during the 1992 drought, the device effectively halved the number of trips and the amount of time to fetch water, provided households with more water, thereby improving hygiene, and increased the involvement of men and children in water collection. Improved water collection, through rain gutters as well as water harvesting in fields are also being promoted.

FORESTRY AND NATURAL RESOURCE MANAGEMENT

Women's knowledge and reliance upon the environment make them the primary managers of natural resources such as forests, water, soil and vegetation. However, they are the principal victims of the deforestation, erosion and degradation scarring Namibia's environment. On a national level, the rural poor compete for natural resources with the demands of Windhoek and other urban centers. Urban residents, along with mining, industrial and commercial users consume proportionately higher levels of water and energy than their rural counterparts. Domestic rural consumption (by 70% of the population) is 85 liters a day/capita, compared to 330 liters a day/capita in urban areas. Irrigation alone accounts for almost 43% of the country's groundwater usage. Similarly, many urban residents continue to cook with fuel wood, relying on wood collected and transported from the rural areas.

Paradoxically, rural poverty further perpetuates the destruction of the resource base. Many women recognize that deforestation and other practices are harmful and even have the knowledge to promote conservation. However, in the absence of economic and technological alternatives, women see no other means of survival. A recent survey of fishing along the Okavango River found that many respondents felt that the use of mosquito nets for fishing is contributing to the decline of fish stocks. Despite this, many continue to use the nets, explaining that they cannot afford to buy meat and can no longer catch enough fish to feed the family with traditional methods.

Namibia is committed to the sustainable utilization and management of its natural resources. A national Green Plan actively calls for the participation of local users in managing and benefitting from the environment. However, to date, few programmes have targeted women. In the Northern regions, the planting and caring of trees is a task undertaken by women. Several NGOs are working with women to establish nurseries, including several managed by community groups, and to encourage tree-planting. Efforts are limited in part by access to water supply and fencing, needed to keep out small animals and protect seedlings against wind.

The influence of South Africa, where commercial forestry is an important part of the economy, has resulted in government forestry programmes orientated towards tree plantations and conservation through restricted use. Prior to independence, forestry in Namibia yielded no revenue and so received little attention. Consequently, forestry is not a well-known discipline in Namibia, resulting in a shortage of trained Namibian staff. Programmes to promote social and agro-forestry have yet to get beyond the planning stages. Women have had little positive contact with government staff from departments concerned with natural resource management. In the Okavango and Caprivi Regions, enforcement of regulations on fishing and harvesting of palm leaves (used for baskets) has led some women to view the Department of Nature Conservation Officers principally as policing authorities. Women are underrepresented on the Forestry field staff and virtually absent from the Nature Conservation Officer core. The enrolment of women in the Forestry programme at Ogongo, and in the proposed Faculty of Agriculture and Natural Resources at the University, should have a significant impact in diversifying the staff of these departments.

INEQUALITY IN ACCESS TO EMPLOYMENT

EMPLOYMENT IN AGRICULTURE

Economic research and policy analysis has typically focused on formal sector employment, overlooking those engaged in subsistence agriculture or in other non-wage earning activities. This focus excludes the majority of women who the census revealed are own account or unpaid family workers. Among the economically active population, 23% of rural women are own account workers, while 33% are unpaid family workers Women constitute over 60% of those employed in agricultural and fishery work; this work employs over 70% of rural women classified as employed.

Moreover, it is likely that the 1991 census, while taking account of subsistence agriculture for the first time, does not fully capture the involvement of women in the work force. Over one-fifth of women classified as homemakers were not considered economically active, an approach which overlooks the participation of many 'homemakers' in agriculture and other productive activities. Seemingly, one strategy to enhancing the livelihoods of women farmers is to support them to produce marketable surpluses. Cash earnings from agriculture could be used to enhance household food security and at higher levels, to invest further in agricultural activities or to support small-scale, non-farm enterprises. However, while agriculture is the largest sector of employment, it is not a major source of income.

Farmers with surplus production to sell must contend with a poorly developed formal market, in part due to the high cost of transporting livestock and produce, particularly from the North. For communal farmers, including women, informal markets are often more profitable and convenient for occasional sales. More importantly, for many households, improving agriculture is secondary in importance to gaining waged jobs. Agricultural productivity is no longer sufficient to ensure household food security, let alone to generate cash income. Instead, households rely on cash income from non-agricultural sources to supplement food production. Thus, off-farm employment and income generation are central components of agricultural and rural development in Namibia. More importantly, strategies to empower rural women must enhance their access to and control over cash income.

FORMAL SECTOR EMPLOYMENT

The expansion of Windhoek and other towns continues to overshadow regional development in Namibia. 42% of jobs in the formal sector are in Windhoek, home to less than 10% of the population. In rural areas, public sector employment constitutes the primary source of employment. Wage-earning opportunities in the private sector are confined to work on commercial farms or in construction or local shops. As a result urbanisation is rising steadily, and growing numbers of migrants are straining housing and social service infrastructure. The situation of school leavers is particularly problematic. The 2,000 new jobs created each year fall far short of an ILO estimate that the creation of 20,000 formal sector jobs in a five year period is needed to curb unemployment.

Many youths are detached from agriculture and other rural activities and view only civil servant posts or salaried positions as acceptable employment. Social problems, such as alcoholism, crime and violence are on the rise, particularly in rural towns. Women are not adequately represented in formal sector employment. In 1988, women comprised 33 % of those formally employed. The 1991 census showed little change, with women accounting for 31% of the formally employed, and 25% of those employed in rural areas. Rural women have higher levels of literacy and educational attainment than rural men, but are less likely to get unskilled jobs, such as in construction. At the same time, they are far less likely to be literate or to have reached secondary school than their urban counterparts and are less likely to obtain professional positions.

The NDT survey of 1800 women in the Owambo Regions found that over 90% of respondents had never been employed in the formal sector. Another study in a nearby location found that men were twice as likely to have a job in the formal sector as women. Women must contend with lower pay, less management responsibility, and the low status attributed to female dominated professions, such as nursing and teaching. Even in these professions, the male to female ratios are reversed at senior levels.

Men outnumber women in management and business occupations. Women make up the large army of domestic workers employed by middle and upper class households in urban towns. Importantly, this category of employment is now protected under the labour act.

Although not well-enforced, the act provides an important framework for action by the recently formed domestic workers union. The new farm workers union will also lobby for improved working conditions and rights of this class of labourers and their families. The situation is more difficult for rural women in formal employment. Those who are employed often lack job security and medical or other employment benefits, in addition to low pay, as low as N$25 month. Pre-schools and crèches, in short supply in the towns, are virtually non-existent in the rural areas. Thus, employed mothers must rely on family support for the care of children. As noted above, leaving children in the care of pensioners and relatives has allowed many women to migrate to urban areas.

The government aims to promote foreign and private sector investment in the communal areas. Commercial enterprises around commodity crops, such as cotton, oilseeds, and sugarcane, are being developed. Options to boost off-farm employment include agro-industries around the processing of food and products as well as non-agricultural manufacturing and services. However, experience so far suggests that many agricultural development schemes offer limited job creation. As a result, improved productivity through subsistence-based land use might yield greater economic returns. There is also potential for employment through public works programmes. Two labour-based road projects have been undertaken in the North, with the first road already completed. Recruitment and hiring policies stressed that women should have an equal opportunity to participate.

At first, communication, channelled through the headmen, failed to reach women. This reflects the persistent division that wage-earning opportunities are for men, while women are expected to take up food for work activities. However, at the urging of the donor, renewed efforts resulted in a labour force of between 28-40% women. However, women were less likely to be promoted to positions of more responsibility. Of note, an informal taboo existed among rural residents of both sexes against the participation of married women who were seen to be supported by their husbands. Thus, the project made only minor inroads in changing attitudes but did improve the wellbeing of women and their families. Some women were able to invest in production or in their own education.

Finally, several pilot programmes are assessing the potential of community-based wildlife programmes to enhance conservation and to generate income for nearby communities. It is too early to judge the effectiveness of this option, although such programmes still require enabling legislation which recognises local rights over land and resources. However, to date, the focus has been exclusively on game, traditionally a male domain. There are few programmes aimed at community-based resource management of trees, plants and fish-resources more utilised by women.

INFORMAL SECTOR AND INCOME GENERATION ACTIVITIES

Unable to find formal jobs, women are engaging in petty trade and other informal sector activities. Unlike in other African countries, most regions in Namibia lack a tradition of entrepreneurial activity. Only since Independence has a lively informal sector, with open markets and home enterprises, begun to emerge. However, as with formal employment, the informal sector has quickly become stratified by gender. Men dominate activities with high profit margins, such as taxi-driving or middle-level trade. Women carry out activities, such as selling cooked food, brewing beer, and making baskets or crafts, with low profit margins and considerable time requirements. Incomes are low, averaging N$50-80 month. However, some women entrepreneurs have turned small-scale activities into lucrative businesses.

For example, women in the Caprivi dominate the marketing of fish, and a number of successful fishmongers own boats, hire fishermen, and provide credit. The production and marketing of baskets also appears to be flourishing, and the informal marketing of large baskets in Owambo extends into South Africa. Many groups have identified the potential of income generating activities to improve the livelihoods of women and their families. Church institutions, NGOs, and government groups, including the Department of Women Affairs and the Directorate of Community Development, are mobilising women around community level projects.

Increasingly, spurred on by the success of initiatives in other towns and villages, women themselves are coming forward to request support for income generation. As a result, projects are blossoming throughout the country.

Yet, to date, a small proportion of income generating activities have enjoyed success in improving the incomes of women and in expanding their sphere of skills and experience. While it is important that projects utilise women's know-how, many activities are centered on tasks traditionally seen as women's work; projects include bakeries, sewing and needlecraft, brick making and gardening. As a result, women learn few new skills and do not always receive training and support in finance and management. In some regions, projects have failed to acknowledge that women in the area do not, in fact, have a tradition of needlework, sewing, gardening, etc. Emphasizing "women's work" reinforces gender patterns, which may be acceptable if the enterprise is financially viable.

However, few initiatives are supported with appropriate planning and feasibility studies. Markets in cash-strapped rural areas are particularly weak. People simply do not have the cash to spend. As a result, income-generating projects tend to be concentrated in rural centers, where government employees and other wage earners provide a customer base.

Some rural women are able to sell their goods at livestock auctions or the "pension fairs" which take place on pay out days. Moreover, even rural Namibians have become accustomed to purchasing produce and ready made clothing and products from South Africa. Groups producing clothing and handicraft will also have to compete with the South African market and overcome well-ingrained consumer preferences. Consequently, participants may expend much time and labour only to earn little or no money.

Other constraints to programmes include the lack of affordable materials or the limited availability of natural resources, such as water for gardens or cement, or fuel wood. The burdensome workload of women also inhibits their ability to participate in income generation. An evaluation of community gardens in the North found that the time which women had to put into travelling to and working in the garden diverted their attention away from agricultural tasks.

Moreover, the gardens did not consider women's experience with growing tomatoes and other small vegetables in their homestead, where using rainfed production places less demands on their time. Mobilizing for income generation can also ignore the weak foundations for community organizations.

Many rural communities in Namibia are inexperienced in cooperative or group models. Income generation projects must therefore assess if group participation is feasible or if involvement on an individual basis might be more desirable. Development organizations and community groups are drawing on the growing wealth of experience to redesign income generation activities and improve prospects for success. A number of NGO and government programmes are underway to build capacity in planning, training, management and evaluation of income-generating activities.

PROGRAMMES AND EXPERIMENTS IN SUPPORT OF WOMEN

Although still in the embryonic stages, a range of government and non-government initiatives seek to involve women in leadership and decision-making and to improve their access to resources and services. Programmes and policies aimed at rural women in particular signal a growing recognition of their contribution to household food security and to the well-being of much of the Namibian population.

In its analysis of changes since Namibian Independence, this chapter has highlighted measures which seek to redress political, legal, social and economic imbalances faced by women farmers. Additional trends and programmes of merit are discussed below. It must be stressed that this study does not do justice to the wealth of innovation and experimentation occurring at the grassroots level. Moreover, the value of development Programmes lies as much in the experience and lessons they offer as in the success.

POLICY PLANNING AND RESEARCH

On the most basic level, programmes have aimed to promote awareness and sensitivity to gender issues in government circles and among the general public. An initiative, supported by the Swedish International Development Agency (SIDA), seeks to ensure those women's concerns and priorities are fully integrated into national planning processes. The programme emphasizes training in gender-sensitive planning for civil servants and networking among key Ministries, including MAWRD, and the National Planning Commission (NPC), responsible for development planning in the country. The fledgling inter-ministerial gender network could prove an important forum for urging policy-makers to incorporate gender in national and sectoral planning processes. Similarly, an effort by an NGO, the Namibia National Women's Organization (NANAWO) educated parliamentarians on issues of women and health and urged them to involve women in their constituencies to address these concerns.

Gender-sensitive planning must be backed up by appropriate research and analysis, a process which has only recently begun in Namibia The NPC's Central Statistics Office, in consultation with government departments, research centers and NGOs, has devised a strategy to generate, analyze, present and disseminate gender-specific statistics. This process represents an important step in overcoming the dearth of statistics needed to inform policy. The Ministry of Education and Culture has established a system of gender-based statistics to monitor differential enrolment and retention rates. Other important research initiatives include the research project of the Legal Assistance Centre and the economic and legal study of the Owambo regions, undertaken by the Namibia Development Trust (NDT) and the University Law Faculty.

There are plans to replicate the latter survey in other communal areas. It is envisaged that a new gender research unit at the University of Namibia (UNAM) research centre, the Social Sciences Division, will promote ongoing and systematic research and policy discussion around gender issues. Research findings are also being made accessible and disseminated at the local level Although practice is not widespread, simplified versions of the Division of Rural Development's socio-economic survey of the South and the NDT study have proven useful for promoting awareness of the obstacles faced by rural women and for generating debate on development options. The Owambo survey also formed the basis for designing workshops for rural men and women on the implications of customary law.

The Central Statistics Office is coordinating the production of a simple booklet with data on women and men in Namibia. Despite these steps forward, women farmers remain underrepresented in national-level planning and research, even in sectoral initiatives that target the communal areas. However, soon to commence is a programme supported by the Food and Agriculture Organization and MAWRD to integrate women into agricultural development programmes. An important component of the programme will be to improve national agricultural planning through the development of gender-sensitive data collection and approaches to planning. The programme also aims to train extension staff in socio-economic and gender analysis so that regional experiences and needs flow into agricultural and rural development plans and policies.

PUBLIC AWARENESS

Efforts also aim to make the public aware of women's rights and of gender issues -the relations between men and women. Namibia is fortunate to have supportive leadership. The President and Prime Minister have been two of the nation's most vocal supporters of women, examples which pose a small but significant challenge to the male dominance prevalent in many rural areas. The radio and print media ensure that debate and discussion of the obstacles faced by women reach a wide audience. The Government newspaper, New Era, is mandated to emphasize community and rural development issues and does so in both English and indigenous language articles These efforts are complemented by campaigns and information, such as that prepared by the Legal Assistance Centre to inform local groups of the rights of women and children enshrined in the Constitution.

As noted earlier, the Department of Women's Affairs has simplified and translated the UNCEDAW into Namibian languages to stimulate discussion at all levels. In rural schools, efforts are underway to make the curriculum gender-sensitive and to provide guidance and support to girls to overcome gender-barriers when choosing careers. For example, the NANAWO branch in the Okavango region is encouraging girls in secondary schools to consider non-traditional careers, including agriculture professions. Although not gender-specific, education and media campaigns have also been actively used to educate the public on issues of direct relevance to rural women. Government ministries and NGOs together have produced publications and radio Programmes on topics such as AIDS, wise water use, and the causes of desertification.

LEGAL AND POLICY REFORM

Lively debate and informed planning and research are instrumental to creating the legal and policy environment to support the advancement of rural women. Progress has been limited, in part due to the slow and cumbersome translation of polices into legislation. However, new policies, such as a plan to develop an agriculture bank for the communal areas or a policy to establish conservancies for community-based wildlife management, signal greater attention to the need for a legal and policy framework to underpin rural and agricultural development. These policies display some gender sensitivity and would improve the access of rural women to essential resources.

The Co-operative Act, now under review by Parliament, is a notable example of both participation in the policy process itself and of legislation which can create the conditions for local-level organization and control of credit and other productive resources. An advisory committee of government and NGOs developed the policy through broad consultation, and the committee will become a legally-recognized board once the Act is passed. The policy encourages the development of autonomous co-operatives as vehicles for empowering women and, as discussed earlier, stipulates the participation of women in management structures.

ACCESS TO PRODUCTIVE RESOURCES AND SERVICES

As legal reform and policy development continues, programmes and interventions are targeting rural women at the local level. The Ministry of Agriculture, Water and Rural Development (MAWRD) is implementing several measures aimed at improving extension capacity and outreach to communal farmers in general, and to women farmers in particular. One important initiative in Namibia is the Division of Rural Development's Household Food Security Programme (HFS), closely supported by UNICEF. The programme aims to enhance household food security, particularly for female-headed households, by improving agricultural services and rural development support to women and by reducing the time and labour of women on burdensome tasks.

The programme trained rural development extension staff, now incorporated into the main agricultural service, in communication skills, participatory development, and, importantly, on concepts of household food security and gender. In addition, the extension staffs mobilise local partici-pation, in part through training and support to community-based rural development promoters, most of whom are women. Through the FAO programme noted above, other agricultural extension workers will gain training and experience in participatory and gender-aware approaches. An international NGO, ACORD, is conducting similar training over a five-year period for field workers from farmers associations, the national trade union, and government extension staff.

In addition, a newly formed Home Economics Advisory Board is exploring the potential role of home economists in extension, an involvement intended to aid women and men both in income generation and household resource management. Finally, the Ministry is seeking to shift from the administration of costly services to the provision of extension, research and other farmer support. Over a dozen Agricultural and Rural Development centers have been or are near completion. The decentralised Agricultural and Rural Development centers will facilitate the contact of extension services with women farmers and enhance their access to agricultural services and inputs. In the Caprivi, a committee of nongovernment and government staff is considering how the involvement of the Likwama Farmer's Co-operative in selling seeds and inputs and in providing other services can promote complementarily between the Co-operative and MAWRD. Although this process has not addressed women farmers, this co-operation will improve the participation of local people in the Centers.

These programmes are a central step towards reorienting agricultural services towards women farmers. The HFS programme, as well as efforts by the Rural Development Centre, CCN and Canadian-Namibian Cooperation (CANAMCO) has led to the pilot introduction of appropriate technologies in some villages. The aqua roller was introduced to female-headed households through the HFS programme. In collaboration with NDT, the Rural Development Centre is designing new donkey carts for transporting water and crops. The experiences with these technologies, such as hammer mills for millet and agricultural implements, are leading to new designs, as well as management strategies more suitable for Namibian women.

To date, these projects have been ad hoc and have led to only limited exchange of experience. A UNIFEM-supported initiative, recently underway, will assess technologies of greatest value and relevance to Namibian women on a broader scale. A particularly fruitful area of NGO involvement has been in credit unions and rural savings schemes. Organizations such as the Rural People's Institute for Social Empowerment (RISE) and the Namibia Credit Union League have gained considerable experience-from successes and from shortcomings - in supporting local groups to manage and administer group savings and credit programmes.

Many of the credit unions have helped women to mobilize and invest their cash resources. Also valuable are lessons learned by the Private Sector Foundation, the Institute for Management and Leadership Training, Cooperation for Development and other NGOs providing credit and small loans, and training to women entrepreneurs. Similarly, although not always profitable, income generation activities have enhanced the skills and knowledge of women in management, finance and communication.

NETWORKING

Until recently, government and NGO co-operation was weak, and a lack of development coordination resulted in duplication and inefficient resources. Linkages across sectors, within and between regions, and between government and NGOs are helping to improve service provision, enhance access to policy-making, and stimulate the exchange of ideas and information. For example, the Department of Women Affairs has set up a coordinating structure to facilitate NGO, government and donor participation in nine priority areas under which gender concerns will be addressed. Rural Community programmes constitute one of the areas, and priorities are to implement rural job creation, to reduce the workload of women, to sensitize rural communities to gender issues and to implement projects to reduce malnutrition in rural areas. MAWRD and CCN will be the lead agencies.

Several government Ministries are also seeking to coordinate the use of volunteer promoters in literacy, rural development and community health programmes. Regional rural development committees of Ministry, donor, and NGO staff exist in the Owambo regions and in the South. Similar government-NGO coordination is also being formed around both vocational training and micro-enterprise, where there is an array of diverse, ad-hoc initiatives. In the NGO sector, rural organizations are represented in both of the two umbrella organizations. NGO collaboration and consultation with community-based organizations has led to plans for a national, participatory People's Land Conference, to be held in August

1994. Gender issues are a focal point of the research and preparations for the conference.

PROMOTING LOCAL CAPACITY

The success with which policies and endeavours benefit rural women will only emerge over time and with careful assessment. Achievements must be measured against the backdrop of the nation's recent Independence and relatively brief exposure to democracy and participation. In this sense, it is the promotion and nurturing of grassroots organizations which represents the most significant step towards advancing rural women. A number of programmes seek to strengthen local-level structures and organizations to empower local residents to design, manage and assess development processes in their areas. Developing local capacity takes time, and many communities continue to rely on external funds and technical assistance to implement programmes.

Nevertheless, rural women are being incorporated into decision-making and leadership processes through their involvement in local committees and grassroots organizations. Women are present at all decision-making levels in UNICEF's Integrated Area Based Programme, a regional, multi-sectoral development initiative. Piloted in a district in Owambo, the programme has led to the formation of active committees at the village, district and regional levels as well as sectoral committees around agriculture, water and sanitation and other issues. Women are increasingly involved in the management of water points through community-based Water Point Committees. Other initiatives which seek to involve women in community decision-making structures include CANAMCO's regional rural development programme in the Okavango, and the Sustainable Animal Range Development Programme, with pilot projects in six villages and small towns in the East and South.

While their participation in community organizations is important to promoting gender equality, rural women in Namibia often lack the experience or confidence to accept leadership and decision-making roles. For this reason, some NGOs are supporting the establishment of women only organizations or women-only branches. An affiliated association to the Eastern Epukiro Farmers Association gives Herero women farmers the confidence and autonomy to speak and participate apart from their dominant male counterparts. Similarly, Southern women involved in the regional farmers union have formed the Good Hope Women's Co-operative to better advance their own concerns. Separate organizations could further marginalise women by confining them to stereotypical tasks.

In the absence of training and support in organizational management, some organizations have disintegrated, resulting in frustration and disappointment. However, women-only organizations formed around farming and other mainstream activities appear to enable rural women to assert their knowledge and interest and to gain experience in agriculture and rural development programmes. Independence ushered in financial and technical support from multi-lateral and bi-lateral agencies, many of whom had worked only in the wings with the exiled liberation movement. These agencies have emphasized gender issues in programming and assistance to the government and nongovernment sectors.

For example, international assistance has been central to supporting the Department of Women Affairs and to women's organizations such as NANAWO and Sister Collective. The international community has placed priority on women's rights and helped to promote the initiatives aimed at legal education and reform education and reform initiatives. Several agencies, such as SIDA and the Norwegian aid agency, NORAD, have direct grant-making Programmes for activities which specifically target women. More commonly, donors expect applications for financial support to demonstrate gender-sensitivity in project design, management and evaluation. A number of international agencies request that proposals specifically show how women will benefit or be affected. Some donors also request applicant organizations to specify gender composition of staff and management of boards with a view to redressing imbalances in decision-making posts.

These requirements, together with advocacy and networking, have clearly prompted government ministries and

NGOs to better address gender issues in planning and implementation. This influence and control is two-directional. For Namibian NGOs and groups excluded from policy processes, international agencies also serve as a channel for influencing policy. Many foreign donors help to promote to government the ideas and concerns of women's groups, farmers associations and other Namibian organizations underrepresented in policy processes. A donor co-ordination group on Women in Development is helping to reduce overlap in programming and to better spread resources. Separate sub-committees focus on women in micro-enterprises, women and law, women NGOs, preparations for Beijing, the Department of Women Affairs, and women and training.

However, few donors have translated the focus on gender to support to women farmers. Inversely, technical cooperation in the agricultural sector, even programmes targeting communal farmers, have taken little account of gender issues, and so too, have yielded few benefits to women farmers. Like many of the groups they support, international agencies are Windhoek-based. Those with regional staff are often engaged in infrastructural programmes, such as rural water supply, or micro-enterprise and have limited contact with rural communities. Agricultural projects for women are often confined to horticulture and forestry and preclude crop and livestock production. In addition to the UNICEF and FAO support described above, a notable exception has been the collaboration of the Danish aid agency, DANIDA, with CCN to recruit and train women extension officers and to improve services for women through pilot Agriculture and Development centers in the North.

Finally, Namibian staff in government, NGOs and CBOs has already echoed concerns raised in countries with more experience with donors. These include an emphasis on project-based rather than core-funding, bias towards particular regions and paternalism towards Namibian institutions, who find their autonomy and control over the development agenda compromised. Others worry that donor support perpetuates dependency, and that, in the absence of financial support and strong local capacity, many initiatives will crumble. Namibia faces the complex challenges of redressing social and economic imbalances and forging a climate of democracy in which all are willing and able to participate.

In Namibia, many leaders have recognized the situation of struggle and inequality of women. Greater attention is being given to the role of women in development. The country has demonstrated its commitment to providing better health and education services and to improving conditions in the workplace. The Constitution, together with ongoing legal reform and awareness, is helping to create an environment conducive to women's rights. However, little of this progress has reached rural women, who continue to struggle under heavy workloads, food insecurity, and unequal access to economic resources and opportunities and social services. Rural women are almost entirely absent from public life and their concerns are underrepresented in the organs of government.

Those women farmers constitute the primary food producers and caretakers of children must be recognised. Indeed, taking the needs of women farmers into account is a matter of efficiency as well as equity. Programmes are more likely to succeed if women participate. Improving the food security, productivity and well-being of rural households can reduce the need for costly food aid, curative health care and other crisis interventions. Thus, rural women must be specifically targeted in order to improve their economic and legal status and, in turn, to empower them to participate in development and change. As identified at a consultative workshop on Women and Agriculture, a range of short-term and long-term strategies are needed to promote the advancement of women farmers. While some strategies offer concrete actions, others target changing attitudes and increasing awareness.

Women and Decision-making

1. Affirmative action legislation is expected to be passed by the end of 1994. This measure should be used to ensure

that women are better represented in decision-making positions. There should be provision for greater representation of women as members of parliament and on the regional and national councils. Women's involvement in national and sectoral decision-making can help incorporate gender in planning and can yield long-term results in changing attitudes and priorities.

2. Although some planners and civil servants have received training in gender awareness, there is still a lack of understanding of gender issues. Many government officials and leaders continue to equate gender only with feminism or see it as a woman's issue. Campaigns to create greater gender awareness are needed to ensure that both men and women take responsibility for advancing women's status.
3. NGOs, CBOs and the private sector must also be lobbied to include more women in management positions and in decision-making bodies, such as boards and committees.
4. Educated people and those in positions of authority must set an example by recognizing and respecting women as equals.

Institutions to Advance Women

1. The Department of Women Affairs must be strengthened as a mouthpiece. It should have representation in the Cabinet and have an official presence in the 13 regions.
2. Women's organizations remain urban-based. Professionals working in the rural areas should help mobilize rural women into pressure groups.
3. Farmers associations or affiliated branches of women farmers should be promoted and supported.
4. Rural institutions often cater to interest groups and serve the influential and wealthy. Skills in strategic planning are needed to ensure that rural institutions clearly target and aim to serve women and other marginalised groups.
5. The National Planning Commission should encourage donors and NGOs to be more evenly distributed among the regions. Although some progress has been made, formal

mechanisms are needed to improve coordination among all NGO, private sector, and government institutions working with rural people. These networks should be used to advocate on behalf of the rural poor and to communicate the needs of rural women into policy processes.

Promotion of Women's Rights

1. The country must urgently repeal/amend discriminatory laws. Women should be able to obtain credit and loans in their own right, marriage laws should be amended, and there must be guarantees that women can have equal access and secure rights to land. This process should be expedited through the following strategies:
   A. Greater financial and technical support to the Women and Law Reform Committee could expedite the process of review and recommendations.
   B. Women should be encouraged to challenge unconstitutional laws in the courts in order to set legal precedents.
   C. Namibia's capacity to facilitate legal reform is stretched. A specially-recruited legal drafter is needed to translate recommendations into legal bills.

Understanding Poverty and the Status of Rural Women

1. Socio-economic research is needed to better understand the causes and effects of poverty on rural women and their families.
   A. Research by the government and by institutes such as the Namibian Economic Policy Research Unit should assess the impact of macro-economic and sectoral policies on women.
   B. There is a need for gender-disaggregated statistics within all Ministries and among non-governmental organizations. The upcoming National Comprehensive Agricultural Survey, to be conducted jointly by the CSO and MAWRD, should include gender-based questions and analysis.

C. Research should also evaluate the power-relations and processes at the household level. Topics include: the fluidity of household composition; division of labour within the household; decision-making processes; the changes in interests in power in productive, domestic and reproductive spheres, and patterns of resource allocation within and between households.

D. Greater information on the informal coping strategies of rural women should inform interventions designed to improve access to credit, technology, employment and services.

E. Longitudinal studies are needed to monitor the status of rural poor women over time. Oral histories of women are also an important tool for understanding cultural attitudes, social changes, and the means by which women survive.

F. The role of women in natural resource use and management also needs to be addressed.

Improving Women's Access to Productive Resources and Services

1. Agricultural services should be further decentralised to reach out to the needy, who are not able to reach Agricultural and Rural Development Centers.
2. Extension officers should undertake agricultural needs assessments of women farmers. Extension staff in agriculture, veterinary services, forestry and nature conservation should receive in-service training on participatory and gender-aware development approaches.
3. Many services stress high technological inputs, such as tractor services. Women farmers often cannot afford these services or are not reached by them. Agricultural services can both improve local participation and improve yields by focusing on simple, low cost interventions, such as improved seed bed preparation and straight line sowing and planting.

4. Namibia must develop an appropriate technology base for women's agricultural and domestic tasks. Technologies of use to Namibian women include line makers and weeding tools, simple hand or animal powered mills, and improved food storage. Information and experiences with technology should be disseminated to community groups, NGOs, and extension staff through newsletters and workshops. The Rural Development Centre in the North is a likely candidate for this role.
5. On-farm teals should women farmers. Women should be involved in research on and distribution of improved crop varieties.
6. Veterinary services must be targeted to women farmers.
7. Extension officers have observed that women are more likely to attend and participate in meetings when it is conducted by a woman. MAWRD and other Ministries with extension or field work staff should increase the number of women extension officers. This will entail the following:
   A. Working conditions must be conducive for women to be fieldworkers. Decentralising the agricultural services will reduce the distances which extension officers must travel to meet farmers. Primarily seen as an urban issue, the provision of child care facilities at the extension officer's workplace is also essential.

   B. The agricultural colleges should implement affirmative action enrolment policies. Experience and skills should be taken into account for those women who, due to pregnancy, marriage, or economic reasons, did not obtain the required educational qualifications. Faculty and staff must be sensitized to the cultural and social obstacles faced by women students.

   C. Girls should be encouraged to consider agriculture and environment professions and bursary programmes should assist young women to pursue higher education in agriculture, forestry and natural resources. Extension officers, agricultural teachers and even farmers can serve as mentors to girls in agricultural subjects.

8. Extension officers and NGOs working in rural areas should utilise rural development promoters, many of whom are women, as a liaison to local villages.
9. Credit unions, NGOs and MAWRD, currently developing a rural bank, should exchange ideas and develop creative savings and loan schemes appropriate to the needs of rural women. A campaign should urge rural women to save in banks, post offices or local schemes.
10. Pilot programmes should assess the viability of resource sharing initiatives, such as programmes with draught-animal power, or group ownership of breeding animals.
11. MAWRD should implement gender-based record-keeping and evaluations to assess if agricultural serv-ices,inputs and small loans schemes are reaching women.
12. Rural institutions should improve linkages with the Southern African Development community so that Namibia can learn from the problems and successes of promoting women farmers in neighbouring countries.

Improving Women's Access to Employment and Income-earning Opportunities

1. Women's productive work in agriculture and other 'informal" spheres should be recognized in national statistics and policies.
2. Initiatives to market agricultural produce and livestock production should incorporate rural women.
3. Income-generation activities are often used to mobilize women who have limited experience or inclination to work in groups. Programmes to support income-generation should also work with individual women to develop financially-viable enterprises.
4. Gender-sensitive, labour-based projects, such as the road construction project in the North, should be replicated elsewhere in the country. Except for short-term, drought relief programmes, payment should be in cash, not food.

5. National development planning should give priority to agribusiness and off-farm enterprises which will create wage-earning opportunities for rural women.

5

ZAPU Women in Zambia

The Rhodesian Bush War also known as the Zimbabwe War of Liberation or the Second Chimurenga, was a civil war in what was then the country of Rhodesia, which lasted from July 1964 to 1979. The war and subsequent settlement led to the implementation of universal suffrage, the end of the white minority ruled nation of Rhodesia and the short-lived government of Zimbabwe-Rhodesia, and the creation of the Republic of Zimbabwe under the leadership of Prime Minister Robert Mugabe. The Rhodesian government under Ian Smith and Zimbabwe-Rhodesian government under Abel Muzorewa fought against Robert Mugabe's Zimbabwe African National Union and Joshua Nkomo's Zimbabwe African People's Union.

After World War II, most African colonies sought independence from colonial powers. This stemmed mainly from the wide disparities in wealth possession between blacks and whites. In Rhodesia, Europeans owned most of the fertile land whilst Africans were crowded on barren land. Furthermore, forced labour in white-owned mines and brutal repression against blacks led to widespread motivation for resistance against the minority government. Throughout the 1960s and 70s the Soviet Union and the People's Republic of China trained and funded mainly Communist African armies of liberation to expand their global influence and gain access to natural resources against the backdrop of the Cold War. After the Sino-Soviet Split these two powers were often in competition with each other and hence there were two liberation armies in the

Rhodesian Bush War; ZANLA supported by China and ZIPRA supported by the Soviet Union.

After gaining independence, the Soviet or Chinese backed nationalists would normally form Marxist/Socialist states, aligned with the Communist Bloc. This ensured valuable trade links and strategic influence in the region. This pattern was established earlier in South East Asia with conflicts such as the Vietnam War and Cambodian Civil War and in neighbouring African countries with conflicts such as the Angolan War of Independence, Mozambican War of Independence, Gaddafi in Libya or the 1974 coup in Ethiopia leading to the rule of the Marxist Derg. The ZANLA fighters were mainly Shona and were supported by the People's Republic of China and North Korea, whereas the ZAPU fighters were mainly Ndebele and were supported by the Soviet Union and East Germany. Each group fought separate guerrilla wars against the Rhodesian Security Forces.

Rebels were armed with a wide range of weapons, including Russian grenades, Tokaråv pistols, PPSh sub-machineguns, the Czech M52/57, the French MAS, German Mauser rifles, and MP40 sub-machineguns, but the most common infantry weapon was the AK-47 and the SKS. The nationalist movements also used a variety of Soviet and Chinese-made equipment which eventually included surface-to-air missiles and land mines. The use of ambushes and surprise attacks on civilian convoys and rural farms and villages was a common tactic as these areas were often hard to defend. Nationalists derailed several Rhodesian Railways trains with explosives, and brought down to civilian airliners. In June 1979, the governments of Cuba and Mozambique offered direct military assistance to the Patriotic Front, but Mugabe and Nkomo declined.

The Communist Party of Great Britain actively supported ZAPU. North Korean military officials taught Zimbabwean militants how to use explosives and arms in a camp near Pyongyang. By April 1979, 12,000 ZANLA troops were training in Tanzania, Ethiopia, and Libya. The Bush War overlapped several Cold War conflicts in its neighbouring countries, including Angola's war of independence (1961-1975) and civil war (1975-2002), Mozambique's war of independence (1964-1974) and Mozambican Civil War (1977 to 1992), and Shaba I (1977) and Shaba II (1978).

CIVIL DISOBEDIENCE (1957-1964)

In September 1956, bus fares in Salisbury were raised to the point at which workers were spending between 18% and 30% of their earnings on transportation. The City Youth League responded by boycotting the United Transport Company's buses and succeeded in preventing the price change. On 12 September 1957 members of the Youth League and the defunct ANC formed the Southern Rhodesia African National Congress, led by Joshua Nkomo. The Whitehead administration banned the SRANC in 1959 and arrested 307 leaders, excluding Nkomo who was out of the country, on 29 February in Operation Sunrise. Nkomo, Mugabe, Herbert Chitepo, and Ndabaningi Sithole established the National Democratic Party in January 1960. Nkomo became its leader in October.

An NDP delegation headed by Nkomo attended the constitutional conference in January 1961. While Nkomo initially supported the constitution, he reversed his position after other NDP leaders disagreed. The government banned the NDP in December 1961 and arrested NDP leaders, excluding Nkomo who, again, was out of the country. Nkomo formed the Zimbabwe African People's Union which the Whitehead administration banned in September 1962. The United Federal Party, campaigning on majority rule, lost overwhelmingly in the 1962 general election to the more conservative Rhodesian Front. Nkomo, legally barred from forming a new political party, moved ZAPU's headquarters to Dar es Salaam, Tanzania.

In July 1963 Nkomo suspended Ndabaningi Sithole, Robert Mugabe, Leopold Takawira, and Washington Malianga for their opposition to his continued leadership of ZAPU. On 8 August they announced the establishment of the Zimbabwe African National Union. ZANU members formed a militant wing, the Zimbabwe African National Liberation Army, and sent ZANLA members to the People's Republic of China for training. In July 1964 ZANLA forces assassinated a Rhodesian Front official and the war began.

FIRST PHASE (1964-1972)

The Smith administration detained the ZANU and ZAPU political leadership, headed by Joshua Nkomo and Robert Mugabe, in August 1964. The major political leaders imprisoned were Ndabaningi Sithole, Leopald Takawira, Edgar Tekere, Enos Nkala. Maurice Nyagumbo. In April 1966, the Rhodesian armed forces engaged militants in Sinoia, the first major engagement. The military leaders of ZANLA, which consisted of Dare Rechimurenga, were barrister Herbert Chitepo, and Josiah Tongogara. Militants began launching attacks against Rhodesia in the mid-1960s, first from bases in Zambia and later from Mozambique. The conflict intensified after the Unilateral Declaration of Independence from Britain on 11 November 1965. Sanctions were implemented by the British government after UDI, and member states of the United Nations endorsed the British embargo.

The embargo meant the Rhodesian Forces were hampered by a lack of modern equipment but used other means to receive vital war supplies such as receiving oil, munitions, and arms via the government of apartheid-era South Africa. War material was also obtained through elaborate international smuggling schemes, domestic production, and equipment captured from infiltrating enemy combatants. In the latter months of 1971, the Black Nationalist factions united and formed a coalition which became known as the 'Joint Guerrilla Alliance to Overthrow the Government.'

SECOND PHASE (1972-1979)

The black nationalists operated from secluded bases in neighbouring Zambia and from FRELIMO-controlled areas in the Portuguese colony of Mozambique. These militants made periodic raids into Rhodesia. With the decline of the Portuguese empire from 1974 to 1976, Ian Smith realised Rhodesia was surrounded on three sides by hostile nations and declared a formal state of emergency. Soon Mozambique closed its 800-

mile-long border with Rhodesia, but Rhodesian forces often crossed the border in "hot pursuit" raids, attacking the nationalists and their training camps. In 1976, Rhodesian Selous Scouts destroyed a camp containing many hundreds of trainees, which they claimed was a military target.

The nationalists claimed the site was a refugee camp. The Rhodesians also operated into Zambia after Nkomo's nationalists shot down two unarmed Vickers Viscount civilian airliners with Soviet supplied SAM-7 heat-seeking missiles. In the first incident, Air Rhodesia Flight RH825, ten passengers who survived the crash landing were murdered at the crash scene - the female survivors were raped before being murdered. As the conflict intensified, the United States and Britain attempted to negotiate a peaceful settlement. However this was rejected by the Rhodesian government as they were unwilling to relinquish political and economic control, and the black nationalists were bitterly divided by feudal, tribal and political differences.

The RSF called up part-time soldiers in preparation for a major counter-offensive on 2 May 1976. Militants bombed a railroad bridge over Matetsi River on 7 October 1976 when a train carrying ore passed over. On 3 April 1977 General Peter Walls announced the government would launch a campaign to win the "hearts and minds" of Rhodesia's black citizens. In May 1977 Walls received reports of ZANLA forces massing in the city of Mapai in Gaza Province, Mozambique. Prime Minister Smith gave Walls permission to destroy the base. Walls told the media the Rhodesian forces were changing tactics from contain and hold to search and destroy, "adopting hot pursuit when necessary."

On 30 May 1977, 500 troops passed the border and traveled 60 miles to Mapai, engaging the ZANLA forces with air cover from the Rhodesian Air Force and paratroopers in C-47 Dakotas. The Rhodesian government said the military killed 32 ZANLA fighters and lost one Rhodesian pilot. The Mozambican government disputed the number of casualties, saying it shot down three Rhodesian planes and a helicopter and took several troops prisoner, all of which Minister of Combined Operations

Roger Hawkins denied. The United Nations Security Council denounced the incursion of the "illegal racist minority regime in Southern Rhodesia" into Mozambique in Resolution 411, on 30 June 1977.

Walls announced a day later that the Rhodesian military would occupy Mapai until they had eliminated ZANLA's presence. Kurt Waldheim, the Secretary-General of the United Nations, condemned the incident on 1 June, and Rhodesian forces withdrew. The American, British, and Soviet governments also condemned the raid. Militants bombed a department store in Salisbury on 11 August, killing 11 and injuring 70. They killed sixteen black civilians in eastern Rhodesia on 21 August, burning their homes on a white-owned farm.

In May 1978, 50 civilians were killed in crossfire exchanged between Marxist militants and the Rhodesian military, the highest number of civilians to be killed in an engagement up to that point. In July Patriotic Front members killed 39 black civilians and the Rhodesian government killed 106 militants. On 4 November 1978 Walls said 2,000 Patriotic Front militants had been persuaded to defect and fight for the Rhodesian Security Forces. In reality only 50 militants defected. In 1978 450 ZANLA militants crossed the Mozambique border and attacked the town of Umtali. At the time ZANU said the militants were women, an unusual characteristic, but in 1996 Joyce Mujuru said the vast majority involved was men and ZANU concocted the story to make Western organizations believe women were involved in the fighting.

In retaliation for these acts the Rhodesian Air Force bombed guerrilla camps 125 miles inside Mozambique, using 'fatigued' Canberra B2 aircraft and Hawker Hunters —- actively, but clandestinely, supported by several of the more capable Canberra B(I)12 aircraft of the South African Air Force. A number of joint-force bomber raids on guerrilla encampments and assembly areas in Mozambique and Zambia were mounted in 1978, and extensive air reconnaissance and surveillance of guerrilla encampments and logistical build-up was carried out by the South African Air Force on behalf of the RhAF. The increased effectiveness of the bombing and follow-up 'air mobile' strikes using Dakota-dropped parachutists and helicopter 'air cav' techniques had a significant effect on the development of the conflict, until a successful raid on the Rhodesian strategic fuel reserves in Salisbury forced the decision to explore a negotiated settlement. The conflict continued until 1979 when an agreement was reached on a constitution to transfer power to a majority government – the Lancaster House Agreement.

PERCEPTIONS

The conflict was seen by the nationalist groups and the British government of the time as a war of national and racial liberation. The Rhodesian government saw the conflict as a fight between one parts of the country's population (the whites) on behalf of the whole population (including the black majority) against several externally financed parties made up of predominantly black radicals and communists. The Nationalists saw their country as having been occupied and dominated by a foreign power, namely, Britain, since 1890. The British government, in the person of the Governor General, directly ruled the country from 1923, when it took over from the British South Africa Company. In 1965, Ian Smith's Rhodesian Front party took over the government when it unilaterally declared independence.

The minority Rhodesian government believed they were defending Western values, Christianity, the rule of law and democracy by fighting Communists. They were unwilling to compromise on most political, economic and social inequalities. The Smith administration said the traditional chiefs were the legitimate voice of the black Shona and Ndebele population and that the nationalists were dangerous usurpers. In 1979 the Smith administration attempted to blunt the power of the nationalist cause by acceding to an "Internal Settlement" which ended minority rule, changed the nan of the country to Zimbabwe-Rhodesia, and installed the country's first black head of government, Abel Muzorewa. However, unsatisfied with this and spurred on by Britain's refusal to recognise the new order, the nationalist forces persisted.

The Second Chimurenga/Bush War ended when the white dominated government of Rhodesia returned power to the British government with the 1979 Lancaster House Agreement. The Rhodesian government did so at the behest of both South Africa (its major backer) and the U.S. Although minor multi-ethnic elections had been held on a limited basis in Rhodesia before, elections were held in early 1980. Britain recognised this new government and the newly independent and internationally recognised country was renamed Zimbabwe. Today in Zimbabwe some mourn and some rejoice the death of Joshua Nkomo, a leader of the liberation struggle. The whole day on television there were specials about the history of Zimbabwe, as well as songs, dancing, and tributes to the man whom some called "the King of Matabeleland."

The Zimbabwean national anthem, Ngaikomborerwe Nyika Yezimbabwe, Blessed Be the Land of Zimbabwe, played constantly here in Bulawayo, as well as imbube pieces, a blend of Ndebele and English, by the a cappella group Black Umfolosi. Rachel and Dumy, who work at our hostel, both watched intently and said it was a real shame, and "people in town won't be happy today-everyone will walk around with their heads down." But the white owner, David, came in and raised his hands in the air, saying, "Finally, the opposition leader is dead!" In Harare (then Salisbury), in 1955, some nationalist leaders, dissatisfied with the growing inequality between black Africans and white settlers (the descendants of Cecil Rhodes' Pioneer Column), formed the City Youth League, which gradually became a new organization called the African National Congress (ANC).

Of prime interest in everyone's minds was the Land Husbandry Act of 1951, which had taken land away from Africans and given it to the minority whites. Elected president of the group, young Joshua Nkomo surprised the settler government by calling for majority rule. Banned in 1959, the ANC changed names and operated as a new National Democratic Party (NDP), retaliating with a series of demonstrations, strikes, and sabotage, called Zhii, or vengeful annihilation of the enemy. In 1961, while Nkomo was out of the country, the government banned the NDP. In response, nationalists created yet another group, the Zimbabwe African People's Union (ZAPU), a primarily Ndebele organization. Joshua Nkomo again led this group, and was again banned by Sir Edgar Whitehead. The Rhodesian Front Party's Winston Field was elected in 1962, and he instituted a series of crushing laws, outlawing black assemblies and political debates, and passing a mandatory death sentence for arson.

Nkomo thought about fleeing to Mozambique to head up a government in exile, and around this time disagreements between Nkomo and Robert Mugabe (the current Zimbabwean head of state) led to Mugabe's disgusted resignation. Mugabe went on to form the Zimbabwe African National Union (ZANU), a primarily Shona group. Nkomo pressed on with the struggle as well, and most of the ZANU and ZAPU party leaders continued to be banned or imprisoned for their nationalistic actions. Mounting tensions eventually led to civil war. (Less than a century earlier, in 1896, the Ndebele and Shona had joined to fight the British South Africa Company in the First Chimurenga, the "War of Liberation."

Squashed in 1897, one of the movement's spiritualist leaders had prophesied, "My bones will rise again," in a Second Chimurenga). This Second "War of Liberation" began on April 28th, 1966, now known as Chimurenga Day, with a day-long skirmish between Rhodesian Front soldiers and police against freedom fighters in the city of Chinhoyi: all died except one. In the years that followed, fortified by ZANU training camps in Mozambique and ZAPU bases in Zambia and Tanzania, armed conflict continued, with young women and men trained and fighting as scouts, messengers, spies, and soldiers.

THE ZAPU GUERRILLAS

In 1965, immediately after UDI, the Zimbabwean nationalist leaders were of the opinion that guerrilla warfare could provoke British intervention in Rhodesia. This assumption was based on the fact that the British government had indicated it would intervene militarily only if 'law and order' broke down in Rhodesia. The Zimbabwean nationalist leaders based their military strategy on the idea that, '... all that was necessary to end white domination was to train some guerrillas and send them home with guns: this would not only scare the whites but would ignite a wave of civil disobedience by blacks'. Maxey asserts that the very rigid control and formal censorship of the mass media stopped the rapid spread of mass opposition by reinforcing the appearance of calm. When the Rhodesian government found itself in serious trouble it turned for external help to South Africa.

ZAPU and its military wing ZPRA, with Joshua Nkomo as its leader were based in Zambia. The other nationalist party was the Zimbabwean African National Union (ZANU) and its military wing was the Zimbabwean African National Liberation Army (ZANLA). Both ZANU and the PAC received the bulk of their support from China. The Moaist approach to guerrilla warfare was quite different from the theories of the Soviet Union, which supported both ZAPU and the ANC. One of the major differences between ZAPU and ZANU was the latter's conviction that physical attacks on Whites and their property were necessary. ZAPU started its training schemes shortly after its formation in 1963 and from 1964 onwards Chikerema, its Vice-President went to a number of socialist countries on behalf the organisation to negotiate for increases to ZAPU's training facilities.

By 1966, ZAPU, which was the major Black Nationalist movement, realised that the British government would not intervene in Rhodesia. Celliers argues that ZAPU's armed wing also did not have the ability to force a collapse of law and order and cynically concludes that the major task of the insurgent forces was to convince the OAU of their existence and wish to overthrow the Smith government. This was vital if the black nationalists were to continue receiving political and financial support. It was also apparent that if Rhodesia were to become Zimbabwe, the black majority themselves would have to take up arms to fight for liberation. During the early years of the war, ZPRA bore the full responsibility for the war effort whilst the parent party ZAPU concentrated its efforts on mustering international support. ZANLA played a limited military role at that time.

The nationalist organisations recruited guerrillas from inside Rhodesia and from the large immigrant community living in Zambia, Botswana, Tanzania and even the United Kingdom. The ZPRA cadres were better trained and equipped than ZANLA. One reason for this could be the strong support it received from the USSR, Cuba and the German Democratic Republic (GDR). The Rhodesians found the ZPRA fighters more formidable and more disciplined. It was suggested that over ninety per cent of the fighting men in ZAPU were Ndebele, although they only comprised ten to twenty per cent of the Rhodesian population.

ZAPU commanders denied this tribal bias and Maxey concludes that recruitment appears to have been evenly spread over the country. He further quotes Boywer Bell, who used figures obtained from the Rhodesian authorities, which indicated that deceased guerrillas came from all the Rhodesian tribal groups with a pre-dominance of Ndebele. Boywer Bell concurred with 'ZAPU's claim to be a-tribal…and that its leadership and battle groups are mixed'. Celliers argues that, 'ZAPU had the backing of the Matabeles, who constitute some 19% of Zimbabwe's black population, while ZANU had that of the loosely grouped Shona nations which constituted 77% of the black population'.

ZAPU guerrillas, particularly in the early stages of the war received their training mainly in Russia, Cuba and Algeria, whilst some others received their training in Bulgaria, North Korea and Zaire (Katanga province). At a trial held in Rhodesia in 1968, a ZAPU guerrilla gave a brief description of the training he received in Russia. The classes lasted approximately four months and included a wide range of political and practical topics. Subjects included political science, aspects of intelligence work and the use of codes and ciphers. The guerrillas were given a run-down on the work of the CIA, MI6 and MI5, and the French and Federal German intelligence organisations. On the military side they were taught the use of explosives, hand-grenades, and how to use and assemble guns, rifles and pistols. Both ANC and ZAPU groups had a fairly formal structure with a commander and a political commissar. From 1966 to 1968, they were even dressed in semi-military uniforms.

THE CHIMURENGA WAR IN RHODESIA AFTER UDI

Both ZAPU and ZANU called the Zimbabwean phase of guerrilla warfare Chimurenga, a Shona name derived from the rebellions of 1896-1897. Rhodesian intelligence officers divided the Chimurenga war into three phases. The first phase was from 1964 after Zambian independence when guerrillas began crossing the Zambezi River so as to infiltrate Rhodesia, until the end of Operation Excess in Mashonaland in 1968. During this time, the first military engagement between the Rhodesian security forces and seven ZANLA guerrillas took place on 28 April 1966, near Sinoia, 100-km North West of Harare. This day is now commemorated in Zimbabwe as Chimurenga Day, marking the start of the war.

The Sinoia group of guerrillas was part of three teams, which had entered Rhodesia with the aim of cutting power lines and attacking White farmsteads. A second group murdered a white couple with the surname Viljoen on their farm near Hartley on 16 May 1966. Security forces later captured the insurgents. In total 13 of the 14 original insurgents were either captured or killed by security forces. A little while later another ZANLA infiltration was detected near Sinoia. In the battle that followed seven insurgents were killed and a number captured. The second phase covered the period 1968 until the attack on Altena Farm at the end of 1972. The third phase was the rapid escalation of the war and several international attempts to achieve a negotiated settlement and ended with a cease-fire agreement signed on 21 December 1979. It is in the context of the first phase of the war in Rhodesia that the Wankie campaign took place.

THE ANC-ZAPU ALLIANCE

In 1966, Joe Modise, commander-in-chief of MK based himself in Zambia and with ZAPU military commanders conducted reconnaissance work into Rhodesia. In April 1967 a plan for the prosecution of the armed struggle was put forward. 'After lengthy debates an order was issued that our men and women were to cross the Zambezi towards home'. The decision by the ANC and ZAPU to operate jointly was approved by the ANC Executive in June 1967. Pallo Jordan comments that the Wankie campaign was most probably 'planned and executed by the most militant elements within MK'. Lodge alleges that the SACP Central Committee was totally unaware of the Wankie campaign until news of the military operation hit the world's press.

Shubin disputes this pointing to the unreliability of Lodge's source namely a report in *Ikwezi*. The fact that Chris Hani was a member of the SACP and the political commissar of the Luthuli Detachment made it highly unlikely that the SACP did not know of the plan beforehand. By the middle of 1967, it was apparent that ZAPU's guerilla tactics had made no significant impact on the Rhodesian authorities and the ANC had no success in infiltrating guerrillas back into South Africa. Their plan was to send a joint MK-ZPRA force across the Zambezi River into northwest Rhodesia. This big group would split into two upon reaching the Wankie Game Reserve.

The main MK column would march south, through the Rhodesian bush into South Africa. The second smaller column of MK soldiers would be part of a ZAPU unit. They would move east and set up a base at Lupane inside Rhodesia to commence a guerrilla war against the Ian Smith regime. This base would also provide a future transit base for MK infiltrators en route to South Africa. Chris Hani said MK hoped to build a 'Ho Chi Minh route to South Africa'.

PREPARATIONS FOR THE TRIP HOME

Morodi, a Luthuli Detachment combatant received military training in Egypt after which he spent a year in the Soviet Union. He and some other ANC comrades returned to Zambia in early 1966. In early 1967, Morodi and other MK recruits were all transferred from the Tanzanian camps to Joshua Nkomo's camp outside of Lusaka. Another Luthuli Detachment combatant, Norman Duka, says that in early 1967 the ANC Chief Representative in Dar-es-Salaam told him that the chance to go back home [to South Africa] had arrived. He and two others left by lorry to Zambia. The guerrillas received a further five months of intensive training and political education. Chris Hani explains: A lot of time was allocated for the detachment to be together in the bush to be able to train together in order to ensure that physically we were ready for the rigorous task that lay ahead. But in addition to the physical preparation there was also the political preparation, the need for us to forge an understanding between the forces of Umkhonto we Sizwe and the forces of ZAPU and to understand the historical necessity of the battles of Wankie.

Importantly the diet of the combatants was greatly improved a few months before the campaign and everyone felt healthy. At about this time the ANC President-General, Chief Albert Luthuli died in South Africa. The acting President Oliver Tambo declared a week of mourning and delayed the march of the guerrillas' home. The Luthuli Detachment was thus named in honour of the late ANC President-General. The route chosen for the march home was explained by Morodi: Some of our men who had been sent through Botswana were captured, and they were beaten up and sent back. So we choose that we have to go through Rhodesia, so that when we meet people there - the police or the army - we can be able to fight, because it's not an independent African state and we know it's our enemy. So it was agreed.

Before departing the guerrillas were issued with uniforms of Russian origin, which consisted of a tunic, a long pair of trousers and a hat. The uniform was made of khaki gabardine. Each guerrilla received boots, which had a distinctive 8 pattern on the sole, and which unfortunately would later make it easier for the Rhodesian security forces to track them. Each received a cloth-covered water bottle and a rucksack in which they carried food, private clothing and ammunition. Each guerrilla was given a sub-machine gun with 300 rounds and a semi-automatic rifle with 300 rounds. Some, not all guerrillas received a pistol with 90 rounds of ammunition and each guerrilla was provided with two hand-grenades: defensive and offensive. The day before departure each guerrilla was given a medical check up, and the group prepared for their long march home.

6

Guerilla Girls up in Arms

The Problem with Women in War

WOMEN OF NEPAL: FEUDALISM AND INEQUALITY

Nepal is a desperately poor country where more than 80% of the people live in the countryside without electricity, running water, or basic sanitation. More than half earn less than a $1 a day. Peasants on tiny plots of land live on the edge of deepening poverty, debt and hunger. Women are doubly oppressed. A common proverb in Nepal goes, "To be born as a daughter is having ill fate." The reality behind this saying is that women in Nepal are among the most oppressed on the planet. Feudal tradition and patriarchy subject the women to a life of servitude to fathers, husbands and sons. They have no right to inherit land. With a lot of the men in the cities looking for work, the women do most of the farming—in addition to taking care of the children, cooking, washing, grazing animals and hauling water.

A peasant woman may get up at 4 a.m. and not see the end of her day for 18 hours. Her life expectancy is only 52 years. In one village, I asked a young woman to tell me about her day and she said: "I wake up at 5:00 a.m., prepare a simple soup for the family, get grass for the goat, which takes five hours. Then I have to clean the pots and dishes. I prepare food and eat and then take the goats and cows to graze them and I also gather roots in the forest. Its five o'clock by the time I get back from grazing the animals. Then I have to prepare another meal. I also have to gather firewood from the forest. I finally go to sleep at 9:00 p.m."

Under feudalism, young girls are considered "useful" when they can do chores. But after a woman gets married, she lives with - and serves - her husband's household. So many parents believe that "To get a girl is like watering a neighbor's tree. You have the trouble and expense of nurturing the plant but the fruits are taken by somebody else." This is why most women in Nepal are denied an education. Almost 80% of women here cannot read or write—giving Nepal one of the highest female illiteracy rates in the world. Under feudal tradition, parents "arrange marriages" and children have no say in whom they will marry. Some daughters are married off as child brides before they are even teenagers. Divorce is not allowed. A widow is expected to spend the rest of her life mourning.

Abortion is illegal in Nepal, even if a woman's life is threatened. At least 100 women here are in jail for the "crime" of terminating a pregnancy. And because Nepalese law defines abortion as a form of "homicide," many of these women have long jail sentences. A lot of women also die from unsafe illegal abortions—about 4,000 every year. They come in to local hospitals—their uteruses and intestines punctured by some sharp object like a bamboo stick, even a shard of glass. Worldwide, the percentage of maternal deaths due to unsafe abortions is 13%. In Nepal it is closer to 50%.

Sometimes it's a father, brother or other relative in the village. Sometimes it's the owner of a factory. A woman sold for $600 or $200—the price of a water buffalo or slightly more than a video recorder. Kidnapped and taken to a brothel across the border in India—where they cannot speak the language and are isolated, far from home. Many die in India. Most never make it back to their village. If they do escape and return to Nepal, they are ostracized. A raid of a brothel in Bombay in 1996 of 218 Nepalese girls found that 70% of them were HIV positive.

Every year, as many as 10,000 Nepalese girls, most between the age of 9 and 16, are sold to brothels in India. Some studies estimate that as many as 200,000 Nepalese women now work in India as prostitutes. Most of these women die before their 30th birthday. "Deukis" also contributes to this trafficking of women. This is a system in Nepal in which rich childless families buy girls from poor rural families and offer them to the temples as though they were their own. These girls are forced into prostitution. According to a 1997 UN Special Report on Violence Against Women, 17,000 girls were given as deukis in 1992.

Meanwhile, the Nepalese government treats women who have been kidnapped and sold into sexual slavery as criminals - to be hounded, hunted down and punished. At a seminar organized by an NGO (non-governmental organization) and the Kathmandu police, school teachers and social workers came up with a list of punitive measures for women who "willingly" become prostitutes. These included registration and identity cards for all women between 12 and 35 years old to allow monitoring at a village level; the amendment of laws so that women can be more easily prosecuted for becoming prostitutes; the strengthening of village authority to punish women who come back and induce others to go to India; confiscating property of women who return from brothels; and organizing teachers and students to collect data on women who return with HIV or AIDS.

WOMEN IN THE PEOPLE'S WAR

"Before the initiation of the People's War I did not know anything about politics or parties. But after the initiation [of the armed struggle] one of my relatives suggested I take part in the local cultural group and asked me to go to their rehearsal. I didn't tell my mother or father about this—I only told my older brother who said, 'Go ahead, if you want to die... Can you carry a gun on your shoulder?' I replied, `You didn't give me a chance to study and now I am eager to solve the problems of the people and the nation. I want to fight for liberation. If you won't allow me to go I will rebel." Rachana, an 18-year-old woman guerrilla

Rachana was a member of a squad I traveled with in Rolpa, a district in Western Nepal where the People's War has been the strongest. I remember one afternoon, watching Rachana studying, practicing her reading and writing, her eyes stuck to a dog-eared page in deep concentration. I thought about how this extraordinary scene is being created in guerrilla zones across Nepal. Young peasant women—illiterate, facing nothing but a back-breaking future—leaving their villages, taking up arms, learning to read and write and studying the political and theoretical questions of the revolution they are fighting.

Looking at the status of women in Nepal, it's not hard to see how such brutal and demeaning conditions drive many women into the arms of the revolution. When the People's War began, it was like opening the gates of a prison—with thousands of women rushing forward to join the fight. I heard stories of women leaving their villages—defying backward-thinking fathers and husbands, escaping loveless marriages, and getting out from under the dictatorial thumb of mothers-in-law—to join the people's army. Government repression against the People's War has also inspired many women to join the fight. One 15-year-old woman guerrilla told me:

"500 police raided our village and arrested just about everyone—even the children and old people. My mother was arrested and I was also arrested and kept in custody. There was so much repression by the police, so I joined the cultural team of the party. And because of the exploitation and oppression of the poor masses, and especially that suffered by women, I was inspired to find a way to free the masses from such a situation. I found this was being done by the CPN (Maoist) so I joined the party."

Women are now participating in the armed struggle as fighters and commanders at all the different military levels of squad, platoon, and company. And they are also a big part of the local militias, as well as the revolutionary women's organizations. I will never forget the fire in the eyes of the young woman squad member who told me what it was like to join the armed struggle. She said: "I knew a little about the revolutions in Russia and Peru. And I knew that women there had participated with guns on their shoulders. After some time I became a squad member and picked up the gun like those women.... Now that I'm with the squad, I feel more responsibility to overthrow the reactionaries and make a new Nepal. I see how many women are attracted to the People's War and I'm going to work to recruit more women into the people's army."

TARGETED BY THE GOVERNMENT

At least 2,000 people have already been killed by the police in this war, including 200 women. And many women have also been raped, brutalized and jailed. One woman organizer told me: "After the initiation the reactionaries put a lot of effort into trying to stop women from participating in the People's War. Thousands of women have been raped and many women are in jail. I'll give you one example. During a local election the police came to ask women to participate in the elections. But the women refused. So the police rounded up more than 14 women and raped them all in one place. There was one 12-year-old girl that they raped who was so badly injured she could not even walk for one week."

Many women have lost husbands, sons and daughters. And in almost every village I visited, relatives of revolutionary martyrs came to tell me their stories - full of grief but also pride in the fact that one of their relatives had given their life for the revolution. In traditional Nepalese society, losing a husband can mean economic hardship. A woman without children may have no one to take care of her when she gets old. Children who lose their parents become destitute orphans. But for the revolutionary women who lose their husbands or children there is a larger sense of "family." The party and the people's army make sure the relatives of martyrs are taken care of. Funds are collected for them; they are given a share of land seized by the people's army. And the children of martyrs are taken care of by the larger revolutionary community.

PEOPLE'S POWER, WOMEN'S POWER

The fight for women's equality and liberation is woven into the very fabric of this People's War. And where the revolution is beginning to exercise new people's power, women are seeing some concrete outlines of a new society where the people can get rid of all forms of oppression, including the oppression of women. One woman revolutionary told me: "There have been many changes in people's thinking since the initiation. Fathers and brothers are now involved in things like cooking, getting water, washing dishes. There is also a change in the women's thinking. Before, women were not permitted to do things like make the roof of the house or plow the fields. But now where the People's War is going on, it is easy for women to do this before women didn't make baskets and mats, according to tradition. And women used to think they weren't good enough to do this work. But when we dared to do this work it was easy. So if we dare we can do anything—there's no distinction between men and women."

In areas where the government has lost control, the party is leading the masses to exercise a new people's power. And women are a strong backbone of the people's committees that have been organized to oversee and run various aspects of village life. A woman in Rukum told me: "In our district there have been many changes in the attitudes and practices regarding women. For example we are involved in the judiciary department (one of the people's power committees). And we take part in solving many problems - like cases of second marriages, where we guarantee the right of property for the first wife. People who want to get divorced appeal to the people's court and we decide the case. Most are women who want to get divorced because of beatings or attempted murder, or other abuses. If a woman demands property from her husband when she gets divorced, the court will help her. The court investigates who is right and wrong in each case."

Women are also an important part of building a new self-reliant economy in the areas where there is new people's power. Thousands of women's groups have been organized to support the People's War by carrying out collective farming, raising animals and producing things like socks, gloves, and cloth. Traditionally, women cannot inherit land. But agrarian revolution is central to this People's War and land reform, carried out under the slogan "land to the tiller," also applies the principle of "women's equal right to property." So in the guerrilla zones, many women are getting land in their own name for the very first time.

Many other feudal traditions are being challenged—like the strong preference for sons, the treatment of women as "untouchable" during menstruation, polygamy, arranged marriages, and the belief that widows should mourn for the rest of their lives. Some traditional celebrations are also being transformed by the revolution. For example, the Hindu celebration "Teej" is a day-long fast imposed on women. On this day married women are supposed to pray for the longevity of their husbands and unmarried women are supposed to fast and pray for an eligible husband. Now, this day is being transformed into a day where women feast to strengthen themselves against rape, torture and killings by the police.

Women in Nepal face the same situation that millions and millions of women face around the world. The problems of deep and intense poverty seem insurmountable. The violence against women looks like it will never end. And the weight of tradition - which brutalizes and murders women on a daily basis - appears too powerful to challenge. But the revolutionary women in Nepal are defying all tradition's chains - living and dying to bring about a new world and sending heart and hope to people all over the globe.

CAMBODIAN WOMEN IN THE REVOLUTIONARY WAR FOR THE PEOPLE'S NATIONAL LIBERATION (1973)

Just like the men, Cambodian women, yesterday and today, have contributed greatly to the struggle against foreign aggression in defense of the fatherland. After the anti-national and anti-popular coup d'état on March 18, 1970, the group of traitors Lon Nol, Sirik Matak, and Son Ngoc Thanh sold Cambodia cheap to the U.S. imperialists and allowed them to transform it into a neo-colony and a military base. Since then, with the loss of its independence, neutrality, sovereignty and territorial integrity, Cambodia has been plunged into a most cruel war which brings untold suffering to the women and people of the country.

Applying the Nixon doctrine which consists of making

Indochinese fight Indochinese and Cambodians fight Cambodians, the American imperialists, their lackeys in Saigon and Bangkok, and the group of traitors in Phnom Penh, have perpetrated innumerable crimes against our people. Implementing the policy of "kill all, burn all, destroy all," everywhere the U.S. puppet troops go, they sow mourning, misery and desolation. The enemy every day commits mass slaughter in which neither individuals nor bonzes (Buddhist monks) nor priests are spared, in their pillage and rape that the Phom Penh press and world opinion have convincingly revealed. Every day their planes pour millions of tons of bombs on our territory, killing men, women, old and young indiscriminately, devastating and systematically flattening the houses and rice fields of the peaceful populations, as well as historic monuments such as Angkor Wat, and monasteries.

In the areas provisionally controlled by the enemy, apart from fascist repression, women are still obliged to cope with the high cost of living, a lack of necessary elementary provisions, notably rice, and find it very difficult to make ends meet. To this are added other worries: their husbands and their sons could be conscripted at any moment at all, their daughters kidnapped and raped by the troops of Phnom Penh and Saigon. The American way of life, a depraved society, and prostitution have poisoned the minds of so many girls and women. More than ever, Cambodian women know that the only possible way to free them from this thrall-ring is to join in the struggle with the men, without hesitation or compromise, against the American aggressors and their valets for the national liberation.

At the front, women take part in combat, in medical teams, in destroying every communications, in voluntary work teams. Behind the lines, women play a top-level role. Numerous guerrilla units have been formed entirely of women. Women take charge of various tasks, replacing men who have left for the front: village defense, making booby-traps, agricultural production, planting, medical work, etc... Mothers have shared their children's meals with fighters from FAPLNK (Cambodian People's National Liberation Armed Forces), others have entrusted their young ones to neighbors, in order to fulfill liaison missions. Many other such examples demonstrate the political responsibility of women in Cambodia. While carrying out their national duty, the women of Cambodia are also well aware of their international obligations.

The primordial task which lies before them is to stand in the front line against imperialism, particularly U.S. imperialism. In this, they are offering their worthy contribution to the cause of popular national liberation of the people's of the world, notably those of Asia, Africa and Latin America, which are not yet free of the yoke of colonialism, both old and new. Moreover, women in Cambodia possess a legitimate pride in having helped to improve the conditions of women in general. For, arming themselves with their high revolutionary morality and demonstrating supreme revolutionary heroism, they have achieved exploits which our people hold in high esteem. They are thus contributing to tearing apart those backward perceptions of women which still have currency in the world.

"All our sisters," writes Madame Khieu Ponnary, President of the Association of Democratic Women of Kampuchea, "are determined to lead their just struggle against American imperialism and its puppets, until final victory under the direction of the National United Front of Kampuchea, with the Head of State, Prince Norodom Sihanouk, as president. In this just fight of ours for the ideals of independence, peace, liberty, and progress, we know that we are not alone. From all over the world we receive messages of solidarity. Demonstrations of support are breaking out in all parts of the globe in aid of the just cause of the Cambodian people, and condemning unequivocally the crimes of American imperialism and its valets. May we now take this opportunity to express the deep gratitude of the Association of Democratic Women of Kampuchea to the women of the whole world, without forgetting American women, who, faithful to the same ideals of peace, justice; liberty and progress have spontaneously taken their stand by our side? They have in this way contributed to isolate American imperialism and its valets, and to bring about the triumph of the just cause of the forces for independence, democracy and peace in the world."

YOUNG WOMEN GUERRILLA FIGHTERS OVERRUN AN ENEMY POST

Village T is situated on the edges of the area provisionally controlled by the enemy in Kompong Speu province. A company of puppet troops set up a position there under the orders of their torturer—captain. Since then, the villagers had to cope with all sorts of trials and exactions. For even the shortest journey, they have to seek permission from the commander of the post. Otherwise they would wind up accused of being agents of the "Khmer Rouges" or the "Vietcong—North Vietnamese" and would be subjected to the worst sorts of torture many have come out of such treatment sick, behind, others have gone mad or even died. The families of the prisoners, in order to get their loved ones free, often had to sell what little they had (house, plot of land, buffalo) and even their own children to the torturer-captain the ransom demanded.

The villagers must still pay "loans" in the form of money, rice, pork, poultry, which no one dares try to avoid. Worse still, the traitorous captain and his men embark on orgies of rape against the girls and the women of the village. The inhabitants of this area, victims of exploitation and sorts of robbery by the torturer-captain and his men, have a miserable life full of humiliation. However, despite severe enemy repression day and night, the local branch of FUNK (National United Front of Kampuchea) is still intact, to guide the people in their struggle. In order to free the villagers from the cruel claws of the eager puppets the American imperialist aggressor, the local branch of the FUNK decided to wipe out the enemy position without endangering the population, in conformity with its wishes.

Representatives of the FUNK branches from surrounding villages met secretly to set in motion a plan to attack the position. One question raised, however, stopped everyone short: "How can we attack the enemy if none of us, even the guerrillas, are armed, because of the continual troops searches of the houses and sweeps into the forest?" When a lively discussion of how to find a solution began, a young girl guerrilla interrupted: "We must take the enemy's arms in order to wipe him out." "An excellent idea," everyone nodded. "But how are we going to do it?" they asked. "None of us can even approach the enemy position. How, then, could we possibly get inside?"

The young girl, with a childish smile on her lips, started explaining in detail how her group intended to outwit the enemy. Everyone approved of her well though out plan. A week passed. The carnival atmosphere in village T was quite out of the ordinary. Here, they were putting up a lean-to; there, a kitchen. Over there, they piled up the rice; over there they cut down trees and plants for the decorations. On that day the people from the neighboring villages came to village T in large numbers, some bringing poultry with them, and some bringing vegetables. Festival music could be heard from the end of the village to the other. It seemed that a wedding was about to take peace.

In the barracks, the soldiers also arranged the tables for a feast. Nothing unusual about that and the parents of the bride and bridegroom had come to the quarters to ask the captain's permission for their children to get married. Permission was granted on condition that the parents organize a feast that same day for he and his men. "But," he added, "I want to be served the bride herself and all the bridesmaids will wait on my men. None of the others will be allowed into the barracks today." The parents reluctantly decided to give in to the wishes of the traitor. Three o'clock in the afternoon; twenty people, young and old, men and women, headed towards the barracks, carrying on their heads or on their shoulders the provisions for the feast.

When they arrived in front of the post, the sentry stopped them, and told them to put down their loads. He called to other troops inside and they came out to carry in the provisions. Then the sentry ordered our people to go back to the village immediately. Four-thirty: Ten girls elegantly dressed and accompanied by hefty boys carrying five cases of alcohol, presented themselves at the post. This time, the sentry let the girls in, but stood in the way of the men and ordered them to go back home. At the sight of the lovely ladies, four plain-clothes officers drinking at a table rejoiced. One of them asked the girls:

"You, girls, can you dance the ramvong?"

"Yes, of course we can," they replied.

This set the four shouting and clapping their hands excitedly. Then, the captain gave the order to three of the soldiers to stand guard, one at the entrance and the two others at the lookout, while he told the rest to relax at the tables with their rifles by their side, taking turns to do guard duty.

Hearing this order, the girls begged the commander:

"We are afraid of guns. Monsieur le Capitaine, please don't let your men sit down or dance with us with all those rifles! Otherwise how can we generously give you our attention and our dancing?"

At this, laughter filled the room. The officers wanted to appear gallant.

"My darlings, you have nothing to fear from these rifles. We would never use them on girls as lovely and fresh as you all are right now! If we don't carry our guns, how can we defend you when the Khmers Krahom comes?" (Khmers Krahom is the popular Cambodian term for Khmer Rouges, or Khmer Reds.)

"Yes," replied the prettiest one, "we agree with you, but we only want you to put your rifles in some place where they won't get in the way when we're dancing."

The captain granted the girls' request and told his men to put their rifles in bundles near the tables. Then the party started. First the meal was served. The three prettiest girls waited on the officers, the others on the soldiers. They concentrated on being attentive and thought only of one thing; to make them drink as much as possible. The bell went for the changing of the guard but not one of the merrymaking soldiers took the least notice. They kept on drinking glass after glass and quickly got drunker and drunker. The three angry soldiers on guard came in and sat down at the tables cleared for them by our girls.

The drunken soldiers and officers all shouted and sang loudly. They forgot about dancing. All of a sudden, one of the girls clapped her hands three times. Quick as a flash, without giving the enemy time to work out what was happening; the girls firmly grabbed the gun and pointed them at the soldiers. Simultaneously, one girl fired a shot and ordered the soldiers "Hands up!" They were caught off guard and in no time ten hefty youths, the same ones who had carried the casks of alcohol, charged into the room and tied up the soldiers. The villagers from round about heard the shots and ran towards the post to find out what had happened.

An unexpected but welcome sight met their eyes. They gathered for a meeting in the fields to denounce the crimes committed by the torturer-captain and his whole board, straw dogs for the traitors of Phnom Penh and eager servants of U.S. imperialism. That same night, the guerrillas marched the captive soldiers into the liberated zone and presented them to the local FUNK headquarters. Village T, as well as the surrounding villages was thus liberated and its inhabitants became masters of their lands, their villages and their communes, and they benefited from their newly-won democratic freedoms.

WOMEN AND GIRLS OF SIERRA LEONE

In December 2003, Sierra Leone ended its official disarmament, demobilization, and reintegration (DDR) program. From the time of its initiation in 1998, 72,500 former combatants passed through the program, including 4,751 women (6.5 percent) and 6,787 children (9.4 percent), of whom 506 were girls. From the outset there was recognition of the large presence of child soldiers (up to 50 percent of fighters in rebel forces were believed to be fewer than 18) and women (estimates ranged between 10 and 30 percent) among the various forces, so the program was in principle, designed to include them.

At completion, however, while the program was noted for its effective outreach to male combatants, women and children were underserved. Despite this significant shortcoming, the program has been hailed as a success by the UN, the World Bank, and others and a model upon which other DDR processes could be based. The DDR program also failed to provide support to civilian populations faced with the reality of reintegrating former fighters. Instead, women as individuals and in groups took on the responsibility of assisting these fighters, particularly the children and youth among them, as they returned to civilian life.

The majority of these community-based efforts, however, received little or no aid or recognition from the national and international programs established to guarantee not just successful demobilization, but ultimately effective reintegration and rehabilitation. Outlined here are the rationale for this study, assumptions of the research, an explanation of methodology, and the working definitions that frame this chapter.

RATIONALE

Limited research has been conducted to assess DDR programs' ability to respond to the experiences of women and girls within fighting forces, in Sierra Leone or elsewhere. Still less is known about how programs that do or do not address gender considerations may contribute to or hinder peaceful transitions. Drawing on the Sierra Leone conflict (1991-2000) this chapter uses quantitative and qualitative methods and gender analysis to document and examine women and girl ex-combatants' roles and experiences within the forces and official DDR processes. In addition to a lack of information on the experiences of women and girls in official DDR programs, knowledge is scarce regarding the contributions that women make to official and community-based DDR processes. As conflicts increasingly involve civilian populations, women are more and more often called upon to "unofficially" assist in demobilizing and reintegrating ex-combatants, especially child soldiers.

In Sierra Leone, children constituted half of some of the fighting forces; up to one third of these were girls. This study, therefore, also documents women's previously unrecognized actions to strengthen official and community-based DDR, assist ex-combatants, and contribute to peace building within Sierra Leone and the region. This study rests on the assumption that effective DDR processes are critical for achieving sustainable peace. Further, it presupposes that it is insufficient to prioritize the disarmament and demobilization elements alone at the expense of the reintegration component. Finally, it acknowledges that the burden of reintegration and longer-term rehabilitation is largely placed on the families and communities into which former combatants return; too often official national and international DDR programs overlook this key component. The study does not assume that women are more peaceful than men by nature. Indeed it shows that women play many roles during times of war, ranging from frontline combatants to community peacemakers.

They should therefore be recognized as active agents rather than passive victims in peace processes, including DDR. To exclude their voices and experiences and to ignore their contributions ultimately undermines peace. Throughout August and September 2002 in Sierra Leone, over 60 in-depth interviews were conducted with community leaders, social workers, NGO staff, psychologists, traditional and religious leaders, as well as with government officials, representatives of international organizations and women and girls formerly in the fighting forces. Secondary quantitative data on the fighting forces and their participation in DDR programs with particular emphasis on children and girls was gathered from the Sierra Leone National Center for Disarmament, Demobilization and Reintegration (NCDDR) and the Child Protection Unit of the United Nations Children's Fund (UNICEF), Sierra Leone.

Finally, a survey using quota sampling was used to gather quantitative data. The Sierra Leone survey was a quota sample of girls and young women formerly associated with the fighting forces during the 1991-2002 war. Sub-categories of the study population included captive "wives" of commanders and girls involved in pro-government Civil Defense Forces (CDF). Study sites were selected with the assistance of UNICEF in Sierra Leone and international and local NGOs working with child ex-combatants or war-affected communities in Sierra Leone. The sampling took place in different regions of the country and included the Western Area (the area including and surrounding the capital Freetown) and two of three provinces, the North and the East.

Throughout August and September 2002, surveys were conducted in a variety of locations including remote villages, "suburbs" of urban centers, urban centers, and interim care and training centers for war-affected youth. The survey contained 99 questions pertaining to basic demographic data, entry into the force, roles and experiences within the force, experiences of physical abuses within the respective forces and in community reintegration, experiences of time spent in the army barracks, official disarmament and demobilization, direct community entrance, reintegration, skills training, assistance needs, and current status. Fourteen open-ended questions were included in the survey itself; issues ranged from questions regarding why a girl joined an armed force if she reported joining, skills learned in fighting forces that could assist the respondent now, to difficulties and assistance during reintegration.

Just as scholars have identified the "lifecycle" of conflict, current thinking in the field identifies a lifecycle of peace. The establishment of peace is not a single event, but rather a process characterized by progress and setbacks, successes and failures. Observers of peace processes, including those live in societies with protracted conflict, are all too familiar with premature celebration of ceasefires and peace accords that are later violated. Even if a settlement holds, the transition to a state of peace is a long-term operation. It requires extensive logistical and financial measures to create or reestablish the physical, social, and political infrastructure necessary for the country to transition towards a culture of peace.

Perhaps the most realistic approach to understanding the peace process is to acknowledge that, though negotiations are "the best-known stage in a process of peace," as Anderlini et al. write in Journeys Through Conflict: Narratives and Lessons, It is important to note that these three phases are seldom distinct; they blend into one another in a continuum from ceasefire toward the consolidation of peace. Timelines often blur, for example, when the reintegration phase of DDR ends and the longer-term process of reconstruction begins. International policymakers consider DDR one of the most important steps in any peace process.

The World Bank has defined a successful DDR program as "the key to an effective transition from war to peace." Although each of the three elements of DDR has distinctly different goals and requires independent planning, the phases do overlap and are dependent upon each other. The UN defines disarmament as "...the collection of small arms and light and heavy weapons within a conflict zone." Former combatants are gathered in pre-determined assembly areas, where weapons are confiscated, safely stored, and eventually destroyed. Individuals then receive support in the form of food aid, shelter, clothing, medical attention, basic education, and orientation programs. In addition, censuses are often conducted, and ex-combatants are issued discharge documentation.

Demobilization is both the formal disbanding of military formations and the release of combatants from a "mobilized" state. Discharge of ex-combatants often occurs over a period of time, during which they are usually transported to their home districts or given small transportation grants and the process of initial reinsertion begins. Nicole Ball of the University of Maryland breaks down reintegration into two phases—initial reinsertion and long-term reintegration. Reinsertion refers to the short-term arrival period of an ex-combatant into his/her former home or into a new community. Support during this phase may include basic household goods, land, food supplements, and housing materials. Reintegration takes a long-term approach, to assist the community and the ex-combatant in the difficult transition to civilian life. Assistance during reintegration usually includes job placement services, skills training, credit schemes, scholarships, and rehabilitation programs.

The international community at times refers to a second "R" in DDR, which represents "rehabilitation." This concept encompasses difficult issues, such as the need to address the psychological and emotional aspects of returning home and problems that arise in relation to the wider community. Nearly all DDR programs address rehabilitation in some form, but the most often-used acronym for the process is DDR. Security sector reform—such as dismantling and restructuring the military and constructing a new civilian police force—is often included in discussions surrounding disarmament, demobilization, and reintegration. For the purposes of this paper, DDR will only include the processes defined above and will not address issues pertaining to security sector reform.

The term "gender" refers to the socially constructed— as opposed to biologically determined—identities of men and women. Gender is not the same as "sex," and gender differences are not the same as sex differences. For instance, the ability of women to bear children is a sex, or biologically determined, difference from men; that women, in many societies, are responsible for food preparation and household chores is a gender, or socially constructed, difference. Gender roles are assigned to men and women early in socialization. They cut across public and private spheres; are specific to a given culture at a given time; are affected by other forms of differentiation such as race, ethnicity, and class; and can change in different socio-political and economic contexts within a society.

World Bank literature notes that in any given society, gender shapes the definitions of acceptable responsibilities and functions for men and women in terms of "social and economic activities, access to resources, and decision making authority." It examines how gender considerations are a necessary component of DDR planning and implementation, and how women in Sierra Leone enhanced the DDR process, primarily through their numerous adhoc and local reintegration and rehabilitation programs. Prior to colonization no ethnic tribe dominated the geographic area that is now Sierra Leone. The largest ethnic groups, the Mende and Temne, have long been divided into chiefdoms in the south and the north respectively. A country rich with natural resources— timber, ivory, palm oil, and valuable mineral deposits including gold, bauxite, and diamonds—Sierra Leone fell into British control in the early 1800s.

During its movement to abolish slavery, Great Britain allowed thousands of freed slaves to find refuge in the West African territory, effectively reshaping the demographic composition of Sierra Leone. Other ethnic groups including the

Kono, Limba, Kissi, and Krio migrated into the new British territory. Democratic reforms following World War II established an assembly for the territory led primarily by Paramount Chiefs. Fearing marginalization, the Krio elite, along with other chiefs, created the Sierra Leone People's Party (SLPP), led by Sir Milton Margai, a Mende.

The creation of the Temne-dominated All People's Congress (APC) followed in 1957, splitting the assembly's composition and dividing it ethnically between the Mende (SLPP) of the south and the Temne (APC) of the north. Margai was elected Prime Minister after successful constitutional talks in London in 1960. A year later, Sierra Leone became independent, women gained the right to vote, and a parliamentary system within the British Commonwealth was established. The years after independence gave way to protracted political clashes between the two parties until 1967, when the APC won in a democratic election.

COLD WAR TO CIVIL WAR

Adopting a policy of non-alignment during the Cold War, the Sierra Leone government upheld the colonial practice of emphasizing the export of raw materials over industrial production. Independent mining made up the bulk (80 percent) of economic export from Sierra Leone. Continuing a tradition of maintaining power through asset control and patron systems, by the early 1970s, the APC, with Siaka Stevens as president, controlled 52 percent of the national diamond industry. In 1978, facing increased opposition from professionals and trade unionists, Stevens consolidated his power. He destroyed many of the political institutions established in the British parliamentary system, rendering them ineffective.

Tightening its grip, the APC leadership cut off access to natural resources to those outside its sphere. One result of these actions was increased frustration and unrest among youth and students unable to support them and their families. The political ideals expressed by jobless university students, graduates, and dropouts supplanted the unorganized political frustrations among the uneducated youth, who were sometimes used as thugs by the political leadership. Buoyed by public support, the youth promoted the idea of pan-Africanism, drawing parallels between the colonial past and the post-colonial present. The APC tried to attract distinguished "radicals" among the youth class as potential candidates for the party, but none accepted.

The economy faltered throughout the 1980s, due in part to lost revenues from diamond smuggling. Yet those within the patron system, including politicians, powerful chiefs, and traders, prospered while the average citizen's standard of living continued to decline. Government expenditures on health and housing dropped and state-sponsored scholarships decreased. Looking for allies to overcome the West's containment of Muamar Qaddafi's regime, Libya eagerly nurtured the political discord among young Sierra Leoneans.

One of those who traveled to Libya was Foday Sankoh, formerly a corporal in the Sierra Leone Army (SLA). It was in a Libyan military training camp that Sankoh met Charles Taylor of the National Patriotic Front of Liberia (NPFL). In 1987, the two agreed to support each other's efforts to overthrow their respective governments. Financiers and recruits were found in the main diamond mines of Sierra Leone, located in the Eastern and Southern Provinces, in some cases more easily accessed from Liberia than from the Sierra Leone capital of Freetown.

In August 1985, the APC named Joseph Saidu Momoh as successor to Stevens after several years of economic decline, increased political opposition, and Stevens' increasingly autocratic approach. Corruption, the collapse of the economy, and heavy cuts in social programs, partly due to International Monetary Fund (IMF) structural adjustment programs, had severely weakened the country. Momoh attempted to re-establish a multi-party government with elections scheduled for 1991. However, armed rebel forces led by Foday Sankoh, calling them the Revolutionary United Front (RUF) and backed by Liberia, launched their first attack into Sierra Leone just prior to the elections, thwarting the president's efforts to stabilize the economy.

Initially, RUF forces consisted of three groups: those trained in Libya with fighting experience in Liberia, young men from

Liberia and Sierra Leone who had little or no work, and seasoned NPFL fighters from Taylor's army. In March 1991, RUF rebels invaded Sierra Leone from Liberia and occupied the eastern regions of the country, securing lucrative diamond reserves. In exchange for weapons, drugs, and supplies, Sierra Leonean diamonds were smuggled into Liberia for sale on the international market, generating millions of dollars annually. Controlling the diamond mines also allowed Sankoh to recruit, forcibly and voluntarily, young miners and locally unemployed men and boys into his fighting forces.

By the mid to late 1990s, global exposure of these "blood diamonds" led to an international outcry against their export and sale and initiated numerous UN investigations and resolutions. Within the first 18 months of RUF attacks, over 400,000 people were internally displaced while hundreds of thousands became refugees. The war quickly came to involve not only Liberia, but also Guinea and Côte D'Ivoire. It destroyed hundreds of hospitals and schools and tens of thousands of homes. Because of a lack of health care, failing schools, and the widespread destruction of infrastructure support systems, the population grew increasingly vulnerable.

The Sierra Leone countryside became militarized as a result of the presence of international forces, widespread proliferation of small arms, and a general suspicion towards one's neighbor, especially in areas protected by local militias. Women and girls reported atrocities committed by all fighting forces during the war. Early in the conflict the RUF perpetrated widespread violence across southern and eastern Sierra Leone. Violence against women and children and general terror in rural and urban centers quickly became cornerstones of the movement and were encouraged by RUF leadership. As government revenues fell from the loss of mineral sales, so too did the salaries and the resolve of the SLA. Soldiers committed gross human rights violations, including rape, mutilations, looting, property destruction, and murder.

They forced women and girls to exchange sex for "protection" and used them as prostitutes. With the rebellion spreading virtually unchecked in the south and east, rebels preyed on civilians for food, supplies, and labor. Subjected to violence by both the RUF and the SLA, local militias known as Civil Defense Forces (CDF) emerged. CDF gained prominence with the rise of the Kamajors, the largest traditional hunting society, in the eastern and southern provinces. Other hunting groups were the Tamaboro, Donso, Kapra and later, the Gbethis in the north. With the exception of the Gbethis, these groups existed prior to the war, relying on perceived magical powers and customary hunting weapons such as spears. Combining skill and valor, these groups at times thwarted RUF offensives.

As the war progressed and the RUF gained ground, the government supplied the CDF with weapons and financial and logistical support. Although under the supervision of Samuel Hinga Norman, who was the deputy defense minister, chairman of the CDF, and a Kamajor, the CDF did not feature prominently in the president's overall war strategy. This was a result of the army's unease at what it perceived as competition from other fighting forces and possibly due to fear of the CDF gaining political leverage over the president's hold on authority. In 1995, the government hired Executive Outcomes (EO), a South African "mercenary" force composed of 2,000 former South African Defense Force combat veterans.

The intervention of EO along with the CDF propped-up the failing Sierra Leonean government. EO's rapid deployment and well-trained soldiers attacked RUF forces and regained control of resource-rich areas. Its military victories allowed local traders to re-establish trade networks and, more importantly, enabled a corporate web of allied mining partners to fence off valuable mining zones, squeezing everyday miners into smaller low-paying illicit operations. With the assistance of local landowners or policemen, these traders kept wages low, forced slave - like labor, and traded diamonds on the informal market.

Those who did not cooperate were removed from political positions and trading zones. Women and Girls in Fighting Forces The presence of women and girls within the former rebel RUF and AFRC fighting forces was known early on in the war. Much less is known about their presence or roles in the SLA or the CDF. Drawing on field-based data and secondary sources, this study concludes that the estimated number of girls and young women in fighting forces was higher than previously reported. This increase is partly due to their presence as fully initiated members of the CDF. Of the study population, nearly all stated "abduction" and "forced recruitment" as their means of entry into the various forces.

Ten-year-old Maria B. was outside her home playing with friends under the moonlight when the RUF attacked. All of them tried to escape, but she was captured. She was told to carry looted items for the rebels and was given a five-gallon container of palm oil; anytime she tried to rest she was beaten. Agnes V. was nine years old and on vacation with her family when rebels attacked the village. After looting the village, the rebels rounded up around 50 people, locked them in a building, and began to set it on fire. A junior commander pleaded with the senior commander to release the young girl. She was then selected by the junior commander to be his captive "wife."

The people remaining in the building were burned. Agnes was forced to be the captive "wife" of the commander for the next nine years. During the commanders' absences from the camp, she was in charge of the military compound, including organizing raids and fighting units. Mariama M. was seven years old when she was captured and spent 10 years with the AFRC/RUF as a fighter. She received basic military and weapons training with machine guns and two-grip pistols. She was trained with approximately 50 other girls and 100 boys. Once recruited, women and girls had numerous roles, including that of frontline fighters. In fact, nearly half (44 percent) of the study population received basic military and weapons training from their commanders or captor "husbands."

However, nearly all women and girls performed additional roles:

- 72 percent as cooks;
- 68 percent as porters;
- 62 percent as assistants for the sick and wounded;
- 60 percent as "wives;"

- 44 percent as food producers;
- 40 percent as messengers between rebel camps;
- 22 percent as spies;
- 18 percent as communications technicians; and
- 14 percent as workers in diamond mines for their commanders or captor husbands.

Notably, all of the study population who reported their primary role as "fighter" also reported that they were forced to be captive "wives." According to Kama F., who at age 15 was an RUF frontline fighter, it was better to be a fighter and the "wife" of a common soldier because you could protect yourself with your own weapon, you had access to food and loot, and your chances of escaping were greater, unlike captive "wives" of commanders who were closely guarded with little chance of escape.

WOMEN AND GIRLS AS FULL MEMBERS OF THE CDF

Official claims that the pro-government CDF were composed only of males are inaccurate. Women and girls were fully initiated members of the CDF. This study focuses on the two largest CDF: the Kamajors and Gbethis.

Although the Kamajors were originally a male-only traditional hunting society, in response to the increased pressure from the RUF it became a self-defense force and enlisted women and girls beginning in the early 1990s and continued this practice throughout the war. The Gbethis, never a traditional male society, were created as one of the CDF in the mid 1990s in response to increased rebel attacks. They enlisted and initiated women and girls where they acted as integrated members of the CDF and were included in all ceremonies, amulets, and scarification. They served as com-manders, frontline fighters, initiators, spiritual leaders, medics, herbalists, spies, and cooks. Ramatu T. was a fighter with the Kamajors and fought alongside other girls and women Kamajors in Kenema and Bo Districts.

Describing her initiation she says, they use native herbs, which you drink and they bathe you in. These herbs make it so you don't feel like returning to your family. The initiator placed charms around my neck so that bullets are deflected, and a special charm to protect against knives and pangas; they will just bounce off my body. After this they gave me my special dress and herbs and charms. I was instructed not to bathe for several days because it would reduce the magic. Later, they rubbed the blood of a human being on my skin, and I found that I was not afraid of anything. I had a strong and fearless heart.

Some women and girls joined the Kamajors and Gbethis at the request of their husbands who were already initiated in the militias. Mamuna K. was married to a Gbethi man who asked her to join for her own protection. Mamuna, who was pregnant, sent her remaining children into Freetown for their safety and joined the Gbethis the same year. Importantly, Mamuna was an herbalist and her role within the Gbethis was to prepare the baths and drinks for those undergoing initiation. Within the group she was regarded as crucial to maintaining the magical powers of the fighting force, as she collected and prepared herbs for the fighters' food and drink. Others were abducted and conscripted by the Kamajors and Gbethis.

At times, women and girls worked with their male counterparts to capture civilian adolescents and children whom they forcibly initiated and trained as fighters. Some "joined" or became "wives" to male CDF fighters as a matter of survival. Mariatu R. agreed to become a "wife" of a fighter and join the Gbethis when an RUF attack on her village left her and her elderly parents as the only survivors. Upon joining, Mariatu was able to bring her parents and herself within the ring of protection offered by the Gbethis. Many adolescents and children "joined" the Kamajors and Gbethis with the approval of their parents.

This was especially the case when the Paramount Chief of the area endorsed a particular unit of the CDF; it then became mandatory that all families contribute a member to the CDF. Dissension was rare. For example, in Kenema Township, Kenema District, where the Kamajors were especially active during the war, the burned homes are not the result of rebel activities. Instead, they belong to families who did not contribute a family member to the Kamajors, and thus were suspected rebel sympathizers. According to one informant, "There is not a house in Kenema [Township] left that did not contribute someone to the Kamajors." Women and girls in the Kamajors and Gbethis observed widespread human rights violations by members of the CDF, including cannibalism, human sacrifice, and sexual abuse. For example, Ramatu T. reported that a common practice among her Kamajor force was for adult Kamajor males to enter a village and capture an adult civilian.

They would then cut the person's throat, turn them upside down, and "squeeze them from toe to head" to drain their blood into a bucket. All members of the fighting party, including the women and girls, would then drink the blood so they would not be afraid during the attack. Perhaps in part because of their participation in such violent acts, as well as their involvement in activities such as warfare, that went against traditionally acceptable roles for females, all young women and girls formerly with the CDF in the study population reported stigmatization, threats, and abuse upon returning to the communities they had fought to protect. The RUF was loosely configured, and camp and command structure varied throughout the country.

In general, a commander held "houses" or compounds in which his or her recruits and captives served. While there were a number of female RUF commanders, the majority were males. Captive "wives" of commanders exerted substantial power within the RUF compounds. These "wives" were predominately girls. When the commander was away, they were in charge of the compound. They kept in communication with the commander and would select and send troops, spies, and support when needed. These girls and young women decided on a daily basis who in the compound would fight, provide reconnaissance, and raid villages for food and loot. Some counseled their captor husbands on war strategies, troop movement, and upcoming attacks. Saramba M. spent five years with the RUF as a commander's "wife."

During that time she distributed weapons to boy and girl fighters prior to village raids and attacks on enemy forces. She also chose boys and girls for spy missions to infiltrate camps of the SLA, CDF, and Economic Community of West African States

Monitoring Group (ECOMOG) and to report on force locations and size. At times, such spying led to the deaths of these children and sexual abuse by male soldiers, particularly in the case of girls who were told to become intimate with the men in these forces to gather information. In the absence of the commander, when food and loot were delivered to the camps, it was brought to his captive "wife." She would then decide how these goods were to be apportioned among those in the compound.

Lynette S. distributed food and loot to groups of boy fighters within her RUF compound to try to persuade them not to harass or sexually abuse the young children in the camp. She expressed deep sympathy for the young children and had a number of strategies she would employ to try and influence her commander "husband" to also look out for the well being of the children. Bodyguards accompanied the commanders' captive "wives," both to provide protection in case of attack on the compound and to prevent their escape. Between four to six children might serve as bodyguards; 25 to 50 percent were girls. Ester C., a commander's "wife," was guarded by six boys and three girls; the youngest boy was six.

They were armed with AK-47s and two-grip pistols. Nearly all bodyguards and the commander's captive "wife" or "wives" carried guns and other weapons. In some cases, as documented in Kono District, commanders' captive "wives" were replaced by new or more favored girls. Subsequently, the rejected "wives" were sent by their commander husbands to the front lines to fight. Ramatu S. and Inna T. described RUF camps in the south with strictly enforced separations between civilians and soldiers. RUF commanders believed that a separation of camps would prevent civilians from witnessing atrocities committed by soldiers or learning about force size and strength should they escape and inform government factions.

Consistent with this strategy, "wives" of commanders or soldiers who were rejected were forbidden from returning to the civilian camps and were instead sent to the front lines. Commanders' "wives" were in charge of Small Boys Units (SBU) and Small Girls Units (SGU). The SBU were made up of boys aged 8-15 used primarily for scouting to prepare attacks and food raids, but were dispatched to execute some of the most violent killings and mutilations. The SGU were made up of similarly aged girls and were used primarily for raiding villages and spying, although they too were sent to fight and commit atrocities. In some cases, commanders' "wives" used loot to mitigate abuse by the SBU or to reward them for not abusing the girls within the compound. In other cases, they could order punishment of the SBU or SGU for "disrupting life in the compound."

Fighters, male and female, had their own "families" within the compound, which consisted of children they had captured and who were under their protection and care. Girl fighters could and did serve as heads of these "families." Food and loot were distributed on the basis of these "families." Much has been said about girls trying to attach themselves to boys or men within the compounds to avoid gang raping. While this appears to be accurate, this study also found that older children and adolescents who were not attached to a "family" were not given food and had to survive as scavengers. Thus, attachment of girls to boys or men was also means to secure food as well as (some) protection against sexual assault.

The presence, roles, and experiences of women and girls within the fighting forces in Sierra Leone has a number of important implications for the design of those processes that seek to build human and national security and peace in the post-conflict period. It is evident that despite their trauma, women and girls showed tremendous agency. They developed a number of skills and strategies that enabled them to survive and regain some control over their lives during their time with the fighting forces.

From the standpoint of DDR programs, however, the need for strict categorization of individuals as "combatants" or "non-combatants," and the reluctance on the part of the international community and local governments to acknowledge that women and girls are integral to the fighting often devalues the multiple roles they play in conflict. This is not only detrimental to disarmament and demobilisation; it also harms the women and girls. By being treated as passive victims or "dependents," they are again stripped of control of their lives and their sense of dignity. Moreover, by not acknowledging the skills and resources that they have attained, DDR processes risk losing tremendous social capital that could be utilized for post-conflict reconstruction.

THE ROLE OF WOMEN IN THE PEACE PROCESS

Throughout the war, rural and urban women from all classes and ethnic groups mobilized to form active organizations, conduct marches, and lead rallies for peace and justice. Many women's organizations participated in peace processes during and after the war, including the Mano River Women's Peace Network, Women's Movement for Peace, Forum of African Women Educationalists (FAWE), Sierra Leone Women's Forum, Network of Women Ministers and Parliamentarians, and the Sierra Leone Women's Movement for Peace. They educated civilians on electoral proceedings, recruited and trained observers, and pressured the military to respect the results of elections. Their efforts were critical in shaping informal and formal peace processes, and in bringing about an eventual end to the conflict.

The first attempt at a ceasefire came in January 1996, after a bloodless coup that overthrew the brief military dictatorship of Valetin Strasser. Brigadier General Maada Bio opened negotiations to cease hostilities with the RUF. Women's groups, led by Women Organized for a Morally Enlightened Nation (WOMEN), pressured Bio's military government, the National Provisional Ruling Council to hold democratic elections. Yet, when elections were held, only five women were on a list of 68 candidates representing the Sierra Leone People's Party (SLPP). Although given the opportunity, the RUF did not submit candidates of its own.

The SLPP won the elections, led by Ahmed Tejan Kabbah. Kabbah's first attempt at brokering a peace plan was the 1996 Abidjan Peace Accord. Drafted between the RUF and the Sierra Leone government, the accord called for a cessation of violence and the transformation of the RUF into a political party, with a power-sharing incentive to entice the RUF to lay down its arms. Although women suffered greatly from the war and were active in civil movements for peace, none were present at the Abidjan negotiations. At the signing of the Abidjan peace accord, some girl captives were released from RUF control as a goodwill gesture. However, mutual distrust in implementing the provisions of the accord, and RUF reluctance to lay down arms without the unconditional departure of EO ultimately led to its failure.

Other contributing factors included the government's belief that military victory remained possible and the RUF's fear of judicial reprisals. The government's failure to consistently pay or supply its soldiers, its increasing dependency on and financial support of the CDF and the high price tag of EO led to the splintering of the SLA. Some soldiers joined the RUF or became part of the new rebel Armed Forces Revolutionary Council (AFRC), which aligned itself with the RUF.

In 1997, the AFRC overthrew President Kabbah's regime. Former Army Major Johnny P. Koroma headed the AFRC in Freetown. Shortly thereafter, the RUF was invited to join the regime. Support for the AFRC came from professionals, civil servants, politicians, and other members of the socio-economic elite who felt alienated from the Kabbah government. Growing concern in the region regarding a joint AFRC/RUF government in Freetown brought about the intervention of the Economic Community of the West African States (ECOWAS) to restore the Kabbah regime. ECOWAS determined to act militarily to prevent further chaos, economic ruin, and violence.

In March 1997, with the approval of the UN, the Nigerian-led ECOMOG, the military wing of ECOWAS, attacked Freetown, forced the AFRC/ RUF regime out and restored Kabbah to power. Key policy objectives of the Kabbah government were to delegitimize the AFRC/RUF, uphold the rule of law, create a competent and trustworthy national army, and defeat the rebellion. Kabbah's restored government continued to rely on ECOMOG for protection, as well as the support of the CDF. ECOMOG's presence, however, contributed to violence against civilians. Violation of women and girls' human rights by ECOMOG soldiers was widespread. Girls desperate for income would prostitute themselves or become "girlfriends" of ECOMOG troops for protection.

ECOMOG soldiers coerced others into spying on enemy camps. Girls were made especially vulnerable during RUF attacks on ECOMOG forces, and it was common for suspected "girlfriends" of ECOMOG soldiers to be targeted by the RUF for torture and murder. At the same time, girls from RUF and AFRC camps would be sent into ECOMOG areas to befriend soldiers, establish sexual relations with them, and collect intelligence. In January 1999, a joint AFRC/RUF attack on Freetown resulted in the deaths of over 5,000 civilians. Thousands more were mutilated and raped, and over 5,000 were abducted, mostly women and girls. Recognizing the improbability of a military victory over the AFRC/RUF, the government sought a peace plan and eventually agreed to the 1999 Lomé accord.

The Young Women's Christian Association (YWCA), as a founding member of the Inter-Religious Council of Sierra Leone, played a leading role in the negotiations that led to the signing of the 1999 Lomé peace accord, officially ending the war (though fighting and unrest continued into 2002). It called for RUF inclusion in a power-sharing government and granted blanket amnesty to gross violators of human rights. In addition to pardoning RUF leader Sankoh, it placed him at the head of the Commission for the Management of Strategic Resources. Two women were involved in the Lomé process, one a member of the government delegation and the other a representative of the RUF.

Although they were not chief negotiators, the final document reflected at least some gender-specific issues as a result of women's participation. For example, Article 28 calls for special attention to victimized women and girls in formulating and implementing rehabilitation, reconstruction, and development programs. The formation of commissions to promote good governance was also called for in the peace accord. Yet within the key entities including the Commission for the Consolidation of Peace, the Commission for the Management of Strategic Resources, National Reconstruction and Development, and the Council of Religious Leaders, there were no women represented at the time of writing.

In October 1999, the United Nations Assistance Mission to Sierra Leone (UNAMSIL) deployed troops to support the implementation of the Lomé peace accord and bolster the government in the DDR process. However, because there were vast areas still under RUF control, UNAMSIL forces were unable to fully restore peace. In particular, fighting in the diamond-rich eastern province persisted. Small RUF raids and offensives against UN troops yielded large numbers of UN weapons and armored vehicles. RUF attacks peaked on May 3, 2000, when 500 UN peace- keepers were taken hostage. Less than a week later, British Special Forces arrived in Freetown, expelled the RUF from the city, and restored a sense of security. Subsequently, British forces trained and armed Sierra Leonean troops and drove the remaining RUF soldiers from their territory, allowing UN peacekeepers to return.

The Lomé accord collapsed when the RUF broke the ceasefire following UNAMSIL's assumption of control of the diamond-rich areas of eastern Sierra Leone. Recruits from Liberia continued to enter the country, facilitating RUF control over the resource-rich region. When Sankoh's intentions of continuing the war despite Lomé surfaced, women assembled in the streets demanding "Not again! Enough is enough!" Their slogan was a response to both the inadequate representation of women after the 1996 elections and Sankoh's tactics, which the women understood to be a means for him to re-arm for war. The women on the streets called for an end to male domination and male-biased decisions within parliament. They were particularly critical of the decision to appoint Sankoh as a minister and repeatedly called attention to the fact that he was refortifying for war. Women's activism reached a high point in 2000 when they ultimately played a catalytic role in bringing an end to the conflict.

A group of elderly women, representing churches and mosques, requested a meeting with Sankoh, who was living in

Freetown. The women came as an interfaith group with an agenda of peace at any cost. Upon arrival they were abused by Sankoh, his guards, and advisors, who refused to listen and mistreated them. The assembled older women stood outside the house of Sankoh, hitched up their skirts, bent over, and bared themselves. In Sierra Leone, such an action by women of this age and standing constitutes the worst curse, sign of shaming, and insult that can be brought upon anyone.

When word of what had happened reached the streets, people were shocked. But they were also mobilized, both because they now had courage to stand up to Sankoh and the RUF, and because they had an obligation to enforce the curse of these respected, senior, religious women. Previously, people had lived in fear of retaliation and violence by the RUF as Sankoh sent death squads to any part of the capital where people spoke out. Yet when such a curse is given, it is the family and society's obligation to back the curse. Men in particular were mobilized to defend the power and honor of the women. May 8, 2000, was set as the date for mass peace protests and demonstrations.

The families of the women, religious organizations, labor and trade unions, and adolescents and school children committed to join the peace protests. Since it appeared that many people would not be going to work or school, the government declared it an unofficial holiday. The mass demonstrations on May 8, 2000 marked the turning point in the conflict. This time the women marched to Sankoh's house with parliamentarians and civil society leaders. Sankoh's guards opened fire, killing a number of the protesters. On May 13, British troops captured and arrested Sankoh, charging him with the murder of unarmed protestors. With the incarceration of Sankoh, the RUF began to splinter, creating a vacuum in which General Issa Sessay became the new RUF leader and eventually the head of the RUFP, a newly formed political party.

The war was officially declared over in January 2002, when hostilities between the CDF and RUF soldiers in eastern Sierra Leone ceased. When the war ended there were approximately 400,000 internally displaced people and up to 500,000 refugees in Guinea, Gambia, Ghana, and Cote D'Ivoire. At least 55 percent of the refugees were women. Women's organizations continue to address these ongoing issues. For example, recognizing the regional dimensions of the conflict, the Mano River Union Women's Network for Peace visits women refugees in Guinea and Liberia encouraging them to become a part of the peace process, addressing problems such as sexual assaults in camps and food short- ages, and, with assistance from the United Nations High Commissioner for Refugees (UNHCR), reuniting women with family members and returning them to their homes in Sierra Leone.

DDR was initiated by the government of the Sierra Leone People's Party (SLPP) in the aftermath of the 1996 Abidjan accords. A National Commission for Reconstruction, Resettlement, and Rehabilitation (NCRRR) was established with a department that had responsibility for disarming the varying factions. In 1998 the department was restructured as the National Committee for Disarmament, Demobilisation, and Reintegration (NCDDR), after which the program began. Its goals were threefold:

1. Collect, register, and destroy all conventional weapons and munitions turned in by combatants;
2. Demobilize the initially estimated 45,000 combatants from the SLA, RUF, AFRC, and the CDF, 12 percent of whom were thought to be women; and
3. Support ex-combatants through demobilization to prepare them for reintegration.

DDR was conducted in three phases, the first beginning in 1998. Phase I was conducted by the NCDDR, chaired by President Kabbah, and ECOMOG, which was mandated to assist in disarmament, weapons collection, and demobilization. In 1999 with the Lomé accords in place, Phase II was initiated, running until April 2000; DDR was conducted by NCDDR and the United Nations Observer Mission to Sierra Leone (UNOMSIL), which was mandated to assist in disarmament and monitoring of demobilization. UNOMSIL was replaced in October 1999 by a significantly larger peacekeeping mission to support the DDR effort. Phase III, which ran from May 2001 to January 2002, was conducted by NCDDR and the new United Nations Assistance Mission in Sierra Leone (UNAMSIL).

Reception centers were established for disarmament and demobilization throughout the country. From September 1998 through May 2001, during Phases I and II, a series of questions and performance of disassembly and reassembly of a gun, usually an AK 47, were used to assess combatants and their DDR eligibility status (combatants 18 years or older). It was believed that the ability to assemble and disassemble a weapon was a good litmus test to determine whether an individual had participated in the conflict as an armed combatant—the requirement for participation in the DDR program. During this time, women accounted for six percent and girls for 0.6 percent of participants. In Phase III (May 18 2001 through January 2002) group disarmament was allowed, meaning a group could bring in weapons together.

This helped marginally to increase women's participation to seven percent and girls to 0.7 percent. Combatants voluntarily presented themselves at the reception centers to disarm and surrender all weapons and ammunition, and to be assessed for eligibility in the program. While officially those under 18 years of age were not required to present a weapon to enter DDR, this study found widespread discrepancy among UN and NCDDR officials and staff of NGOs working within the DDR process as to whether or not children had to turn over a weapon. According to nearly all interviewees who passed through DDR, despite official policy the weapons test was repeatedly administered to children to determine their admission into programs.

Qualifying adults (18 years of age and above) were sent to a demobilization center where they received pre-discharge orientation, their benefits packages, a small amount of resettlement and transportation money, and were discharged. Children (17 years of age and below) were to be sent to Interim Care Centers (ICCs) and could select to enter skills training or an educational program of their choice. Late in the program it was decided that "wives" of (male) ex-combatants could apply for micro-credit to help maintain their families, as the men complained about their inability to sustain families. However for a female applicant to access the loans, she had to be present with a "husband," who was willing to identify her as his wife.

No woman could claim benefits alone, regardless of the number of children she cared for. If women had been permitted to apply alone, it could have enabled them to abdicate their "relationships." But this was not considered by senior DDR officials, one of whom said that "even if they were raped and abducted, 70 percent of the women and girls wanted to be with their 'husbands'." The DDR program in Sierra Leone is widely seen as a success and considered to have been sensitive to the needs of female and child combatants.

During a visit to Sierra Leone by UN Under-Secretary-General and Special Representative of the Secretary-General for Children and Armed Conflict, Olara Otunno, a UN statement was released noting that "since the Sierra Leonean conflict ended in January 2002 an ambitious programme for the demobilization and reintegration of 7,000 child ex-combatants has [reunited] 97 percent of them with their families and communities." In March of 2002, in an interview with IRIN news, when asked about female ex-combatants, Dr. Francis Kai-Kai, Executive Secretary of the NCDDR stated "we had about eight percent of them. In the designed program we made every provision for the female ex-combatant."

However, this study finds this claim difficult to substantiate when compared to actual experiences of women and girl ex-combatants through interviews and NCDDR data. The estimated number of all forces was 137,865 of whom 12,056 were assumed to be girls. Yet, and data drawn from UNICEF and NCDDR indicate, there is substantial disparity between the numbers of girls within the forces and those entering DDR programs, thus calling into question the design, implementation, and success of these programs. Despite official policy, the possession of an AK-47 (even with a group) and knowledge of its assembly and disassembly was repeatedly used by disarmament administrators to determine entry into the program, even for those under 18. This proved to be a particular problem for women and girls who did not always have a weapon in their possession.

There was a perception among them that a weapon was required for everyone seeking entry into the DDR program, and, indeed, among those in this study's sample, all who entered into DDR (half the study population) were asked to turn in a weapon and perform the weapons test. The security was bad." Second, female ex-combatants, particularly women and girls from the CDF, reported fearing RUF former fighters housed at the centers. Christiana R. left an adult center due to the sleeping accommodations. "As a woman," she said, "I could not stay there." With regard to children in particular, young women and girls explained that interviews conducted by DDR and ICC staff in the presence of other children and youth did not protect their affiliation with regard to fighting force. CDF girls reported immediate threats to their lives when RUF youth became aware of their affiliation, and they left the ICCs shortly thereafter.

For example, Bintu O. was interviewed in a room where other adolescents stood around looking in. As soon as it was known that she was a Kamajor, the former RUF children began to threaten her, and she left the center that evening. Third, there was the widely perpetuated myth that women and girls were not involved in the CDF. This denial was propagated by influential figures such as then Deputy Minister of Defense and National Coordinator of the CDF Samuel Hinga Norman, who was himself a Kamajor. For some women and perceived requirement kept some who would have qualified from attempting to enter the program. Of the study group that did not go through DDR, 46 percent cited not having a weapon as the basis for their lack of participation. There were several reasons girl ex-combatants found themselves without weapons at this critical time.

Although they had been in the fighting forces, many in the CDF were ordered to hand in their weapons prior to demobilization and were then left behind as the men were transported to the assembly centers. Other girls indicated that their guns were taken away by their commanders and handed to male fighters. Additionally, many who were not "primarily" fighters had used weapons from a communal source but did not possess a gun themselves. In further discussion, interviewees revealed six key concerns that affected their attitudes towards DDR and the reasons they chose not to join or remain in programs. First, some girls and young women indicated they did not know about DDR or felt there was nothing to gain by going to the centers. Twenty-one percent of the sample that did not go through DDR reportedly feared reprisals at the centers and thus avoided the entire process. Other respondents perceived the facilities to be dangerous with large numbers of men and inadequate protection.

At the end of the war, Norman was promoted to Minister of Internal Security, which caused a number of this study's informants to insist that they remain anonymous when discussing issues of women and girls within the CDF. Recently, however, the Prosecutor for the Sierra Leone Special Court ordered the arrest of Norman and he is currently awaiting charges of crimes against humanity and war crimes, including for the use of child soldiers within the CDF. Fourth, there was a mistaken belief that children in the CDF were not separated from their families and communities. As a result, many were not classified by UNICEF and international NGOs as "separated children" and therefore could not receive other forms of aid.

This is significant, as a number of UN, government, and NGO programs and benefits were designated for "separated children," including child combatants. It was not uncommon for NGOs to report that they did not work with children in the CDF "since they were never separated," and particularly with girls, since there was the assumption that the CDF did not include female members. However, among the women and girls interviewed for this study, some with the Kamajors and Gbethis, had spent significant time away from their families and communities, including traveling the length of the country to fight with other CDF.

Fifth, over-classification of girls and young women abducted by the RUF, AFRC, and SLA as "camp followers," "sex-slaves," and "wives" by some within the international community and the Sierra Leone government prevented the establishment of DDR programs to address their actual lived experiences. According to DDR officials, "wives," including those abducted, were to be explicitly excluded from formal entrance into DDR. The focus of DDR was on the main fighting forces, and "minority" groups would not be taken into consideration. However, since women and girls frequently played multiple roles, narrow classification of them as "wives" resulted in programmatic errors.

Of the study population, 60 percent reported having served as a "wife," yet only eight percent reported this as their primary role. Additionally, in the case of the CDF in particular, there was the erroneous belief that male CDF fighters could not have sexual or casual contact with a girl or woman; it was largely considered impossible for female members of the CDF to exist in the category of CDF "wife" or "sex slave."This myth gained international legitimacy in October 1998 when a boy Kamajor refused to shake the hand of UNICEF head Carol Bellamy "because he was not allowed to touch a woman."

This story was widely circulated and repeated in contexts that helped strengthen the belief that women and girls were not included in the CDF. However, among Sierra Leoneans, it was understood that interactions with members of the opposite sex, including sexual relations, were permitted for both male and female members of the Kamajors and Gbethis. It was common, especially among those Kamajors and Gbethis who were married to each other or lived together. The only caveat was that sexual contact nullified the perceived magical powers of a fighter's charms, and thus after such contact, fighters had to reapply the charms to regain these supposed powers.

Finally, it is important to note that cultural notions of childhood in Sierra Leone affected the way in which young women and girls engaged with the DDR program. In many rural and urban areas, childhood and adulthood are defined not by chronological age but by actions undertaken by the person, such as a boy harvesting and making palm wine or a girl having a baby. When girls who had borne children arrived to disarm, some entered the programs as women since this is how they were now "culturally" defined. Indeed, it was reported to the researchers by those in charge of DDR programs and officials who screened participants that it was not uncommon for girls under 18 with children to enter DDR as women. Thus they did not benefit from the programs that were established for child combatants, and were largely left unsupported since the DDR program did not have adequate mechanisms to address the needs of women in the forces.

For those who did enter the DDR process (i.e. half of the study sample) many noted the paucity of supplies, particularly in terms of their physical needs as women. At the ICCs where child combatants and "separated children" were taken and demobilization centers where adults were taken, 43 percent reported not receiving adequate clothing; 54 percent did not receive proper sanitation materials, including soap, shampoo, and feminine hygiene products; and 23 percent did not have access to medical care when requested. Women respondents also reported very poor conditions at adult demobilization centers.

In terms of the length of their stay at demobilization centers, the young women and girls surveyed had experiences that contradicted official claims. For example, while UN data indicate that nearly all children remained in the centers for at least six months, among those surveyed for this study, only 20 percent had remained for that length of time. Finally, only 44 percent of the sample reported receiving the benefits they were promised in demobilization. In particular, lack of financial payment was noted as a leading cause of rising tension among child ex-combatants and resulted in rioting, strikes, and attacks against NGO staff and property in 2002.

IN THE REINTEGRATION PHASE

As in many war-torn countries, the reintegration of ex-combatants in Sierra Leone is complex and sensitive. For the young women and girls, in particular, there is a range of issues that create concern. In response to an open-ended question, 50 percent of the study population named material deprivation, including lack of food, clothing, and housing, as the greatest challenge for their reintegration. Others noted separation from family, rejection, and abuse by family or community, fear of a return to war, and the inability to attend school as major concerns. When asked what factors helped to mitigate these issues, responses included the end of the war, support from their community or family, and support from NGOs.

However, the most critical and often identified need was for education—a core component of most DDR programs for children. Seventy-five percent of the study population indicated a desire to attend school and gain literacy skills. Forty-nine percent stated that skills training would be essential to their successful reintegration. Sierra Leone ranks among the lowest countries in the world in female literacy and education. Purposeful destruction of schools by the fighting forces further devastated the education system. Well-meaning social workers associated with implementing DDR programs at times discouraged or prevented older ex-combatant girls and girl mothers from entering school, instead urging them to attend skills trainings. They argued that since so many of these young women now had children and few had husbands to assist with income, they would need to develop skills rather than continued education to support them. At the same time, a number of women and girl mothers were unable to attend skills trainings because of a lack of adequate care for their children (this is related to stigmatism and rejection by families who may welcome a girl back, but not her child or children).

There is also a misperception that the older girls and young women considered themselves too old to attend school. Thus, while education was an option for those who went through official DDR, many of the young women and older girls were discouraged to pursue that option. Notably, this argument was not put forward to adolescent boys or men. NGO records themselves reveal unbalanced ratios of boys and girls enrolled in education programs. The reintegration of children and youth from fighting forces is a significant factor in any peace process. Yet few resources and limited time are given to the "R" in DDR.

While significant research is being done on the need to support long-term reintegration and rehabilitation processes, in most cases, the burden of caring for ex-combatants still falls to individuals and communities.

Women in Sierra Leone, though under resourced and unheralded, have filled in these programmatic gaps and done much to reintegrate former combatants, particularly women and child soldiers. Working alone, as leaders and members of NGOs, and through the Ministry of Social Welfare, Gender, and Children's Affairs, women have taken in and cared for child soldiers, provided women and child former fighters with critical services and training, and thereby worked to normalize and bring stability to their communities and their nation. Shellac Davies, a leading peacemaker in Sierra Leone, has observed the trauma inflicted on child soldiers and the mixed responses they receive in their home communities.

At the end of the war, the attachment between commanders and the child rebels disintegrated, but children often felt that they couldn't go home. "The children were in a dilemma," says Davies. "Mothers who survived the mans-laughter but were witnesses to the evil acts committed by their children virtually disowned them. 'A child who committed such an atrocity could not have been born from my womb,' many mothers were known to have said." However, Davies has documented the work of some women and mothers to reintegrate the very children who committed the atrocities. It was these women who "realized that the children involved in the war were both victims and perpetrators."

She goes on to describe how the children's violence was the result of their own victimization at the hands of commanders: urged by their commanders within the rebel movement, they were known to have committed most of the atrocities experienced during the war. Those children under the influence of drugs obeyed commands to kill their parents, burn down houses, and amputate the limbs of their siblings and other members of the community.

In the Bo District (south central Sierra Leone), a group of women decided to take back those children and youth from the fighting forces between the ages of 6 and 25. "The women claimed that such a move was their own contribution to upholding the peace," says Davies adding, "It should be noted that some of those women had lost their own children and relatives as a result of the war." Women in Makeni (Bambali District, north central Sierra Leone) also organized themselves to care for children coming out of the fighting forces. Women in this region, known as the rebel stronghold, experienced the realities of the rebel war in particularly brutal ways. They were forced to become "wives" of the commanders, rape was a weapon of war used against them, and they were forced into various functions including acting as human shields for rebels during attacks.

"The women there knew those children who committed atrocities in Makeni and its environs," says Davies. "Some of those young boys and youths were urged to rape women who could pass as their mothers, aunts, or elder sisters." Despite these experiences, in their pursuit of peace the women were willing to play a pivotal role in the re-integration of these child ex-combatants. Davies notes: "If the peace so far achieved is to prove meaningful and sustainable then society has to take up its responsibility of caring for its children." As individuals and through collective action, women in communities are leading efforts to reintegrate women and girl ex-combatants. "The women argued that if those children were left uncared for now that peace has been achieved they would easily revert to their old ways," says Davies. "They argued that left abandoned these child ex-combatants would have nothing positive to do and or think, and will prove a threat to the fragile peace now in existence."

Fifty-five percent of the study population indicated that women in the community had played a significant role in their reintegration. This is noteworthy as it was higher than their responses for being assisted by traditional healers (14 percent), traditional leaders (20 percent), international aid workers (32 percent), health workers (51 percent), and on par with religious leaders and social workers, many of whom are women. Interviewees noted that women in the community provided them with helpful guidance, shared meager resources, and, perhaps most importantly, helped to facilitate skills training and education by providing childcare, clothes, or food. The basic assistance given in the form of childcare was critical in enabling many ex-combatants to enter skills training programs.

AT THE COMMUNITY LEVEL

As staff of NGOs working to reintegrate combatants, women contributed to building peace throughout the country at the grassroots level. For example, Esther A., a reintegration and HIV/AIDS program officer with a local NGO that works with child ex-combatants and war-affected children, was captured by the RUF along with three of her siblings. She watched as her siblings, all university graduates, were killed.

She narrowly escaped. After all that has happened to me, I still want to work with these children. Really the past is not easy; you cannot force people to tell their stories. I share my story with the children. I share my losses. They see this reality that they, the RUF, were the ones who took my beloved people, and yet I am here helping them. You can forgive, but you can never forget.

Esther's colleague, Ramatu S. was trained as a teacher before joining an NGO as a psychosocial supervisor for child combatants. In addition to her full workdays with children and adolescents and caring for her own two children, Ramatu has taken five girl mothers with their children and two foster children, all former members of fighting forces, into her home so they have a place to live and recover. With regard to women's collective action, the Luawa Skills Training Center (LSTC) in Kailahun, the Women's Progressive Movement (WPM) in Freetown and Caritas-Makeni has been innovative in their efforts in the Makeni area.

Founded by six women, LSTC now has 120 members. It serves as a reintegration program and assists women abductees, ex-combatants, and victims in their efforts at independent living. The organization offers tailoring and garra tie-dying classes. Once women learn the skills and sell their products, they are required to give some of their earnings back to the organization.

WPM was founded in 1998. Its mission is to find abducted children, provide financial and medical assistance, and help women become independent. When the parents of abducted children cannot be found or their relatives shun them, members of WPM adopt them. Today, nearly every member has taken on at least one child and in many cases, several.

Affiliated with the Catholic Church, locally based NGO Caritas-Makeni operates in central Sierra Leone with a staff comprised mostly of nuns and female social workers. In a country with a 60 percent Muslim population this organization has been effective in reaching beyond Catholic communities. In their programs in the Districts of Port Loko, Tonkolili, and Bombali, it has instituted programs that allow for girl mothers to bring their children to skills training or to care for them while their mothers attend school. They provide a room and mat for the child to sleep on and food for the mother and child during the day. This contributes to higher retention rates in the programs and helps prevent their involvement in illicit activities such as prostitution, which is on the rise. Caritas-Makeni also offers a program on alternative income generation for those who have entered the sex trade and reproductive health and safe sex education.

AT THE NATIONAL LEVEL

Women in international and national NGOs are also working with young women and girls to incorporate them into their skills training programs. National women's organizations such as the Progressive Women's Association (PROWA) and the Forum for African Women Educationalists (FAWE) are among the groups running skills training centers, which include education for basic literacy. With branches across Africa, FAWE established its Sierra Leone chapter in 1995 during the war. It is now a national women's organization with branches throughout the country. It offers a range of training programs to girl and women ex-combatants including tailoring, carpentry, tie dying, and masonry.

FAWE has rebuilt schools and community centers that were destroyed and in some areas, has constructed and opened schools for girls. Some of its programs cater to girl mothers and other vulnerable girl populations with the aim of increasing literacy and education. FAWE is the only organization to accept pregnant girls into the classroom. In March 1999 FAWE began the Rape Victims Program. Their projects include radio programming, visits with school children, counseling, and referrals to team doctors. Female survivors who became pregnant were given pre- and post-natal care by the organization.

FAWE has partnered with over 30 ministerial and government agencies, UN agencies, international and local NGOs to carry out their work. PROWA is operating in the Kono District, an area that has been heavily impacted by the war and where, at the time of publication, few international NGOs were active. PROWA was one of the few organizations in the area to offer skills training to female ex-combatants. Additionally, it is one of the few organizations that encourages and allows pregnant girls to participate in their programs. Since Kono was the last area to disarm and an RUF stronghold, many girls who recently came out of the bush are in Kono and in need of assistance, thus increasing the importance of the efforts of this women's group.

The UN Development Fund for Women (UNIFEM) has focused its support for women in Sierra Leone at various levels, working with other UN agencies, with national ministries, and with community-level official and non-government organizations to ensure gender-sensitive policies. In particular, UNIFEM has worked to ensure that special attention is given in the Truth and Reconciliation process to crimes against women, and that the needs and concerns of female survivors are addressed. In addition, the Ministry of Social Welfare, Gender, and Children's Affairs, due in part to the advocacy efforts and technical support of UNIFEM, recently received government approval and funding for a gender directorate.

The ministry works with UN agencies and international and local NGOs to provide accelerated education and skills training for ex-combatant children. UNICEF, in partnership with the Sierra Leone government, and local and international NGOs, has developed model programs for encouraging the schooling and reintegration of former child combatants. To summarize, communities that receive ex-combatant children (who benefited from DDR and elect to attend school) into the education system are "rewarded" by receiving books, supplies, and sports equipment. Schools and communities receive materials based on the number of ex-combatants they accept. Thus, ex-combatants are not perceived as "benefiting" from violent behavior in the fighting forces; instead all children in the school benefit by having their peers return.

At the same time, accelerated schooling is offered for older child ex-combatants who have missed school years due to the war. In partnership with the United States Agency for International Development (USAID), UNICEF has developed targeted programs for young mothers, combining childcare and food with vocational training and basic literacy skills. There is also a focus on training women in non-traditional skills such as welding, carpentry, and the construction of houses. These initiatives, led by individuals, communities, NGOs, and national mechanisms, and in some cases, supported by international aid, are relatively small and inexpensive compared to official DDR efforts.

Yet their impact is notable: Over 65 percent of the study population said that women have reached out to help them and that they would be interested in joining a women's organization to assist others. By being over-classified as "dependents," the real experiences of women and girls were not acknowledged and they were precluded from receiving benefits provided to other combatants. This assumption—that women and girls were victims only, with no significant role in either the execution of war or the building of peace—is detrimental for their future and could adversely affect the country's recovery.

First, as observed during 2002, the exclusion of child and female combatants from official DDR processes can lead to increased levels of insecurity. For in the same way that disaffected male youths and ex-fighters might lead rebellions and form militias, so can women and girls. In 2002, riots increased, particularly among former child and adolescent combatants, and ICCs were attacked. Social workers reported that adolescent women and girls were sometimes the leaders of these protests. Without support or care from their former "partners" or "husbands," their own families, the community, or the state, many of the young women— particularly those with children born as a result of their captivity—resorted to civil unrest as a means of accessing basic goods for the survival of their children.

For these young women and girls, the stakes are, in effect, greater than for some of the men and boys. Second, the exclusion of women and girls from official programs and assistance has significant social consequences including poverty, crime, and prostitution. Inevitably it also leads to an increase in HIV/AIDS. Moreover, the exclusion of single mothers means the exclusion of their children. Thus the emergence of another generation of disaffected marginalized youth is possible. Third, despite the horrors they endured, the women and girls showed tremendous agency and initiative during their times in the forces.

Within the confines of their environment they regained some control of their own lives by developing skills to ensure their survival and strategies to protect others. Yet when the DDR program was implemented, there was virtually no recognition of the multiple roles they played or skills they gained. Many have ambitions for education and independence. They feel tremendous responsibility for their offspring and aspire to give them better lives.

The presence, roles, and experiences of women and girls within the fighting forces in Sierra Leone are more complex than previously reported. This inaccurate assessment resulted in operational and programmatic errors on the part of the UN, multilateral organizations, international NGOs, donor governments, and the government of Sierra Leone. In short, the inadequate attention to women and girls, coupled with a lack of gender sensitivity regarding their particular circumstances and needs, had a detrimental impact on the DDR process as a whole. Bias in design and implementation of DDR programs resulted in the near exclusion of women and girls from DDR programs and benefits, with those within the SLA and the CDF particularly marginalized.

Disarmament and demobilization camps and procedures were constructed to attract large numbers of male fighters and did not give adequate attention to ensuring that the human rights of women and girls were protected and preserved. The efforts of child protection agencies operating in Sierra Leone are among the best to date. Still, due to biases within the DDR program, alternative approaches must be sought to address the needs and rights of the many excluded women and girls that potentially fall under the umbrella of war-affected children and youth. A range of factors including inadequate funding resulted in limitations to reintegration and longer-term rehabilitation elements of the programme.

Yet the successful reintegration of ex-combatants is an essential component of national and human security, necessary to build sustainable peace. Some international programs have recognized the need to address reintegration from the ex-combatants'. and the community's perspectives. In addition, there is growing understanding that financial assistance alone is not sufficient for effective reintegration, that the needs and aspirations of ex-combatants and their families must be addressed, and that local support systems, psychosocial services, and other referral centers should be established to assist all ex-combatants in their efforts to return to a peaceful and productive lifestyle. But while these efforts are developing, it is critical to ensure that women and girls are fully integrated, and that there is greater understanding of the roles they played in the war.

International human rights laws oblige national, and particularly international, actors to ensure that women are treated equal to men. Finally, women have held leadership roles throughout Sierra Leone's history. During the war, despite the widespread violence, women were fundamental to the reorganization of civil society, mass mobilization for peace, and the eventual cessation of the war. Women's organizations such as the YWCA played central roles in the processes that led to the signing of the Lomé peace accord.

The YWCA of Sierra Leone openly encourages women to "unite and initiate programs for self sufficiency and take up leadership roles in our communities and country as a whole." National organizations such as FAWE and PROWA are rebuilding schools and educating children including ex-combatants. Local community members and informal networks and groups support some of those who did not pass through DDR programs or receive benefits. Women, individually and collectively, are playing important roles in assisting in the material, social, and cultural reintegration of former fighters.

Women's commitment to rehabilitating ex-combatants is a matter of basic survival. Unlike the international community, they have no "exit strategy." If the peace fails, violence returns to their doorsteps. But such groups are under tremendous pressure. They have meager resources. Their work is often undocumented and unacknowledged in official processes, and they receive limited support from the international community and donor governments.

7

Sex and Equality

Lobola, Osibisa Camp

ZIMBABWEAN WOMEN'S LIBERATION STRUGGLE

In revolutionary war situations there is often no defined front line and both women and children can come directly under attack: thus the stereotyped image of men going off to war, and women staying at home away from the conflict, has to be radically revised. In such revolutionary conflicts, women are not merely victims but also actively work side-by-side with men in support of the war effort. The position of women in liberation struggles shows that wars have to be judged not just from the position of men, but also from the position of women who incessantly struggle to sustain the force of the revolution. This chapter argues, therefore, that the story of a liberation struggle cannot be complete without an analysis of the role women play in guerrilla warfare revolutions.

Using an African feminist approach to women and war, this chapter explores the involvement and the terms of women's participation in the guerrilla war in Zimbabwe. The discussion analyses the suffering caused to Zimbabwe women former freedom fighters not only by the imposition of war, but also by the male centered demands of the nationalist movement, the Zimbabwean male fighters, and the Zimbabwean society as a whole during and after Zimbabwe's war of liberation. Focusing on the role of women fighters in Zimbabwe, this article argues that in revolutionary struggles, women encounter conflict in different ways to men. As armed conflicts affect the revolutionary cadres and non-participatory civilians, the coping strategies adopted under the pressure differ by, and to a large degree, are determined by gender.

For women, vulnerability caused by their physical stature and their position in society increases the burdens placed on them making gender an important element in the determination of coping strategies. Yet despite these problems, progressive gender role changes and fluidity also occur in these contexts. As feminist critic on women and the revolution, Stephanie Urdang, points out, "conflict accentuates resourcefulness in the adoption of coping and survival strategies." The paper draws the bulk of its evidence from oral testimonies captured and recorded during 1980-2001 by researchers on women's involvement in the struggle.

Through their voices and collective life stories, the paper shows the extent and nature of the suffering endured by female combatants. The discussion adds to the importance of understanding the dynamics of socio-cultural historical realities in which a war is fought, and furthermore serves as an attempt to acknowledge the level of human suffering and the trauma that occurs during a revolution. The paper reveals, however, that beyond all this, Zimbabwean female cadres, like women in any revolution, have resilience and courage, even in harsh unyielding environments.

The involvement of Zimbabwean women in the revolution dated back before the 1960s to the 1890s, when six years after the occupation of what was then Southern Rhodesia by the British South Africa Company, the Shona and Ndebele people rose up against the foreign invaders. When this happened, women were involved in significant numbers and roles in the struggle that came to be known as the First Liberation War. Nehanda Nyasikana, a woman, purposefully took up arms and through the spirit that possessed her is said to have divinated military advice to the Shona people. She was eventually arrested for the killing of Native Commissioner Pollard and was sentenced to be hanged, but at her death, she stated that her bones would rise again in the fight against colonialism. Eighty years later, in 1976, the spirit of Nehanda inspired guerrilla fighters during the Second Chimurenga, through possessed spirit mediums.

There were a number of stimuli for Zimbabwe's second liberation war. Among the most serious was the scarcity of land among Africans, unfair labour relations, lack of employment, and burdensome tax obligations. By 1960, Africans in Southern Rhodesia started making radical demands, which resulted in the formation of nationalist political parties. The National Democratic Party (NDP) was formed in early 1960, the Zimbabwe African People's Union (ZAPU) in 1962 and the Zimbabwe African National Union (ZANU) in 1963, splitting off from ZAPU. In 1960, women in the NDP organized a demonstration against the Rhodesian government which had ruled that only fifteen out of sixty-five-parliamentary seats be allocated to Africans. Women, seeing this as the cementing of white domination, joined men in the protests against white rule and took to the streets. Immediately after, in 1961, NDP was banned and according to Ngwabi Bhebe, the women's actions had been the catalyst that had shifted the struggle to a more militant level.

After the women's strike, leading nationalists began to recognize the potential role of women in the organizational structure of the struggle. When Ian Smith, then Prime Minister, took more drastic measures and declared the independence of Rhodesia from Britain in the Unilateral Declaration of Independence (UDI) in 1965, it worsened the living conditions of the Africans both in rural and urban areas. Much of the pressure of this fell on women, resulting in their support of the armed struggle for African majority rule. Samora Machel, then president of neighbouring Mozambique, admitted the ultimate need to involve women in the revolutionary struggle. "The liberation of women," he said "is a fundamental necessity for the revolution, the guarantee of its continuity and the precondition for its victory."

In addition, Robert Mugabe, the post-revolutionary President of Zimbabwe pointed out that "Without women's full participation, the struggle for a social, political, economic and cultural independence of a country may not be achieved." Yet despite recognition of the role of women during the war of liberation, feminist critics have noted that after the struggle Zimbabwean women ex-combatants felt, and still feel, betrayed by the post-colonial government.

UNDER PRE-COLONIAL AND COLONIAL PATRIARCHY

The link between the revolution and the involvement of women in liberation struggles can be easily understood. Women in colonial Zimbabwe under traditional and colonial patriarchal rule had no control over the economy; their powerlessness was grounded in traditional African cultures as well as in Colonial/Victorian/Christian concepts of "woman." First, pre-colonial customary law practices such as marriage and motherhood put women at a disadvantage. Traditional practices largely dictated what became culturally accepted rights and duties of spouses. Because of various marriage rituals in the African tradition such as gift marriage, widow inheritance, forced childhood marriage, polygamy, bride-wealth and inheritance all favoured men, women were first and foremost regarded as wives and mothers, then as individuals. For example, women were required to have a male representative (brother, father, husband) in a public transaction and this rendered them perpetual minors before the law.

And because women were seen as subservient, abuse against them in the form of rape, economic subservience, forced dependence of children and relatives, domestic abuse, and murder by husbands was rampant. The arrival of colonialism encouraged the movement of African men to towns as workers, but controlled the migration of women, thus shifting the distribution of power and economy in favour of men. Not only were women kept away from the cash flow, but as African men entered settler employment in towns, the women left behind had to fill in as *de facto* heads of households. This resulted in increased workloads for women but little remuneration. Women worked up to sixteen hours a day, carrying out their customary tasks as well as those tasks traditionally allocated to their now absent spouses.

Nakanyike Musisi, an African feminist scholar argues, therefore, that during the pre-colonial and colonial period, African women "become an extension of African male bodies," living in circumstances that were different, if not worse, than those of their male counterparts, with women's lack of participation in the cash economy shifting their traditionally circumscribed power to positions in which autonomy was almost impossible. In addition to the perception of what was "womanly" in the traditional culture, the "cult of domesticity," a hypothesis introduced by Victorian Christian colonisers, further entrenched what became perceived as the woman's role. The "cult of domesticity" envisioned women as docile, modest creatures, good mothers and wives: the gender that was supportive of its mate.

An idle wife, confined to the home, was seen as a mark of "gentility," and of a man's ability to support his family. Thus African men and women, aspiring to be at the level of their colonial masters, began to encourage women's docility as a mark of civilisation. The concept of "leisured" wife as proof of "gentility" explains, for example, why most wives of African leaders did not compete to ascend the social and political ladder at the same time as their husbands. It is against this backdrop that at the inception of the revolutionary struggle, Zimbabwean women, like their counterparts in Mozambique, Angola, and Guinea-Bissau, joined the armed struggle. Their hope was that with the revolution, gender equality would be certain. Women who could not conform to tradition saw the revolution as an opportunity to escape difficult situations.

Yet feminist critics argue that at the end of the struggle, women's status actually fell as nationalist leaders and nationalist-oriented societies, in the quest of preserving tradition, expected women to be guardians of culture and respectability, or mistresses of the emerging ruling elites, or wives and mothers, recruiters for political parties, and labourers for the new market economy, while men were engaged in competition for political power in the state and the accumulation of wealth.

THE ZIMBABWEAN WAR AND GENDER EQUALITY

Zimbabwe's liberation struggle was based among other ideologies on Marxism, and contemporary Marxism encouraged the participation of women in the revolutionary vanguard, arguing that women's oppression was a consequence of the class-based and colonial exploitation against which such movements would struggle. Zimbabwean guerrilla movements, in embracing this ideology, were implying that women's rights would be a self-evident part of a future democratic society. Urdang argues, indeed, that Marxist ideologies which preach equality helped women to see themselves as advancing into traditionally male-controlled spheres such as those of decision-making. We find that, among the other crucial objectives that women hoped to achieve through the struggle, gaining equal rights for themselves was among the most important. Yet ironically, among accounts analysing the reasons why women join revolutionary struggles, many highlight the official reasons at the expense of more private and personal motives.

A feminist critique of women and war will show, however, that we cannot overlook the fact that women also participate in war for personal reasons. The Zimbabwean war offered a way out both for the suppressed groups of people and for individuals, including women. The inclusion of women in a guerrilla war, therefore, is not just a way to increase the number of soldiers in general and to have them serve in roles exclusive to women as male leaders might see it, but joining the liberation war is also for women an act of seeking their own emancipation. Thus, when on the eve of independence the post-colonial government downplayed the promises of freedom and liberty that engaging in war had held for women, Zimbabwean women fighters felt betrayed. Some women former fighters in Zimbabwe interviewed by Bhebe and Ranger agreed that they joined the liberation movement in order to improve conditions for themselves and for their families.

The ideology of equality simply appealed to young women

as it did to young men. The revolutionary struggle offered both access to a different status such as an opportunity to equal terms of achievements, equality before the law, and the right to choose. Nhamo, in an interview with Tanya Lyons in 2002, recalled that her reasons were more personal. She joined the war to uplift herself. After completing three years of school, she joined the nationalist fs"On joining the war, females fighters are ready to put on new gender roles; those considered traditionally belonging to men." The assumption is that the new roles will bring about gender equality. Zimbabwe's narratives of the revolutionary struggle show that the concept of women becoming equal to men was a major concern among female fighters. The idea that women who were fighting like men were now equal to men was equally voiced.

Robert Mugabe, then leader of the ZANU Popular Front army wing, affirmed the fact that women had risen to the status of men:

Our women fighters have demonstrated beyond all doubt that they are as capable as men and deserve equal treatment, both in regard to training and appointments. It is because of their proven performance that we have agreed to constitute a Women's Detachment with its own commander who should become a member of the High Command. It is also necessary that we should promote more women to the High Command.

Given this understanding, female fighters often pushed themselves to demonstrate their capability, and because the perception of their roles was influenced by the demands of the system they operated in, female fighters became victims of heated pressure to live up to the standards of men. Understandably, because war reflected traditionally male values, there was therefore a strong drive for women's dedication to be measured against their equality to men. Instinctively, women fighters were pushed to take on male roles; this was essential to their assertiveness. But feminist critics on war and women have argued that the question of equality between women and men in the training camps is problematic when we consider the differences between what most women were actually engaged in during the war, and the expected criteria that are used to indicate whether women had actually been men's equals, or whether they had been successful soldiers.

Research on women and war, from Africa and elsewhere, has shown that only a few women are given the privilege, in war situations, to operate formally in traditionally male domains. The majority of the women's work tends to consist in helping the men to be the soldiers they want to be. Thus women in war situations simply help men achieve their goals. Accordingly, most women are forced to fill all kinds of auxiliary functions so that the war can go on. Thus, in the Zimbabwean revolutionary movement, women fighters were to make sure that supplies reached the guerrillas by providing the supply line: a very important role, but one often unrecognised, or at least treated as secondary.

Nhamo, in her interview with Lyons, recalled:

One of the important roles that were played by female combatants was in the transportation of ammunition between Mozambique and Zimbabwe. Carrying ammunition was dangerous but necessary, and women often faced ambushes and attacks from Rhodesian soldiers. Our job was mainly to carry weapons to the border.

Yet, Maria, another ZANU ex-combatant in an interview with Lyons said, "I think we were just like men!" and Sekai maintained, "Women carried more than men to the front, we all suffered equally in the camps. When there was not enough food to go around, it was divided equally among the recruits." By 1970, a good number of women had been fully incorporated into the war while at the front acclamations pointed to the crucial role of women in the camps, yet ironically research shows that up to the year 1973, females were not considered candidates for military training. Male cadres were reluctant to train women for the frontline duties because they believed that their job was to serve men. These were reactions shaped by a traditional perception of women, and as a consequence, many women and children in the camps were killed because women in camps had no combat skills, no guns and no ammunition.

Thus Nhamo remembered,

I went running because I had not been trained, then I had no tactics I knew, I [had] no practice with a gun shooting and the shock of it and everything. As you are running you would actually feel the bullets "whoosh," and you'd see the other guy in front of you falling, you'd see the whole head coming off....

It was not until 1976, when human rights activist groups mounted pressure on ZANU and ZAPU that eventually women were allowed into combat training. This was reluctantly done because according to Bhebe and Lyons, even after receiving military training, many women were still not dispatched to the front to fight. It seemed most likely that women's training was mainly to give them survival skills and to remove the pressure mounting on the liberation movements from activist groups to train women, and did not have much to do with valuing women's contribution.

Monica was distressed by this action and in an interview with Lyons she pointed out:

I was appointed, "to [guard a camp], as much as I wanted to go to the front, since I had come to fight the enemy. They always wanted people who would look after the camps. We were given our rifles to go and guard the women in this camp, Osibisa. All our camps had guards.

Feminist critics have further argued, therefore, that while the system measured women's achievements in terms of their success in engaging in traditionally male activities, nationalist leaders encouraged women to participate in more traditional female roles. Jane Ngwenya, ZAPU's National Secretary for Women's Affairs admitted that women in the ZAPU camp were fighting differently than men. Her argument was that women were being groomed to remain as traditional as possible, despite the demands of their situation and despite what women themselves valued as important to them.

So we are fighting side by side with our men; we are not left behind. While our men are holding guns and deployed outside to fight, women are fighting in another wing of the struggle, because they try to help themselves through self-help schemes. They have trained themselves; they are prepared for a new Zimbabwe. In short, Ngwenya boasted of the domestic capabilities of women rather than their combat abilities, thus even a female member of the leadership was framing ZAPU women fighters' involvement in the struggle firmly in terms of the traditional female roles rather than advancing their claim to be fitted to meet the demands of warfare.

Margaret Dongo, a well-known Zimbabwean female ex-combatant activist in an interview with Bhebe and Ranger, while talking of the failed role of women, could not help but draw attention to the shortcomings of the Nationalists' attitudes:

> Real battles were fought by men. Our role as women was that we were carriers of ammunition, which was actually heavier than instituting the war itself. There was a tendency to say the women's specialty is in the kitchen. [Yet] Women and men received the same military or political training. It is only [when it came to] power sharing, or making decisions, that women could not participate.

Thus Judith Stiehm, who has done extensive research on women in the US armed forces, argues that female soldiers challenge deeply anchored preconceptions of gender identity. Cross-culturally and historically, combat has been reserved for men as an arena in which they can test, prove, and be rewarded for their virility. The presence of women alters the military when service can no longer be seen as a way of demonstrating manhood. To allow women into a male bastion threatens it as an arena for demonstrating masculinity and, among other things, achieving the prestige of belonging to such an organisation.

It seems clear that nationalist leaders, both male and female, were thus having problems with allowing women to participate in spheres that traditionally belonged to men; hence, women's contributions were largely confined to being carriers of ammunition and caretakers of children, the sick, and the aged in spite of the rigorous military and political training that females had received. This obviously denied women the opportunity to distinguish themselves in terms of male designations of heroism.

War feminist critics Irene Tinker and Mama Amina have pointed out that because Zimbabwe's revolutionary struggle was rooted in nationalist and Marxist ideologies that are basically patriarchal in nature, it did not necessarily embrace gender principles. It was difficult, therefore, to have women assume leadership roles in a structure that had no design for allowing such an operation. These feminist critics thus argue that while Marxist and nationalist theories identify oppression based on class and race, they fail to recognise that class-based capitalist oppression is not synonymous with the oppression of women. As a result, nationalist leaders tend to lack gender analysis. This lack of analysis rendered women in war powerless, resulting in the further oppression of female combatants.

The failure by nationalists to take up the gender issues during the time of the revolutionary struggle, however, diluted the claims made by nationalist movements that they were training women to liberate society. The revolution's standpoint in the war zone simply expanded upon pre-war domestic duties that designated women as mothers and servers of the nation. Perceived as natural teachers and nurturers, women were expected to rally support among the war population; nursing the injured. Thus generally, with the exception of a limited number of women fighters who were connected to powerful men, relatively few women were engaged in the real battles compared to men.

Reflectively, it can been argued that while the liberation struggle in theory paved the way for the increased social and political involvement of women, the actual participation that would have achieved female emancipation was tightly constrained. Thus despite the need for female participation, nationalist leaders and male cadres did not acknowledge women as their equals. Psychologically, men still expected women to stay at home and perform chores which were customarily prescribed as the domestic domain. A female combatant, Catherine Nyamandwe, remembered being advised by guerrillas to "return home because if girls left for Mozambique, no one would cook for male freedom fighters."

ZANLA and ZIPRA nationalist leaders, far from transforming colonial or traditional gender roles during the war actually enmeshed male dominance into the revolutionary ethos, by continually allocating women to perform tasks long-associated with their feminine roles. And at the end of the war, these tasks were merely seen to have been merely women's patriotic duty and not in any way equal to actual engagement in the struggle, thus making it very difficult for women to receive compensation since only those who had fought in real combat were being recognised.

SEXUALITY IN THE CAMPS

Another major frustration that came up among female combatants was that of sexuality and morality. A large number of young women had by 1976 joined the ZAPU and ZANU camps which were traditionally male-led and male zones. The problem that arose was that even though they enlisted women, nationalist leaders expected women fighters to remain docile and passive. But with the sense of liberation brought by the act of joining the movement, women became more open to their own sexual needs. Yet the thinking among the nationalists was that women should not behave in ways identified traditionally with males.

Affairs in military camps were seen as disrupting productivity and the blame was squarely laid on women. They were characterised as luring men from their duties while, on the other hand, men's behaviour was condoned; their actions seen as normal (for males). In the end, sexual relationships among cadres became a moral issue for female commanders, and a political and military problem for the High Commanders. To female leaders such as Teurai Ropa Nhongo, the main problem was that by being sexually assertive, young women were "misbehaving," and this was bad for the revolution.

In response to such complaints by women leaders, the ZANU Defence Secretariat held a rally in July 1978, to discuss the "problems of women." It concluded that not only was such activity by women "misbehaviour," but it was to be blamed for a rise in pregnancies and venereal diseases. Women were now perceived as wild, sexually weak, or diseased, and therefore a threat to the established order. This conforms to a pattern of patriarchal behaviour, as identified by Anne McClintock: the victimisation of women and the destruction of the female sense of selfhood. Patriarchy, she argues, essentially diminishes opportunity for identity formation in its subjects. The impact of this exertion of patriarchal power, albeit by female as well as male leaders, was that Zimbabwean female combatants were now being pulled from all sides, confronted with conflicting loyalties, and being objectified in terms of their sexuality.

As a result, they began to feel diminished, since they were now either characterised as morally debauched, or as sexually predisposed to give pleasure, and in either category, made to feel guilty for it or to feel that they were traitors to the liberation cause. To punish women and to control their "immoral" behaviour, contraceptives were made unavailable to them, and marriages between couples enforced. The traditional practice of bride-wealth was introduced, though earlier some leaders of ZANU High Command and the Department of Women's Affairs had called for the abolition of bride-wealth in order to promote the liberation of women. Naomi Nhiwatiwa had given reports to the international world on how ZANU P.F. was abolishing lobola ("bride-price" or "bride-wealth"), since such acts were abusive to women.

Yet at the same time, ZANU officials were continuing to keep records of marriages so that bride-wealth could be claimed by the women's parents at independence. ZANU High Commanders claimed with some fanfare to their international audience that they were taking the liberation line, but simultaneously they were at pains to point out in more domestic forums that ZANU P.F. would not go against African customary practices: they were anxious not to lose the support of Zimbabwean villagers. The rhetoric of gender emancipation did not reflect much commitment from nationalist leaders.

Feminist critics have argued, therefore, that the persistent support for bride-wealth claims by nationalist leaders during and after the liberation war reveals the nationalists' unwillingness radically to change the social and economic position of women. In addition to enforcing bride-price, sexual liaisons between men and women were condemned and contraceptives banned. The reasons given were that contraceptives were immoral and that they encouraged promiscuity. Yet as African feminists have pointed out, family planning was common even among traditionalists. A close analysis reveals that the actions of the leaders did not have much to do with the preservation of good military order and discipline, but were more concerned with the concept of "decency and morality," that the nationalists felt were being undermined.

We see that women revolutionaries, who enrolled to be fighters, were exhorted by their own leadership to marry and be the mothers of the next generation of soldiers even though motherhood meant exclusion from active duty. It is not surprising that many women engaged in the struggle found themselves becoming frustrated. As if to frustrate women cadres further, women fighters who became pregnant were sent to the women and children's camp in Mozambique where they were made to take up feminine occupations such as knitting and sewing. Yet a critical analysis of events in the camps shows that women's projects which emphasised sewing and cookery were basically rooted in the British colonialist policy that set out to train boys to be assistant clerks for the white administrators while training girls to be good homemakers.

The "cult of domesticity" had informed the views of most elite nationalists before the war and provided the rationale and the justification for the marginalisation of women from active engagement in the war and from allowing them the visibility they needed. In general, nationalist leaders both male and female, introduced laws and regulations in the military camps that protected their middle-class interests. These laws however, re-defined and reconstructed gender roles and gender relations to the traditional/colonial private/public dichotomy just as in the constructs of colonial times, because this best suited and reinforced their superiority. We further see that while women had to undergo restrictions, men's sexuality was never challenged even though some female cadres demanded that men too be punished for immoral behaviour.

Thus, as feminist critic Karin Koen notes, these notions of masculinity and femininity among leaders eventually permeate the attitudes of entire cultures and societies in such a way that male aggression is sometimes seen as natural and inevitable. Sadly, such notions of masculinity and femininity are also reflected in the ways governments and politics are conceptualized and structured; thus Zimbabwean society failed at the end of the war to question the wrongs that had been done to women. According to Tanya Lyons, another issue of concern during wartime is that of sexual abuse not only of women civilians, but even of women fighters.

In contrast to the official rhetoric that exhorted women in military camps to be "decent women and not use contraceptives," an examination of internal ZANU documents and interviews with female ex-combatants reveal that sexual abuse of women fighters by male guerrillas was rampant with perpetrators ranging from the lowest ranks to the highest leadership. Reports indicate that senior officers in the camps forced themselves upon young female combatants, black and white soldiers on their female victims, while guerrillas demanded sexual gratification from their female counterparts.

Rudo, an ex-combatant, on being asked by Bhebe about sexual violence against women in war times lamented;

> When there is a rape or somebody has been raped, there was no mother to tell that somebody had abused you. There was no law, there was no justice where you could report to—there was no court of law. If you fell pregnant no one assisted you.

Thus as Koen argues, "In the absence of normal social structures, men impose their will on women of their choice." Patriarchal attitudes by male nationalists exposed female women cadres to sexual violence by allowing male cadres to claim control over female fighters. Moreover, as Nhongo-Simbanegavi argues, just as the male cadres had exploited the female fighters who had given their lives to serve the country, male cadres at the front similarly exploited the civilian population. One of the chimbwidos (young girls that helped freedom fighters in the war) pointed out that many freedom fighters used pungwes (night-long meetings in which guerrillas politicised villagers) as opportunities to sexually assault women and girls. The editors of the collection Women of Resilience: The Voices of Women Ex-Combatants, argue that the girls had to contend with different men every week, every month. Monica, in an interview in that volume, speaks of this aspect of the plight of women fighters during the liberation struggle;

I have never talked to anybody about this. [It] is very difficult for me to relate because [the war] was very difficult.

Researchers on sexual violence during the struggle show that there is much reluctance from female ex-combatants to discuss sexual abuse during the war. Most feel that it is humiliating to talk about it, while others simply do not want to deal with those issues psychologically. Others, however, like Freedom Nyambuya and Margaret Dongo, have pointed out in their interviews with Lyons and Bhebe, that it would be better if the truth was told. Dongo said, "Women ex-combatants were raped and it is time that Zimbabwe accepted the truth and let what really happened during the war be known."

WOMEN FIGHTERS RETURN TO PEACETIME SOCIETY

At the end of the war, post-colonial governments made it their practice to hide the truth away from the Zimbabwean nation. Instead of letting the truth be told, we see that soon after the war, large posters appeared with the striking image of a woman warrior carrying an AK47 in her hands and a baby on her back. The symbol depicted men and women as equal and it has become a rallying symbol and an icon that has been adopted worldwide. In addition, highlighting the notion of the revolutionary war as a liberating process, the women's movement in Zimbabwe often used female guerrilla's experiences of fighting side by side with their men as the basis for demanding women's rights.

The female as revolutionary symbol came to be used as a weapon to advocate for gender equality in legislation, and to help the Zimbabwe liberation movements gain popularity. Yet as much as the women's party wing was making gains, not much was seen in terms of gains for women ex-fighters. First, the movement was led by nationalist women leaders who were more middle class than the proletariat; hence it specifically ignored the issue of women ex-combatants who were mainly members of the peasantry. None of the issues that affected these women as an individual or as a group were tackled as such.

It was as if women ex-combatants never existed as a separate group of fighters. Thus as Amina Mama has argued, it is because of class differences that bourgeois women did not press for gender equity for peasant former freedom fighters. Most of the integrationist attempts put forward was, in fact, largely designed to benefit the bourgeoisie, the elite—both male and female.

The result is that today some elite female members of the bourgeoisie have made even more gains and have moved up the political power ladder ahead of some men. And that is as far as women's power gains go. The poor were completely left out while women who became politically powerful and successful such as Joyce Mujuru, the current Zimbabwean vice-president, Tenjiwe Lesabe, Sally Mugabe, the late wife of President Mugabe, Florence Chitauro, Ruth Chinamano, Jane Mutasa, Oppah Muchinginguri, and Edna Madzongwe, all had ties to ruling-class males.

Tanya Lyons has thus pointed out that;

At the National Heroes' Acre in Harare there is only one woman buried: Sally Mugabe, late wife of the President. There has been some public debate as a result. But most discussion of "what it means to be a hero in Zimbabwe" has focused on whether soccer heroes should also be buried there. While there are quite a few empty plots left, there has not been any talk of whether women ex-combatants should receive burial at Heroes' Acre.

As Gwendolyn Mikell has argued, this is perhaps the reason why feminism cannot attribute the condition of all women to a universal experience. For Zimbabwean women ex-fighters, their experiences are that the disadvantaged poor women's conditions are mediated by class status, and status in the hierarchy. For example, despite the Legal Age Majority Act (LAMA) passed at independence, by 1988 some legal institutions, such as the Deeds Registry Office, still operated as if women were minors under the law, especially since the elite classes are not governed by common laws. As Chimedza on the case of Zimbabwe has observed, up to 1988 Section 15 of the prior Deeds Registry Act still continued to limit the ability of women to control land. The Act required that a married woman have her deed attested by a registrar or a legal practitioner and state the name of her husband to establish that she was indeed married.

The husband was to assist her in executing any deed or document required or permitted to be registered in the deeds registry, unless proof is produced to satisfy the registrar that she had the legal capacity to execute it without the assistance of her husband. Yet while laws involving the peasantry took forever to change, those concerning the distribution of salaries at professional levels, which was the concern for middle class women, were quickly changed and women started getting salaries equal to those of men. As a result, while middle-class women gained momentum, peasant women were not integrated directly into the cash economy, and resettlement permits are still most often granted to male heads of households, effectively defining women as agricultural labourers, rather than farmers in their own right. Former combatant Rudo pointed out in 1995, "[As a female ex combatant,] you can't be proud. ...we don't want to be identified because we are living in poverty."

While there may have been attempts at the time of independence to provide women's political representation in decision-making institutions, there were several barriers. Firstly, because very few women ex-combatants were in influential positions, women former freedom fighters had little input into designing gender equity policies that stipulated who they became after the war and what gains they received. There was in general a fundamental mismatch between the needs of women ex-fighters and those of the elite civil societies, yet since it was middle-class women who were elected into power, it was middle-class values which were used to dictate what actually came to be drafted into the constitution. Second, because women freedom fighters were not represented as a specific group, with specific needs, those needs were not fully articulated. Where an attempt was made, lack of finance, lack of gender awareness, or lack of political all prevented progress.

The political rhetoric claimed that women in Zimbabwe because of their involvement in the war had raised themselves to the level of men, yet real-life accounts of these women reveal that upon their return to civil society, women former fighters were not only denied the feeling of living up to the image of a "superwoman" that the posters depicted, they suffered disadvantages. For example, although most female ex-fighters were not really engaged in front-line battles as research has shown, on their return to civil society they were indiscriminately labelled "killers"—a concept with strong negative connotations within traditional Zimbabwean societies. No-one in the government sought to educate the populace not to pull former fighters down to the level of murderers.

Zimbabwean society in general looked down upon female involvement during the war, thus one female ex-fighter cited in Lyons felt disgruntled when she found out that, "As far as most of the men are concerned, when you [a female combatant] come back, you are out; they hardly want you to come near their children." Zimbabweans saw these women ex-fighters as unfit to be wives and mothers, despite the significant roles they had played in liberating the nation. Women ex-fighters hence experienced a lot of tension in their lives as they found themselves considered somewhere between heroines and "unclean women."

It is clear that this was a serious attack on their self-esteem, so when feminist researchers have encouraged these women to tell their story or to express their plight, most of them have attempted to hide their past, or to change their stories, because acknowledging their defeat would be to admit the dashing of their hopes and the futility of their efforts and sacrifices. Acknowledging their pain would be accepting defeat. Most have decided therefore that they did not want to be seen as failures, of losers, and as a result chose to go on with their lives in silence without making noise, willing their pain to go away.

Yet this disillusionment has caused a lot of bitterness and resentment among women ex-combatants. Rudo, one of the former fighters interviewed by Bhebe and Ranger, thus asked, "How could I have been called a 'terrorist,' and yet today I can't be called a hero?" Despite having been part of a revolutionary insurgency, under harsh conditions, Zimbabwean women combatants, upon returning to civil society, were expected to fit smoothly into civilian life as if nothing had happened. Most were expected to pick up their role as uneducated peasant women and forget all the education and the experience they had acquired. How were they to explain the rape, the sleepless nights with no food and no water, the threats to their lives? How would they gain recognition that their struggles were worthwhile?

At the eve of Zimbabwe's independence, governments were being constantly challenged by the United Nations and other organisations to push towards gender equality but because, for most Zimbabweans, this ran counter to existing social norms regarding gender roles, husbands, local authorities and other male members felt threatened. For example, in one public address, Robert Mugabe, the president, in response to the passage of progressive legislation by Zimbabwe's parliament, warned women against Western influences such as feminism. He defined emancipation for women as the ability to return to pre-colonial African traditions, and urged women to remain patriotic to the state and to nationalism.

Yet as Cynthia Enloe has noted, it is impossible for female former fighters to return to previous modes of behaviour when their social values have been deeply affected by their experiences—and this internal conflict is not just unique to Zimbabweans, but is characteristic of the situation of female soldiers all over the world. Many ex-combatants experience a sense of lost time. Besides the feelings of being marginalised, female ex-fighters unlike their male counterparts, who can do whatever they may wish to make up for this sense of lost time, women former fighters have less scope to do anything about their own "lost time." Elise Fredrikke Barth argues, therefore, that the pain of war lingers on as time fails to heal the violence.

In addition, Koen has noted that the attainment of justice and the healing of pain in post-conflict situations are hard to establish if women and girls are not granted the benefit of institutional justice. In the case of Zimbabwean women former fighters, however, we see that the pain of women ex-fighters is further aggravated by the fact that there was no justice given. Rape has remained a national male privilege denying women closure to their nightmare. And because rape committed against women during the war went unchallenged, it normalised negative attitudes about women and rape.

In addition to their social plight, a major predicament faced by women in most guerrilla movements is that women have difficulties in actually verifying their actions. In Zimbabwe, compensation for war veterans was conditional on proof of having been engaged in active fighting, and roles other than that of direct involvement in battle were considered secondary to the war effort. Women fighters thus became dependant on men in order to confirm their veteran status. Watteville found that men became the ones responsible for establishing the women's rank, and their contribution as soldiers.

This obviously placed women in vulnerable situations as sexual abuse took place with men using this to get sexual favours. Thus in 1998, when over fifty thousand ex-combatants in Zimbabwe were awarded Z$50,000 plus Z$2000 a month as war veterans' compensation, it has been very difficult to find out how many women, if any, benefited from this scheme. Research shows, however, that by the year 2000, twenty years after independence, many women had not formally had their rank confirmed.

Thus as Lyons asserts:

Today, most [combatants] ... are busy surviving, making business deals, growing maize or ground nuts, or selling vegetables on street corners. Demobilization payments are long spent and they wait patiently for compensation from the government but - even if compensation were available - many couldn't afford the bus fare to town centers to register for such compensation. The "symbolic payment" - parades, memorials - is also long past due.

The irony, as Barth, Enloe, and Lyons have pointed out, is that Zimbabwe female ex-combatants cannot protest their predicament torn between betraying the very revolution they fought so hard for and claiming their rights. Women who attempt to establish their own participation by articulating their own agenda are quickly seen as undermining the revolution and thus being unpatriotic.

This chapter has argued that while women's resilience in revolutionary wars is beyond doubt, for Zimbabwean women however, the resilience did not translate into gender equality, in the military camps and in post-revolutionary society. The post-war status of women ex-fighters in Zimbabwe is unfortunately determined by individual women's positions in that society. This factor is crucial in defining the women's roles in the economy, in politics, and in decision making processes towards their emancipation.

Women ex-combatants in Zimbabwe have to fight harder for resources that some of their male counterparts take for granted. For example, women who fought in the war find access to employment often limited, since most women female fighters employed by the government are put into the rebuilding of social services occupations generally considered an extension of women's traditional domestic duties, which pay very low salaries. Thus women's increased participation in the formal employment sector has not, by any degree, challenged the gender conservatism that characterised the colonial period.

Today, for example, for Zimbabweans, every feminist request for policy change which might ensure the advance of women is regarded as anti-African and anti-tradition, while gains in female emancipation made at independence have slowly dwindled away. Thus feminist critics Alexander and Mohanty have noted that resistance cannot be determined by formal political programmes and military struggles, but by the practices of everyday life as people attempt to resist and alter power relations that inhibit gender equal participation.

For most revolutions, when the war for liberation is over, the rights of women become secondary to many other priorities. In Zimbabwe, structural adjustment programmes by the International Monetary Fund and the World Bank introduced in 1985, and the Anglo-American sanctions imposed on Zimbabwe in 2000, compounded the problem for women former freedom fighters. Scarce resources have had to be spent in countering forces that are threatening the existence of the government. At first the government created new laws in order to overcome the inequality of women, but later, considering other issues more vital, abandoned their promises concerning women's issues. This made it more difficult for most of the women fighters to realise their dreams.

While there is no doubt that female freedom fighters have met with unjust treatment, the war has had deep-seated significance on their lives. Women who were politically active before the war became even more militant during the war. Those who were not equally radical became involved in politics in ways they would never have had in the absence of their war experiences. As Koen maintains, consequently, there were many cases among these women of commitments to socialist or revolutionary beliefs carrying well over after the war. Today, some of these women stand out as compelling examples of strength in the face of hardship and despair. They still see the post-war era as the right time to move society to grant the equal participation of all of its citizens.

For most feminist critics of war, how women ex-freedom fighters motivate themselves and others around them, and how they continue their struggle after the war that betrayed them is over, will always be a wonder. Yet, while the war years for women were stressful, exhausting, and oftentimes frightful, many feminist critics at the same time feel that a sense of excitement and courage was developed in women fighters in a way that shaped their new and independent roles. Barth found that most women ex-fighters never lost sight of the fact that during the war; they took part in the struggle for freedom to an equal degree to men. This, as feminist writers of war maintain, has had empowering effects in the way women, Zimbabwe women ex-fighters included, have come to demand their rights against men and against governments in post-colonial states.

WOMEN, THE NATION AND THE DOMESTIC

The First World/Third World dichotomy has been troubled. Some people feel that this distinction (along with the developing/developed or less developed/more developed) implies that Third World countries should aspire to be more like First World countries. Instead of trying to be more like First World countries, less developed countries should try to maintain their unique culture. Likewise, non-Western and non-industrialized define these countries entirely in terms of First World or Western expectations.

Naming this population is important, so as not to gloss over the differences between First and Third World women, or between men and women in the Third World. As you will read, Third World Women have some particular health needs that must be considered in the economic, political, and social contexts of their lives. If we choose to name Third World women as a group, we want to understand the experiences they share. To understand the common experiences of Third World women it is important to look at the meaning given to the experience. Chandra Talpade Mohanty, a scholar who writes about Third World Women, uses an example of wearing veils in Muslim countries.

In some instances, women are forced to wear veils because of their religion. In other times, women have chosen to put on veils to unite with other women against unfair practices in a workplace. Grouping all of these women who wear veils ignores the meaning given to wearing veils within these two very different contexts. Since these women give different meanings to wearing a veil, it is not possible to say "women in Muslim countries are oppressed because they wear veils". It is not the practice of wearing veils, but the meaning given to wearing veils that can be oppressive. According to Mohanty, women should be grouped according to the meaning they give their common experiences. It is the meaning of their experience that makes them similar to others, not necessarily the experience itself. Looking for the meaning given to these experiences can help us understand the non-Western cultural contexts of the experience.

Domestic violence is the physical or psychological abuse of one partner of a marital relationship by the other. In most cases, women are at the receiving end of domestic violence, which could be a single instance in the heat of the moment or continuing sadistic behavior arousing serious concerns. Though it is a universal phenomenon, domestic violence is more prevalent in economically backward and marginalized sections of society. Women of socio-economically backward societies are exceptionally hardworking and they do hard manual labor together with men and also manage household chores and rearing of children. Ironically, men perpetrating domestic violence appear to interpret this as slave mentality.

Reasons galore promote this enduring evil. First of all, there is something called manly ego. Gender stereotyping has endowed the male with invincibility in the context of a sexual relationship. Then, for those with a bad temper, it is a very convenient way of venting their anger without fear of retaliation. The psyche of some men simply accepts violence as a way of life. In many families, men are the sole or primary earning members. So, mere survival necessity forces women to put up with brutalities. For women with children, this economic security is extra important, since they would be risking the children's future also by ending a marriage. Besides, many women are worried about the trauma that divorce could inflict on children. Society's expectations are also conducive to women putting up with abuse. Friends and relatives always try to save a marriage rather than help to break it up. They force her to look at the overall picture of the welfare of the family. This is more so in third world countries and rural setups. Many customary laws promote this stance, even where the law of the land could be different.

In war-torn countries men tend to be more violent due to continuous exposure to violence. Poverty and resultant low esteem also make men more violent. But ironically, exposure to violence seems to make women more resilient to it. Finally, an unprotected woman is an easy target of anti-social elements. This also forces her to put up with domestic violence. The fight against domestic violence has to start from women's empowerment, by making her economically independent. Women of developed countries suffer comparatively less from domestic violence as they have wider choices, are less dependent on man for survival, and have better recourse to law.

Law, society, and NGOs should join hands to find solutions for the malady. Laws of the land can help by making domestic violence a strong ground for divorce, by making it a criminal offense, by recognizing marital rape, by simplifying the process of divorce and by not differentiating between males and females in inheritance rights. Governments often have problems with budgets and prioritization and they should do their best to see that domestic violence is not their last concern. Society should not look down on a single woman.

There should be enough grass root level workers to reach out to victims of domestic violence. NGOs should provide emergency shelters for battered women. They should help in their rehabilitation by providing vocational training, micro-credit facilities, and employment opportunities. There may not be a fool-proof remedy for domestic violence, for part of the reason is entrenched in man's genes itself. But changing laws and woman's increased self-reliance can surely decrease its incidence. Anyway, women who are combatants, karate black belts, and sumo wrestlers, might find solutions in their own way.

WOMEN IN DEVELOPING NATIONS

If everyone shared common beliefs about literacy, its purpose and its meaning, the complex problem of unequal literacy levels among genders might not exist. Unfortunately, due to prejudices and stereotypes, not all members of society have been given equal access to an education. In countries all across the world statistics show men achieve higher levels of literacy than women. These discrepancies in literacy levels directly reflect society's stereotypical perceptions of women and their role in society. In developing countries especially, the gap between gender literacy levels is extremely large. Because of the noticeable difference between literacy levels among men and women, the United Nations declared 1990 to be International Literacy Year with female illiteracy its focal point.

At that time, neither estimates showed that one third of all women could not read nor write. UNESCO, one of literacy's leading sponsors, declared the "lack of advancement in the education of women and girls are 'the heart of the problem of illiteracy'". The problem is particularly bad in developing countries. According to one United Nations report "females have higher rates of illiteracy than males in all of the developing regions...For the least developed group as a whole, female illiteracy is 73 per cent and male, 53 per cent".

In many developing countries the gap between male and female literacy levels exists because women have been discouraged from receiving the same educational benefits of men. A survey of Third World countries "reveals, women in these nations face a wide range of prejudices. In work, health, education, and law, Third World women are second-class citizens". Women also suffer from "decreased spending on education due to economic constraints" and "traditional attitudes about women's role in society". Many cultures view the male as the authority figure and women as their inferiors. In this type of environment, women's education is viewed as a threat to the way of life.

"Parents may fear that education will harm their daughters' marriage prospects", or that their daughter's dowry will have to increase. Studies show that educated women marry educated men, and educated men require larger dowries for their wives. Even an uneducated man will demand a larger dowry for literate women. This occurs because the men fear that educated women might "expose their ignorance and, above all, challenge their power position within the family".

The concept of a relationship between education and social status is an important one in discussions about literacy. Historically education has been used by the dominant group in a society as a tool to maintain their superior position. By denying women an education, men can maintain a superior position over them. Education will empower women with the ability to question authority, ask informed questions, and search for solutions. In many countries this will topple traditional gender relations; educated women will inevitably fight for their equality. "The dilemma for both men and women is how to reconcile the man's self-image as dominant authority to the women's self-image as an equal".

Despite the threat to their gendered traditions, there has been a trend to increase the educational level of women in developing countries. "The experience of over two decades of development efforts around the world has shown that countries which place the emphasis upon the private economic sector achieve the best development results. This means that, especially for the least developed countries, the women's path to development is the best path. Emphasis upon the problems, concerns, and capacities of women is the bright hope of the development future". With increased literacy, women will be able to influence the economic, social, and human aspects of their community. Education 'can enhance a society's ability to overcome poverty, increase incomes, improve health and nutrition, and reduce family size'.

By making education available to all members of society, a nation can create a larger and more skilled labor force. Education endows a person with self-confidence, the ability to make educated choices, understand directions, and develops new concepts. These skills are the driving force behind technological and economic advancement. Also, by becoming part of the labor force, women will be able to add to their family's income, allowing many families to raise their standard of living. Statistics show "that in most parts of the world where the standard of living is high, literacy is equally high among men and women. On the contrary, where the standard of living is lower, fewer people - especially women - are educated". These facts alone are an incentive for governments to create a national policy which will overcome illiteracy.

A questionnaire distributed by the World YMCA in 1988

confirms the hypothesis that providing females with an education promotes a nation's economy. The survey shows that women who receive literary training "are better equipped to search for jobs and can therefore earn more. They realize that they can do some jobs which are traditionally considered to be for men only [, and] they are more able to run small businesses and keep records on their own". Educating women allows a country to tap into a previously unused resource, thus heightening the level of production the country can achieve. The campaign for women's education is not based solely on the economic benefits it will provide. Many women are beginning to realize the impact education will have on their lives.

Not long ago a group of newly literate women from the south coast of Kenya were explaining the advantages of their recently acquired skills in reading, writing and calculation. Now they could sign their names they had more control over money transactions. They could read medical prescriptions and instructions. "Our eyes have been opened, "said one of them, expressing the new sense of pride and increased self-reliance they all felt. The benefits of women's education extend to all aspects of society. Besides contributing to a nation's economy, educated women are an asset to a nation's private sector.

"Women's education is also associated with quantifiable increases in home output - in the form of better health and nutrition, more attention given to each child, and so on - despite the fact that better-educated women are likely to spend less time in the home". Educated women tend to marry later in life and have fewer children. Also there is an inverse correlation between the level of education and child mortality rates. Women who have had an opportunity to educate themselves are more aware of prenatal health care, hygiene, and nutritional practices. "'For every year of mothers' education, child mortality is reduced 7 to 9 per cent'".

The greater amount of knowledge a women possesses, the more she can influence and contribute to her society. Through education women gain "political awareness, participation and organizational skills" which enables them to become effective community leaders. It is also proven that educated women have a profound effect on future generations. A key strategy behind continuing women's education is encouraging females in professional positions, such as teaching. The success of these women will provide young girls with role models of their same sex who will motivate and excite these girls to educate themselves.

Many developing nations have recognized these benefits of women's education and adopted mass literacy programs. These programs were implemented in countries "where both the state and the people concerned expected literacy to be one of many factors which would improve social, political, and economic conditions and help develop human and material resources". Unfortunately, despite women's desire for education, these campaigns have had difficulty encouraging women to participate. Some women are "overburdened with domestic tasks such as cooking and cleaning, fetching water and firewood, as well as farming and earning money". Others are "directly discouraged by the attitudes of men".

Literacy campaigns, however, are beginning to have an impact on many communities. Where these programs have the full support of national and local leaders they have been effective in reducing illiteracy. The reason why this support [is] so important was explained by one woman who was asked what her husband thought about her participation in literacy classes. "Yes, he grumbles a bit, as men do, "she said."Some men are very worried, and they don't let their wives attend classes. But it's too late, I think. When the Area Commissioner held a meeting here both men and women were asked to come. We didn't dare, in the beginning but the cell leader had brought his wife and she came back to fetch us. The Area Commissioner had complained that so few women were present and said that he would not start the meeting until everyone had met up.

These mass literacy campaigns, supported by the government officials and local leaders, have had excellent success in reaching out and educating thousands of illiterate women. Expanding women's education has become an important objective for developing countries. The benefits are undeniable, educated women contribute positively to every aspect of society. Within the community they add to the labor force, increasing GNP, and ultimately increasing a country's level of income. In the home they promote health care, and education, creating a standard for the future. For developing nations to continue to grow it is crucial that they provide education to the entire population.

8

The Telling of History in Zimbabwe

Highlighting women's conspicuous absence in the media coverage, negotiations, and resolutions during the Zimbabwe crisis, Pumla Dineo Gqola outlines the extent to which we have grown accustomed to the near total elision of women's lives, contributions and agency from significant political events. Drawing upon her recent experiences with a group of South African women on a feminist solidarity trip to Zimbabwe, the author concludes the Mugabe-Tsvangirai power-sharing agreement and its 'gender neutral' language to be blind to women's struggles.

Over the last week, news of the agreement signed by Robert Mugabe, Morgan Tsvangirai and Arthur Mutambara has received repeated airplay. As well it should. Indeed, radio station listeners have been calling in to comment on the perceived vindication of the now former South African president in the eyes of the international community now that there has been success in Zimbabwe. All of this has been seen as further evidence that African solutions work best for African problems. Significantly, this narrative has continued to permeate the contributions of even those callers who are more critical of Mbeki's other stances. We have, therefore, been reminded that although there may be solutions in Zimbabwe, and maybe next in Darfur, problems at home abound.

As I listened to the live coverage of the signing, I was

struck by consistent absences in the reporting as well as in what could not comfortably be used in the interest of the celebrated moment. One reporter, live outside the venue in Harare, noted that even as the ink was drying on the paperwork, a group of MDC women approached him to say they had been attacked by ZANU-PF male youths moments before. I was somewhat relieved that this was a radio, rather than a television broadcast because I did not want to see more brutalised bodies. I could not help noticing that this information was quickly passed over. I recoil from the sight of more bruised and bloodied bodies not because of what Gail Smith has called 'compassion fatigue in relation to the crisis in Zimbabwe,' but because there are other ways to make sense of our continent. A.C. Fick insists that when we privilege particular forms of evidence over others 'we run the risk of giving the former more power than they already have in our world.'

Therefore, we trap ourselves in a certain cycle, since 'we are educated to understand the world in particular terms.' Furthermore, we remain so accustomed to our particular view that we completely miss the presence of other events and 'critical languages' in the very same moment in which we attempt to understand. Part of what we have grown accustomed to is the near total elision of women's lives, contributions and agency from large political events. Consequently, I turned away from the coverage I had been obsessively following in between teaching, and reflected on what was unfolding through other events I have access to. Sometimes it helps to turn away in order to better make sense of what we are in the midst of. This is the approach I brought to my reading of the text of the power-sharing agreement signed on Monday 15 September.

In August, I formed part of a group of South African women who went on a feminist solidarity trip to Zimbabwe. The excursion was coordinated by activist and international relations and development expert Bunie Matlanyane Sexwale, and divided into a group that went to Harare and one that flew to Bulawayo. My group, the Harare group, included the essayist Gail Smith, as well as poets Lebogang Mashile and Gertrude Fester. We went to have conversations with a variety of women's and civil society groups; unionists, students, health activists, law and human rights activists and so on. This trip clarified many of the niggling questions that had been plaguing me in previous years. The Johannesburg office of the Crisis in Zimbabwe Coalition had made the trip possible, also offering us insights into what we might encounter upon arrival. Among us, Bunie was the only feminist who was personally familiar with the different Zimbabwean epochs.

To the extent that it had been impossible to live in South Africa without reflecting on Zimbabwe constantly, the trip followed numerous conversations with people more familiar than I with the crisis in Zimbabwe. Two artist friends, one a filmmaker and the second a novelist, who had grown up in Zimbabwe as South Africans in exile, noted upon returning from visits recently that this was a different Zimbabwe from the one they knew. There was sadness in one's eyes and anger etched onto the face of the other. My child's day-mother, herself Zimbabwean, had remarked upon return from an earlier trip that her homeland made her despair. Colleagues commented on how fatigued they were at being asked to comment about their home country at every turn. I was careful to listen to information volunteered, but not to pry and further exhaust them. Only one said 'things are not the worst they have ever been.'

I had questions raised by other areas of information as well. Where were the women in all the coverage of Zimbabwe, in the negotiations, in the interviews broadcast, among the experts explaining and helping the continent and the world make sense of the crisis? I know from reading, watching and from interactions with feminists from the continent over the years that Zimbabwe has a very strong women's movement. How is it that I was hearing so little about what women were doing, when they were not being brutalised, inside Zimbabwe?

The trip was to help me grapple better with some of these struggles. Unfortunately, it also raised many more. Very few of the new questions are addressed in the resolution we are all invited to celebrate. The Harare we arrived in at the end of August brought different worlds into collision. In a very public sense, it was the Harare in which the (Women of Zimbabwe Arise) WOZA 14 trial was scheduled to start, after many postponements. These are women considered so dangerous that the Zimbabwean State imagines their varied activism treasonous. This was also the Harare which staged the opening of the new parliament, during which MDC leaders, among them the leader of Senate Sekai Holland, shouted for Mugabe to go back to the talks so much that he was visibly flustered as he tried to open parliament.

When Holland agreed to meet us in a public place, with unionist and former MDC Women's Assembly Chair, Lucia Matibenga, the disbelief was palpable on the faces of many young Zimbabweans in the Harare CBD location where we met. There was no question that both women were recognised. As they explained to us, it was unusual for powerful Zimbabwean politicians to be seen in a food court. Holland and Matibenga had both been driven underground by the physical and other attacks instigated by ZANU-PF and other agents of state sanctioned violence. They shared some of these experiences with us. But more so, and interspaced with a wicked sense of humour shared by both, they articulated a very clear vision for a new Zimbabwe. These were women who demonstrated what Pregs Govender has called 'insubordinated spirit', in their actions, incisive analysis of power and in rising after being personally attacked. I was saddened by the fact that as powerful and active as they have been, even these women's names were often lost in the reporting of what occurs in Zimbabwe.

I wonder how much of such voices we will hear in the future, given the bizarre half-protected freedom of speech as articulated in Article 19 of the agreement signed on Monday. Recognising the necessity for freedom of speech in Zimbabwe, the article nonetheless opens doors for dismissing certain media outlets if they are 'foreign government funded external radio stations broadcasting into Zimbabwe' since these 'are not in Zimbabwe's national interest.' What about radio stations operated by Zimbabweans in exile as one of the few ways to contest state-controlled media outlets? So what if another government or its agencies fund them? What if that government is Botswana's? How will the stated desire to ensure 'the opening up of the airwaves and ensuring the operation of as many media houses as possible' translate in a context where ZANU-PF youths allegedly attack people outside the signing?

Further down the same article, I had to laugh as I read 'the public and private media shall refrain from using abusive language that may incite hostility, political intolerance and ethnic hatred or that unfairly undermines political parties and other organisations.' Perhaps there is hope for the Zimbabwean Broadcasting Corporation, whose evening television bulletins were peppered with Mugabe pronouncing on the immaturity of MDC MPs, their unsuitability to lead, and on this being the worst parliament he had ever presided over. However, that was the end of August when we watched aghast, and everything had changed now that it was September and the agreement had been signed.

What would that change mean, when Article 18 of the agreement, which focuses on the security of persons and prevention of violence, conflates state-sanctioned brutality against citizens after the elections with violence by unarmed people? There is no mention of the brutality of the military, even though this emerged in many of the conversations we had with women on our visit. The army was credited with hunting people down, militia and the formal army tortured, killed, maimed and raped. What happens to this memory? How do people just move forward? Many women's organisations reported on how women were forced to pay for reintegration into their communities after surviving previous post-election displacement. Given that the violence between the powerful and ordinary citizens is falsely equated in this agreement, what happens to the scars?

Where do these women, whose houses have often been razed to the ground and their means of livelihood destroyed while their children are raped or driven into exile, fit into the 'gender neutral' language of the agreement? History teaches us that 'gender neutral language' is very often blind to women's lives. Yet, women in Zimbabwe, like in South Africa, are the majority. They are the majority of the displaced, raped, tortured and burnt alive, and of the people sleeping in the safe houses all over Harare. They are also the majority of those who resisted and voted for change. Writing of another African context, Pregs Govender has recently reminded us in her Julius Nyerere Lecture on Lifelong Learning at the University of the Western Cape last week that, the links between 'the militari-sation of society and the increased levels of violence against women across borders and in homes' are not just clear but also backed up by much research at academic and trans-national levels.

Is the Zimbabwean crisis over? Can it be over when there is no recognition of the results from the March elections or of how people suffered for the choices they made? It is not inconceivable, given the absence of a clear call for accountability for perpetrators of violence in Article 18, that the president of Zimbabwe may claim the power vested in him under Article 19 to both 'declare war' against his enemies as in the past, as well as 'grant pardons, respite, substitute less severe punishment and suspend or remit sentences, on the advice of the Cabinet' which he chairs. Is it conceivable that he will bring the rapists and the men who destroyed the livelihoods of men to book? Perhaps I am pessimistic at what should be a moment of great joy. However, the questions remain in the aftermath of the signing: where are the women?

When we met Netsai Mushonga, the co-ordinator of the Women's Coalition of Zimbabwe, she reminded us of the necessity to come up with new paradigms for thinking about vigilance. The automatic equation of violence with militancy is an unfortunate southern African inheritance. In an article written long before our meeting, and far before the agreement, Mushonga had written: 'Democracy for women in Zimbabwe can be summarized in two key capacities: participation in decision-making at all levels, and equal access to resources.' The Agreement is vague on this. Pregs Govender could have been speaking directly to this statement when she remarked last week: "one of the central features of patriarchal authoritarian systems is the way in which we stop thinking for ourselves and begin to depend on the political leader, the expert, the husband or the priest."

This is also a statement for those of us who watch as Zimbabwe changes, and who feel solidarity and search for ways to assist and support meaningful change. I am not entirely convinced that the agreement, which mentions women only three times - in relation to access to land, entitlement to full citizenship and gender equity, as well as the need to appoint women to 'strategic Cabinet posts' - goes far enough. These are important recognitions, and reflections on South Africa's recent past illustrate how difficult it is to get any gender recognition into a negotiation process. The presence of these acknowledgements is no small matter.

However, it seems that much ended up on the negotiation floors given the demands that were shared with us by various women's groups and individual women. It would be a travesty if this southern African country continues to revel in our most uncomfortable heritages as a region, that of downplaying women's lives and pretending women exist as nothing but victims. Our trip showed that women are organising across class and education status in ways that directly intervene in the crisis, and the manner in which the state's courts and violent men responded was a clear recognition of the power of such women. Yet, this agreement that we are all invited to celebrate falls short of this recognition of women's multi-faceted activisms. On the importance of telling stories carefully, Veronique Tadjo argues: 'We live in a community and in trying to tell one story in particular, I have to rely on other stories. Our destinies cross, we meet people; they enter our lives, then exit, to be replaced by others, etc. Our existence is layered by an amazing number of stories. So that's why I move in and out.' Would it not be a remarkable thing if this were true of the Zimbabwean Agreement and the future it ushers in?

PATRIOTIC HISTORY AND THE ZIMBABWEAN PAST

Mudenge was not only speaking as foreign affairs minister, longing to widen diplomatic participation. He also gave a message of warning to the MDC:

Both the sovereignty of the state and the institution of

Mutapaship suffered a mortal blow from which they never really recovered. Depending on foreign influence to come to power has a costly price tag, often too dear for the nation, and sometimes even for the puppet. And though patriotic history is so focussed on Rhodes and the British and the first Chimurenga of 1896 it does appeal also to an earlier Zimbabwean past. Perhaps the best example of this is the televised ceremony presided over by Robert Mugabe at which two halves of a long separate Zimbabwe bird were re-united, one half having been returned to Zimbabwe by the German government.

The 'multi-million dollar ceremony' aroused much criticism even in Zimbabwe. 'It was quite noble for the German government to return the Zimbabwe bird carving', wrote Fidelis Mashavakure to the Standard on 6 June 2003. 'Surely the bird is of some historical significance to present day Zimbabweans and generations to come'. Yet the government had 'over-dramatised' the event:

It was astonishing to see women religiously kneeling down in honour of a stone carving. It was even more astonishing to see the President lead the gathering in sloganeering over the carving. Does the carving belong to Zanu PF or Zimbabwe? The millions of dollars used for this event could have bought food for starving people.. State television and radio could have been used for covering reports on the concerns of the impoverished population. But it was criticism in the South African press which outraged the Zimbabwean government.

The Sunday Times in South Africa satirised the ceremony, saying that Mugabe had a 'bird in his head'. Outraged, the Zimbabwe Minister of Information, Jonathan Moyo, himself responsible for co-ordinating the patriotic history campaign in Zimbabwe's media, sent an official protest to the South African government. The re-uniting of the bird had been 'a historic moment in the reconstruction of the country's heritage' and for the ceremony to be 'ridiculed and insulted by a newspaper is mind-boggling'. Mahoso too seized on the occasion:

The white racist columnist, Hogarth, wrote a column called 'Our Bob's got birds on the brain', which was a savage attack on the entire African process of 'remembering', that is the process of remobilising African memory by reconnecting symbols, communities, movements and people as the South's answer to Northern driven globalisation, reviving their memory of a world without apartheid. The West feared this process, hence the destruction of Iraqi antiquities and 'spitting' on the Zimbabwe bird.

Joost Fontein's recent Edinburgh doctoral thesis, 'The Silence of Great Zimbabwe', offers a fascinating analysis of the current historiographical struggle over the monument. He argues that the African peoples who live around Great Zimbabwe are just as much excluded from it today as they were by Rhodesian curators. Today the monument is interpreted by elite nationalists and by academic archaeologists who jointly ignore the sacredness of Great Zimbabwe to the locals. Fontein describes how local spirit mediums, in alliance with ex-combatants, have constructed their own 'African memory'. Theirs, too, is a kind of patriotic history, and certainly a product of 'deep ancestral memory'. But they were given no role in the elaboration of the patriotic history of the ZANU/PF regime.

The ceremony of the re-uniting of the Zimbabwe bird, though it took place after Fontein completed his thesis, fits perfectly into his argument. The present academic curator of Great Zimbabwe, Dr Edward Matenga, is author of The Soapstone Birds of Great Zimbabwe. It was Matenga who publicised the existence of the lower half of a Zimbabwe bird in the Museum fur Volkerkunde in Berlin and who proclaimed: 'Zimbabwe has a plan to recover the specimen in Berlin and allow it to return home to roost!' Matenga's book has a foreword by Stan Mudenge, who hails it as a contribution to 'authentic national history'. The recent ceremony was a fulfilment of Matenga's agenda as well as of Mugabe's and Mudenge's.

There are other signs of tension between a local, radical, war-veterans' agenda and the agenda of state patriotic history. In early 2002, for example, war veterans in Matabeleland launched a campaign for the removal of Rhodes's grave from the Matopos. The veterans' leader, Andrew Ndlovu declared that 'we cannot find peace when we are keeping a white demon in our midst. It is the very core of our problems. His grave should be returned to the British'. Ndlovu's demand seemed the logical conclusion of Mugabe's ancestral vision of Rhodes as a demonic spirit continuing to possess Tony Blair! And indeed this sort of patriotic demand is continuing to be made in the state press. On 29 October 2003, for example, Caesar Zvayi renewed the call for Rhodes to be removed:

> The Matopo Hills, which today are a tourist attraction ... were a very sacred shrine in the pre-colonial halcyon days and believed to be the earthly residence of God and his high priests and priestesses ... This was the sacred Njelele, Matonjeni, Mabweadziva, Mwarindidzimu, which today has been desecrated as the burial place of a white bandit, who was rabidly racist ... Can the powers that be please do something about this sacrilege and mollify the spirits of the land.

Yet here arises one of the paradoxes of patriotic history. Mahoso is hostile both to the colonial legacy and to bogus universalism. But the one international agency he admires is UNESCO, remembering its attempts to create a new international information order and how these led to attacks on UNESCO by Britain and the United States. As Fontein shows, Zimbabwean archaeologists and oral historians have taken a leading role in the development of UNESCO's new doctrine of 'cultural landscape' as a key criteria for the declaration of World Heritage sites. And on 3 July 2003 the World Heritage Committee of UNESCO endorsed the Zimbabwe government's application and carried through the inscription of the Matopos Hills as a World Heritage site. As the non-government Sunday paper, the Standard, tactlessly but triumphantly reported on 6 July: 'Matobo Hills, where Cecil John Rhodes is buried, have won UNESCO's World Heritage listing'. And indeed the listing does indeed mean that Rhodes's grave is safe.

Robert Mugabe's address on 29 October to the 14th General Assembly and Scientific Symposium of the International Council on Monument and Sites, meeting for the first time in Africa at the Victoria Falls, presented an altogether more sophisticated version of patriotic history and its relation to world heritage:

Zimbabwe was committed to preserving its heritage ...Zimbabweans had, through the agrarian reform programme, found joy because their greatest heritage - land - had been returned to them. 'Now that land has returned to the people, they were able once more, to enjoy the physical and spiritual communion that was once theirs. For it must be borne in mind that the non-physical or intangible heritage is an equally strong expression of a people, manifesting itself through oral traditions, language, social practices and traditional craftsman - ship'. The objectives of ICOMOS were synonymous with Zimbabwe's philosophy. Cde Mugabe said Zimbabwe valued Heritage so much that even the graves of the country's colonialists such as Cecil John Rhodes were being preserved. 'We accept history as a reality'.

PATRIOTIC HISTORY

Zimbabwean patriotic history, then, is a complex phenomenon. It ranges from the brutal over-simplifications of the militia camps, through presidential campaign speeches, through the work of ministerial historians, to the sophistications of Mahoso, and to addresses to world conservationists. It is equally variously propagated - in courses taught by war veterans in the camps, in collections of Mugabe's speeches, in Chigwedere's syllabi and textbooks in the schools, on state television and radio, and in the writings of Mahoso and others in the state-controlled press. As we have seen, it is proclaimed as a remedy for the failures of parents and teachers and especially of universities to instill the revolutionary spirit. As we have also seen, in moments like the Zimbabwe bird ceremony or the declaration of the Matopos as a World Heritage site patriotic history and academic archaeology fit together very well.

The academic custodianship of National Museums and Monuments seems assured. But what are the intentions of the various makers of patriotic history towards the lukewarm universities? Here there is certainly pressure from below. There is a good deal of evidence that there is a project to take patriotic history all the way up from the militia camps to the universities. Already headmasters and College lecturers, if not yet university professors, have been instructed in patriotic history by war veterans. The radical veteran, Joseph Chinotimba, told headmasters in Masvingo that 'to be in harmony with the government you must go for the training. You can only be patriotic if you undergo this course.'

War veterans have taken over entry procedures at Teacher Training Colleges so as to ensure that only their candidates are accepted. Courses in journalism are to be restricted to entrants who have completed militia training. It has also been announced that only those who have completed national service will be accepted into polytechnics and universities or as entrants into the civil service. And in November 2002 it was declared that all tertiary level students would be obliged to take a compulsory course in patriotism, to be called for some reason National Strategic Studies:

The course will cover topics such as the history of the liberation struggle, nationalism, the importance of the land reform programme and other related matters.

In March 2003 there was an attempt to launch such a course at the Bulawayo Polytechnic. Students at the Poly declared a boycott of all classes and asked for support from all other tertiary institutions so as 'to save tomorrow's generation from brainwashing'.

And yet one wonders whether the Zimbabwe government will really try to carry these policies through. At the moment there are not nearly enough - let alone enough qualified - National Service graduates to fill all tertiary places. If they are to have any effect, courses in National Strategic Studies will have to be taught by competent lecturers. It seems more likely that the government will try to co-opt university history lecturers and to establish a relationship with them like that between Mugabe and the Museum staff at Great Zimbabwe. There are some signs of this. At Heroes weekend this year the Chronicle deplored the ignorance amongst youth about Zimbabwe's liberation:

Sadly, a major stumbling block in this regard has been the dearth of books that give a true account of our history, especially the history of the liberation war. We have relied too much on books written by hostile and clearly biased white supremacists that have often wrongly depicted the liberation struggle as a war between barbaric black Africans and white Rhodesian emissaries of civilization. As long as all story-tellers remain bigoted and narrow-minded whites. There will never be a black hero.

The editorial ends with a mingled entreaty and invitation:

What are the level-headed historians in Zimbabwe doing about this? Surely they cannot sit and watch while racists distort the history of our people for cheap political gain. Remember, truth hates delay.

As though in response to this entreaty it was announced on October 16 2003 that 'a partnership agreement aimed at gathering and documenting the country's history' had been signed by the National Archives of Zimbabwe, the Department of National Museums and Monuments of Zimbabwe and the University of Zimbabwe's history department. The project is entitled 'Oral History: From the First to the Second Chimurenga'; it is a 'response to a challenge thrown to the three institutions by President Mugabe to record for posterity the facts of the national struggle.'

The Secretary for Home Affairs, Melusi Matshiya, said that the results 'would be made available to future generations through the Liberation War Museum to be constructed at the National Heroes Acre'. The chairman of the UZ History Department, Dr Ken Manungo, said: 'We hope we will have maximum co-operation from the Government as there is nothing more important than being available to tell what happened.' Manungo said he was 'grateful to the Government because they are going to fund this project'; History students at UZ 'will carry out the necessary interviews and research'.

Depending on how it is carried out and presented this could be a perfectly valid research project. But it is obviously has a very different emphasis from the series of projects carried out at UZ in the 1990s under the rubric of 'Democracy and Human Rights', directed by Professor Ngwabi Bhebe and funded by SAREC. It is still more different from the 'post-nationalist' historiography which was beginning to emerge at the university in the early twenty-first century.

NATIONALIST HISTORIOGRAPHY AND THE HISTORY OF THE NATION

If the editorial in the Chronicle offered role to 'level-headed' black historians, it strikingly ignored the contributions already made by Zimbabwean nationalist historians and histo-rians of the nation. It is certainly not true, for example, that there is nothing to read about the liberation struggle except books by white historians, leaving aside for the moment whether these have all been 'bigoted, narrow-minded and racist'.

The best book on the war is in fact the work of Zimbabwe's most distinguished and productive historian, Professor Ngwabi Bhebe. Bhebe is indeed the outstanding example of a scholar who has written both nationalist history and the history of the nation. It cannot be said that Professor Bhebe has been cast aside in Zimbabwe's era of patriotic history. He is, after all, Vice Chancellor of the state university of the Midlands. Still, it is significant that the Chronicle chose to ignore his work. Professor Bhebe's nationalist historiography and still more his history of the nation is too level-headed and inclusive to be what the paper is looking for.

Plainly I ought to confront the Chronicle's attack on 'bigoted and narrow-minded' white authors of the books which Zimbabwean students read about the first and second chimurenga. I was in Bulawayo when I saw the editorial and my first impulse was to write a letter to them asking 'Do you mean me?' But then I thought they probably did! And yet patriotic history's relationship with my work is more complicated than merely saying it is 'white' or, heaven forfend, 'British'. The Chronicle itself, for instance, carried a whole page article in 2002 showing that 'historians' confirmed the government's case on land alienation. It drew heavily on my

Voices from the Rocks and from the collaborative Violence and Memory to show that 'even' a white historian had documented evictions from the land.

Of course it did not make any use of the last parts of these books which deal with the Matabeleland repression in the 1980s and with the failure of the Zimbabwean government to re-distribute the huge areas of land which fell into its hands in southern Matabeleland in the mid 1980s. Every so often I have tried myself to insert the last third of these books into the contemporary debate. Thus I published a letter in the Daily News on 12 April 2000: 'In Matobo district the majority of the white farms and ranches have been in the hands of government for nearly 15 years. Therefore, if there has not been a just redistribution of land in this part of Matabeleland South, this has not been because of white farmers or British vested interests. It has been, alas, because the people in power have used the land for their own profit rather than for the relief of ordinary people and their cattle herds. The people of Matobo are still waiting'.

Yet sometimes even the last part of my writings gets in to the government press. In June 2003 the Herald carried much to my surprise a whole page entitled 'Ranger re-examines colonial myths'. The first two-thirds of my 'social history' documented the force and fraud of Rhodes, the seizure of the land, the rise of nationalism, etc. So far so good. But the Herald made the mistake of printing the final third, thus presenting its surprised readers with 'the horrors of independence'; with the Fifth Brigade 'savaging the civilian population'; with the rise of a vigorous civil society and a critical church; with 'the megalomania of an aging and unpopular president'. My piece ended:

> The confrontation between the old revolutionary rhetoric (and history) and the new realities of a complex plural society threw Zimbabwean intellectuals and artists into turmoil. Their whole approach to Zimbabwe's national identity and to its history had to be thought through all over again.

Patriotic history is more complex than it at first appears and even on occasion - as with Mugabe's speech to ICOMOS - flexible. Nevertheless because of its narrow focus it has a certain force and simplicity. Critical responses to it have been much more scattered. Some critics have focused on Mugabe's appeal to pre-colonial glories. Many stress the gulf between this appeal and the sterile unprofitability of national monuments. Patriotic history elevates Great Zimbabwe but also, they say, empties it and devalues it. The hostility to whites aroused by patriotic history lessons in the militia camps - which has led to attacks on roadside curio sellers because they cater for and attracts whites - has depressed the tourist trade:

'Great Zimbabwe is now just a heap of stones with no benefit for us', cursed the empty-handed Jerina, as she arrived at home, her arms folded behind her back. A few kilometers away from her hunger-stricken homestead, a disappointed fisherman folded his nets. When things were normal this was the time for him to cast his nets at the shores of Lake Mutirikwa in anticipation of a major catch that would meet an ever increasing demand for fresh fish. 'Will Great Zimbabwe ever rise and be great for us?' the fisherman muttered to himself ...It was not only Jerina and the fisherman who went home empty-handed. In fact it is now the order of the day for drought wracked villagers in Chief Mugabe's area in Masvingo who were earning a living through selling their various wares to tourists who thronged the Great Zimbabwe monuments on a daily basis to explore the mysteries buried at the world acclaimed heritage site. The villagers now sing the blues as the monuments have lost their lustre. Tawanda Magara, a stone carver, said GZ now had a different meaning to him altogether. 'In the past when we saw the GZ monuments we realised that we would always make money since visitors would always come to discover the mystique associated with them. Now we see them just as any other heap of stones. They don't make any difference to our lives.

Others have criticised the disproportionate focus the Mugabe regime has placed on 'heritage' in the midst of economic crisis. 'Patriotism' and 'Heritage', they say, is 'the last refuge of the scoundrels' that are ruining the nation. In May 2002 a Zimbabwean in the Diasporas, Dr T.Mangwende, cited Dr Johnson's definition in his response to criticisms made by

Mugabe of 'young professionals who have forgotten that it was Zanu PF that liberated the country'. Mangwende admitted that he was himself a beneficiary of the 'splendid efforts in education during the early 1980s' but declared himself grateful that these were now 'helping me see through your ruinous policies'. Mangwende claimed that all Zimbabweans were 'number one when it comes to patriotism' but that ZANU/PF itself was dealing in 'rubbished patriotism used to justify the training of wholesale murderers':

It is a sheer waste of time and resources to set up colleges to supposedly teach 'patriotism' to the youth when the teacher needs intensive lessons in 'patriotism'. The President knows more than anyone else that the country is in a mess and there is no point in touring the ruins to assess damage. Still on the subject of 'patriotism', some young Zimbabweans referred to the other half of the recently returned bird as 'just a piece of stone'. Yes, it is patriotic to refer to this 'half' as just a piece of stone given the situation that Zimbabweans find themselves in. If a country is ravaged to the point that it cannot provide basics to its citizens, cultural symbols are the first to lose their value and meaning.

The true symbols of the new Zimbabwe were queues and Mugabe ought to visit them. 'I wish the President well in his tour of man-made ruins'. It is not only the pre-colonial emphases of patriotic history which are criticised. Its account of the 'second chimurenga', the guerrilla war of the 1960s and 1970s, is also repudiated:

Every day in the state-controlled media one hears of distortions of the history of this country. We are frequently nauseated by endless propaganda about how freedom fighters were always winning battles against Rhodesia forces and how lots of helicopters and planes were downed during such engagements. A lot of young men and women sacrificed their lives for this country but that is no reason to lie than an outright military victory was achieved on the battlefield in 1979 [when] not even a single settlement, including those at the borders had fallen to the liberation forces [and] white farmers were able to continue farming even in the remotest hot-spots. War is a serious affair with a high price to pay. Real heroes do not lie and trivialise the pain of war.

The narrowness of patriotic history and its division of Zimbabweans into revolutionaries and 'sell-outs' has been attacked by many critics, not least, as we have seen, by the church leaders in their condemnation of the youth militia. Its narrowness is other ways has also been effectively condemned. In August 2003 Erikana Haurovi wrote to the press to bemoan 'the high levels of environmental degradation which are occurring everywhere'. These demanded practical solutions, but 'Zimbabwe has adopted a strange paradigm in solving its environmental crisis':

> I have noted with great amazement the fact that whenever people sense danger they are reminded of some historical achievement. People are forced to remember the harshness of the historical colonial past whenever some crisis emerges. [Yet] a degraded environment will never recover despite the high level of praise it receives. Such an environment can never offer subsistence to man despite the level of high political achievement which may have occurred in the area two to three decades ago. The indoctrinative sentiments being echoed by the State propaganda machinery seems to be telling the country that no matter how degraded your environment is, political history will save us.

The message seems to say 'never worry about the prevailing drought, political history will intervene. Stop worrying about the polluted water, polluted air, extinction of species, declining soil fertility, siltation of rivers ... since all this is set to be solved by political history'.

Haurovi found that all 'state channels of disseminating information' were 'singing the same chorus in unison, elevating political history as an indisputable saviour'. But 'let us protect our environment first and then enjoy talking about our political history. Political history is nothing when we are living in misery and uncertainty.' But these varying criticisms do not amount to an alternative historical narrative capable of displacing patriotic history. Their authors are left to share Zichanaka

Munyika's hope in a future 'when Zanu PF's stranglehold on Zimbabwe will end and the history of this country will be debated freely by all shades of opinion for the benefit of our children'.

There are signs, admittedly, of more systematic historiographical dissent. One of these centers around the events of Matabeleland in the 1980s, part of the past which patriotic history excludes. As Mugabe himself declared in December 2002: 'Whatever remains were historical differences. These remain as history of our country and we can't bring ugly history into the present affairs and rewrite that ugly history. No.' Instead ZANU/PF has sought to turn December 22, the day of the Unity Accord between ZANU and ZAPU in 1987, into a national anniversary.

In response the Zimbabwe Liberators Peace Platform, the organisation of critical ex-combatants, has announced that Unity Day should be kept as a day of national mourning. Max Mnkandla, information secretary of the ZLPP, called on Zimbabweans 'not to be fooled into celebrating an accord which legitimated the slaughter of their kith and kin'. Instead of expensive celebrations 'an upright government' would spend money on exhumations and reburials.' History itself needed to be exhumed. On December 22, said Mnkandla, 'we shall be in our black robes, remembering those who perished and lie in mass graves'.

And if Matabeleland in the 1980s is one of the large omissions of patriotic history so, too, is the history of the towns and of the trade unions. Patriotic history sees townspeople as 'those without totems' and the state press from time to time carries bewildered articles about why urban populations are so unpatriotic. The role of trade unionism is largely excluded from the new narrative of nationalism. The most articulate protest against these exclusions has come from the veteran journalist, Bill Saidi. Saidi quotes from a ZAPU central committee report in 1984: 'In the period leading up to the first national organisation of resistance to colonial rule, the workers of Zimbabwe led the way to unity in their struggle to form the first trade unions'.

According to ZAPU, 'this development of a working class was an important foundation for the resurgence of the people's resistance ... The workers have fought many battles and taught the people many useful lessons. One of these lessons was the value of unity'. Yet, says Saidi, after the 1987 Unity Agreement the workers dropped out of political discourse. How, he asks, 'did the workers lose out? ... Today the most important people to Zanu PF are not the workers but the so-called war veterans.'

The MDC emerged from the trade union movement and obtains most of its support from the towns. One might have expected it to have developed a counter-narrative against patriotic history which re-instated the workers and made urban history once again central to Zimbabwe's modern experience. One might have expected it also to try to overcome what Brian Raftopolous has diagnosed as the main weakness of the trade unions in the 1950s and early 1960s, namely their failure to articulate rural grievances and aspirations. In the earlier period this weakness allowed political nationalism to dominate and eventually to absorb radical trade unionism.

Today the divergence between an urban MDC and a rural ZANU/PF yawns dangerously wide. But the MDC has made very little of trade union or worker history, perhaps because it believes that it already enjoys the support of the towns and of labour. Nor has it made much of a show of articulating rural grievances and aspirations. It does not possess a coherent land policy. It has been all too easy for ZANU/PF to depict the MDC as globalised and a-historical.

In any case ZANU/PF controls all television and radio; now, with the closure of the Daily News, it commands virtually all the press; and it is able to determine what kind of history is taught in schools. It is virtually impossible for critics to develop a counter-narrative in any systematic way. The spokesmen of Zimbabwean civil society, however, increasingly feel the need for this. The Crisis Coalition and the NGOs have appealed to international norms of human rights: precisely those, in fact, that Mahoso has criticised as bogus universalism. It is not a policy which has worked, as the recent refusal of the United

Nations Human Rights Commission to discuss a motion censuring Zimbabwe reveals all too clearly. In the week of this refusal a spokesman for the Crisis Coalition told a gathering in London that it was essential to develop a new narrative which roots human rights in Zimbabwe's own history.

It must have become clear that history is at the centre of politics in Zimbabwe far more than in any other southern African country. But how can academic historians make an impact in the debate? Let me return at the end of this review to the University of Zimbabwe and to its aspirant pluralist and post-nationalist historians. These have refused to go on radio or television. But if their voices have not been heard as advocates of patriotic history, they have not been heard in any other way either. Zimbabwe is a country in which books have much less effect than radio, TV or the press. But even if academic books and articles made an impact the University of Zimbabwe is effectively gagged. Printing costs have raised so rapidly that the UZ publications department cannot afford to publish any of the admirable monographs and collections it has accepted without massive subsidy.

Among other things this means that a very large edited collection on Zimbabwe's political economy remains unpublished. Even my own edited collection, Nationalism, Democracy and Human Rights - which might be said to provide some of the building blocks for a counter narrative - has only seen the light of day after two successive subsidies. And even then only 100 copies have been produced! The university's journal, Zambezia, has not been published for several months. All the external agencies which used to subsidise research and publication have withdrawn. The university is mute.

Bibliography

Andrews, Peggy. *Sisters Listening to Sisters: Women of the World Share Stories of Personal Empowerment.* Bergin and Garvey, 1996.

Awkward, Michael. *Negotiating Difference: Race, Gender, and the Politics of Positionality.* University of Chicago Press, 1995.

Bannerji, Himani. *Thinking Through: Essays on Feminism, Marxism, and Anti-Racism.* Women's Press, 1995.

Basu, Amrita, ed. *The Challenge of Local Feminisms: Women's Movements in Global Perspective.* Westview Press, 1995.

Butler, Judith and Joan W. Scott, ed. *Feminists Theorize the Political.* Routledge, 1992.

Carver, Terrell and Veronique Mottier, ed. *Politics of Sexuality.* NY: Routledge, 1998.

Chapman, Jennifer. *Politics, Feminism and the Reformation of Gender.* Routledge, 1992.

Chapman, Jenny. *Politics, Feminism and the Reformation of Gender.* Routledge, 1993.

Cocks, Joan. *The Oppositional Imagination: Feminism, Critique, and PoliticalTheory.* (out of print)

Elshtain, Jean Bethke. *Meditations on Modern Political Thought: Masculine/Feminine Themes from Luther to Arendt.* Penn State Univ. Press, 1992.

Fowlkes, Diane L. *White Political Women: Paths from Privilege to Empowerment.* Univ. of Tennessee Press, 1992.

Fraser, Nancy. *Justice Interruptus: Critical Reflections on the "Postsocialist" Condition.* Routledge, 1997.

Gottfried, Heidi, ed. *Feminism and Social Change: Bridging Theory and Practice.* Univ. of Illinois Press, 1996.

Hughes-Freeland, Felicia and Nickie Charles, ed. *Practising Feminism: Identity, Difference and Power.* Routledge, 1996.

Jones, Kathleen B., ed. *Citizenship in Feminism: Identity, Action, and Locale.* Indiana University Press, 1998.

Kenney, Sally J. and Helen Kinsella, ed. *Politics and Feminist Standpoint Theories.* Haworth Press, 1997.

King, Katie. *Theory in Its Feminist Travels: Conversations in U.S. Women's Movements.* Indiana Univ. Press, 1994.

Meehan, Elizabeth and Selma Sevenhuijsen, ed. *Equality Politics and Gender.* Sage, 1991.

Meyers, Diana Tietjens, ed. *Feminist Social Thought: A Reader.* Routledge, 1997.

Naples, Nancy A., ed. *Community Activism and Feminist Politics: Organizing Across Race, Class, and Gender.* Routledge, 1997

Okin, Susan Moller. *Women in Western Political Thought.* Princeton Univ. Press, 1992.

Pascall, Gillian. *Social Policy: A New Feminist Analysis.* 1997.

Pateman, Carole and Elizabeth Gross, ed. *Feminist Challenges: Social and Political Theory.* Northeastern Univ. Press, 1987.

Phillips, Anne. *Engendering Democracy.* Penn State Univ. Press, 1991.

Phillips, Anne. *Feminism and Politics.* Oxford, 1998.

Randall, Vicky and Georgina Waylen, ed. *Gender, Politics and the State.* NY: Routledge, 1998.

Rocheleau, Dianne, Barbara Thomas-Slayter, and Esther Wangari, ed. *Femininst Political Ecology: Global Issues and Local Experiences.* 1996.

Sapiro, Virginia. *A Vindication of Political Virtue: The Political Theory of Mary Wollstonecraft*. Univ. of Chicago Press, 1992.

Simon, Sherry. *Gender in Translation: Cultural Identity and the Politics of Transmission*. Routledge, 1996.

Sunstein, Cass R., ed. *Feminism and Political Theory*. Univ. of Chicago Press, 1990.

Thomas, Sue and Clyde Wilcox, ed. *Women and Elective Office*. Oxford, 1997.

Waring, Wendy, ed. *By, For and About: Feminist Cultural Politics*. Women's Press, 1994.

Warren, Karen J. and Duane L. Cady, ed. *Bringing Peace Home: Feminism, Violence, and Nature*. Indiana Univ. Press, 1996.

Wolf, Naomi. *Fire with Fire: The New Female Power and How It Will Change the 21st Century*. Fawcett Books, 1993.

Young, Iris Marion. *Justice and the Politics of Difference*. Princeton, 1998.

Young, Stacey. *Changing the wor(l)d: Discourse, Politics, and the Feminist Movement*. Routledge, 1997.

Zack, Naomi, ed. *American Mixed Race: The Culture of Microdiversity*. Rowman and Littlefield, 1995.

Index